Unfinished Rebellions

DeVere Pentony

Robert Smith

Richard Axen

OKA

UNFINISHED REBELLIONS

Jossey-Bass Inc., Publishers
615 Montgomery Street · San Francisco · 1971

UNFINISHED REBELLIONS
DeVere Pentony, Robert Smith, and Richard Axen

Copyright © 1971 by Jossey-Bass, Inc., Publishers

Jossey-Bass, Inc., Publishers
615 Montgomery Street
San Francisco, California 94111

Library of Congress Catalog Card Number 72-148658

International Standard Book Number ISBN 0-87589-095-4

Manufactured in the United States of America
Composed and printed by York Composition Company, Inc.
Bound by Chas. H. Bohn & Co., Inc.

JACKET DESIGN BY JANE OKA, MILL VALLEY

FIRST EDITION

Code 7111

THE JOSSEY-BASS SERIES IN HIGHER EDUCATION

General Editors

JOSEPH AXELROD
*San Francisco State College
and University of California, Berkeley*

MERVIN B. FREEDMAN
*San Francisco State College
and Wright Institute, Berkeley*

Preface

When we embarked on this study of the crisis events that have engulfed San Francisco State College in the past few years, we had two primary purposes: to define the events in a detailed case study and to analyze the issues underlying these events. In our earlier book, *By Any Means Necessary,* we described the events. *Unfinished Rebellions* presents insights gleaned from the dilemmas of the college.

    Unfinished Rebellions begins by focusing on the many issues raised by the multiple roles that colleges and universities in the United States have been attempting to play. Focusing on roles helps place the rest of the book in perspective. San Francisco State cannot be viewed properly as an aberration in higher education. Many of the issues dramatized on its campus and discussed in detail in this book are part of the broader questions of the purpose and thrust of American education. Although the book does not specifically treat each of the issues raised in the opening chapter, we felt it desirable to provide some general background to facilitate understanding of the analysis of issues which follows.

    In the chapter on student initiative for educational reform, we portray the traditional ways of the college directly challenged as never before. The student-stimulated experimental college, with its courses in Zen basketball and world government, sharply—often humorously—raised the question of whether our educational establishment had so structured its courses and interests that its curriculum was failing in its primary mission of teaching what was worth knowing. Similarly, the growth of student-run programs of community involvement, tutoring,

Preface

draft counseling, and so on, were basic criticisms of the role we had been playing or failing to play. Perhaps even more important, the effort to develop human interaction and concern in these courses cried clearly for a modification of the lonely impersonality which is a by-product of our traditional system.

The chapter on radical ideology and strategies focuses on the radical end of the reformist-radical continuum. Many students no longer accept without thought or question the ideology presented in the schoolroom. Their examination of democratic values has led some to develop radical ideologies and strategies. In this chapter we describe and analyze this revival of radical ideology as it challenges the way colleges have been run.

The dilemma of racism in a land supposedly based on respect for human dignity and equality came sharply and massively into view on the San Francisco State College campus. The chapter on minority education chronicles and analyzes the drive of minority ethnic groups to induce the college to respond to their desperate needs.

The chapter on student justice emphasizes the nature of our disarray and the difficulties of obtaining consensus on the limits of academic conduct once a clash over basic values begins. The question remains however whether large sections of the student constituency consider these limits legitimate on substantive or even procedural grounds.

The successes and failures of the San Francisco State faculty in making the academic corporation a self-governing community are chronicled in the chapter on crisis management through faculty governance. The chapter demonstrates how deeply the patterns of the corporate model are entrenched in the minds of the public, legislators, trustees, and top educational managers.

Although the ethical and behavioral relationship of the student to the college may understandably be vague and rather imprecise, one might expect that the system of rights, obligations, and procedures of the faculty would be more developed and less open to misunderstanding and abuse than it now is. The chapter on professional and unprofessional ethics suggests that this expectation was not borne out at San Francisco State College. In raising questions about the codes of behavior appropriate for those who make their careers in the college or university, the chapter seeks to stimulate thinking about the limits of conduct that are needed.

The next two chapters focus intently on the interrelationships between the college and the wider community, particularly during times of college crisis. Two patterns of college-community interaction, chosen because of their great impact on the college, are described and analyzed in the chapter on intervention by the police and media. Perhaps no issue in recent times has been more controversial than that of calling police onto campus. When, how, why, if, and where the police shall be used are questions that touch the campus in many areas and that raise the issue of the place of the college or university in society. Is the college merely one of the many subordinate institutions in society answering directly to the governmental or quasi-governmental minions of the body politic? Or is it or should it be something unique, requiring special kinds of interrelationships with the community outside its walls? By describing the dilemmas posed by emergency police action on campus and examining the factors that led to massive police participation in the affairs of San Francisco State College, we can make recommendations for the future.

The educational effort is difficult under placid circumstances and nearly impossible when dramatic events outrun or distort the facts, altering drastically the relationship of the campus to the society around it. The garbled, often sensationalized, communication links among the trustees, the campus, and the community lead us to question how the attentive publics can be truly informed of the facts so that they can play their roles as patrons in an enlightened and productive manner.

Rarely in the discussion of the interrelationships between society and a public institution is it possible to gain a firsthand look at the pressures that operate on chief administrative officers as they attempt to guide the institution through divisive times. The chapter on public reaction provides that opportunity. In doing so, it demonstrates how emotional, unthinking, and punitive some segments of the patron public have become in the present period. It also dramatizes the growing disparity of value orientation among students, faculty, trustees, and sections of the public.

Finally, we conclude *Unfinished Rebellions* with a chapter in which we reflect on the meaning of the experiences and issues discussed in the preceding pages. Where are we heading? What are our prospects? What is to be done?

The events that occurred at San Francisco State foreshadowed developments that have not yet been played out on other campuses.

Here in dramatic microcosm arose most of the problems and dilemmas of our higher educational system and indeed of the broader society in which it is enmeshed. We make recommendations and proposals for approaching the problems, and we try, above all, to place the complexity of the issues before the public, so that people of interest and goodwill can perceive clearly the urgent need for imaginative attacks on the problems.

We acknowledge with gratitude the unremitting efforts and responsibilities assumed by Sandra Standifird, Diana Crosetti, and Lorraine de la Fuente, who shared in the administration of the project and prepared the manuscript, and the patient cooperation of many students, faculty, staff members, and administrators who provided materials, agreed to extensive interviews, and read portions of the manuscript. Louis Heilbron, former chairman of the board of trustees, provided us with major insights from the perspective of a participant on the board.

We are especially indebted to three agencies, the Statewide Academic Senate of the California State Colleges and the Danforth and Rosenberg Foundations, which provided substantial support for us and our research assistants. The San Francisco Consortium also lent its support as a repository of funds. (None of the collaborating organizations and individuals bear responsibility for the content of this book.)

San Francisco   DeVere Pentony
January 1971   Robert Smith
                                                  Richard Axen

Contents

Unfinished Rebellions

ONE

The Many Lives
of the College

As the student enters college to begin his undergraduate days, he enters not one institution but many. An American college is a multisplintered thing. Although the beginnings of American higher education can easily be traced to efforts of early American religious institutions to train prospective clergymen, those schools developed, at first very slowly and then quite rapidly, into places of confusing and often contradictory role complexity. By the beginning of the twentieth century the goal of education for all had moved upward, first to the level of high school graduate and then to the level of college graduate. Fifty years later parents of even the most deprived socioeconomic classes could consider the goal of a college education for their children as a reasonable one. The passage of the GI Bill of Rights after World War II finally put a college education within easy reach of the masses for the first time. In a way reminiscent of the great land rush days of the nineteenth century, the rush to the colleges was on. The reasons for this rush are complex and involve considerations of status, employment, industrialization, the ebb and flow of the labor market, war, and a host of other variables.

We begin this study of a college in crisis by attempting to place San Francisco State College in the context of American higher education in 1969. A brief analysis of the American college as it has developed is presented in this chapter in order to set the stage. The discussion of issues and problems rising out of the crisis of the American college is dramatized by the events at San Francisco State College.

There are many ways to describe the modern American college and people with various perspectives have done so (Goodman, Riesman and Jencks, Friedenberg, Kerr, Hayden, Freedman, and so on). We have chosen to portray it as an institution living at least nine different lives all at once. Each portrayal is followed by a brief examination of the purpose and function of that aspect of the institution. We raise questions about the thrust of American higher education today, questions to which we return in our examination of the issues raised at San Francisco State in its period of crisis.

Life 1: As Explorer

Although it seems not always to have been so, the college has become an arena where at least some faculty and students are engaged in explorations on the behavior and value frontiers. From the supergalactic to the subatomic, the search for knowledge about social and natural phenomena goes on in the laboratories, classrooms, libraries, offices, and dormitories of the college. The range of questions examined is astounding: Why war? Why universe? Whither population growth? How genes? Why disease? How to know? When ecological balance? Why aggression? Why authority? Why famine amidst plenty? What of cultural variations? How brain? How learn? The proliferation of knowledge about how things and people behave is astounding. The knowledge revolution seems to threaten man's ability to digest and use it.

Similarly, on the value front, students and faculty raise and examine questions of standards of action. How have people in the past answered questions about proper conduct? What is the good life? How should people relate to one another? What do we expect will be the guiding values of the future? What is beautiful and what is just from the perspectives of yesterday, today, and tomorrow? In its ideal state the American college is a place for asking any and all questions of taste and value. No question is profane; no idea is too dangerous; and no answer is to be suppressed. The walls of the academy are to be strong enough to withstand the repressing volleys of enforced orthodoxy.

The lives of explorers have traditionally been filled with danger, excitement, and frequent disappointment. So it is with the college. Particularly as college life leads into the uncharted seas of knowledge and the rough waters of value conflict, the college finds itself continually struggling with those who have vested interest in knowledge as it is and ways of behaving as they are. And although this struggle may be exciting in the deepest sense, its frustrations and disappointments are many. The college, moved as it is by ideas, is really no short term match for those who are powered by guns and money. While there may be nothing so powerful as an idea whose time has come, the birthing and nurturing of an idea is often a risky business filled with awesome threats of censorship, suppression, and even prison.

In this context the American college, connected to the ways of affluence, seems particularly vulnerable. Even though moved by ideas, the men of the college are kept alive by an ability to gain life-sustaining income from the society at large. This means that society has a continuing ability to force the exploring college to concern itself with the impact of its adventures into inner and outer worlds. Explorers have frequently had to depend on patrons to fund their adventures, and the explorer at the college is similarly dependent on patronage. In modern America, the public is the patron. The money that keeps the college open comes increasingly from the taxes on the general public. The folk wisdom which comments that it is those who pay the piper that call the tune suggests an underlying reality of American higher education. The hallowed freedom of inquiry is constantly in danger of colliding head on with the folk freedom of support. Because the United States is in the throes of the postindustrial system change with all its strangeness, frustration, and suspicion, one could expect a heightening of tension between the explorers and the patrons. The mettle, the power of persuasion, and the devotion of the college explorer is being tested as never before.

While the patron public may be threatening with increasing intensity to limit the freedom to explore on the knowledge and value frontiers, an attack from within the intellectual citadel has already begun. Starting from the assumption that no freedom is absolute, there are some who are wondering aloud if some limits should not be placed on that freedom of any inquiry which contributes to the destructiveness or debasement of life. This attack is seen most starkly in the contention that the college should cease all explorations that aid directly or indirectly in discovering more effective weapons of massive destruction. But it is also found among those who deplore some of the investigations of human behavior, particularly in the intimate fields of sexual conduct. Perhaps for the first time since the Dark Ages the hard won freedom to inquire is being questioned by the inquirers themselves.

From a somewhat different perspective, this questioning seems to translate into a criticism of the explorers as people who are too much interested in exploration for knowledge and not sufficiently interested in the social and individual consequences of these explorations. Thus, the anthropologist who studies the cultural patterns of the urban Indian is maligned for concentrating on the discovery rather than on proposing ways to solve acculturative problems. The political scientist who focuses on the study of political behavior is seen as a defender of things as they are rather than as a user of his critical intelligence to propose things as they should be. In these instances and many others, there is an implicit rejection of the freedom of the explorer to choose his own far horizons. While many perceptive people have argued that there is no necessary contradiction between the empirical and normative efforts, there can be little doubt that faculty and student demands for relevant education are grounded on the belief that what is needed is action against evil, not further study of the nature of evil or soil analysis of material from the moon. The scholar is being pressured to bring his scholarship down from his ivory tower to serve the immediate cause of the good, the true, and the beautiful.

However, for many who live this life of the college, the choice between knowledge for its own sake and knowledge for society is false and leads to the destruction of the college as a place of exploration. Knowing indeed that the observer cannot be completely separated from the observed and that one's experiences shape his understanding, some college explorers prefer to hold on to the assumptions of objectivity and dispassionate analysis of natural and social behavior. They do so with the shadowy hope that they can find how things work, often with a feeling that such knowledge and particularly the scholarly style of rational argument and humane persuasion will contribute to successful strategies for change, control, and adjustment. Thus these explorers seek not an escape from the responsibility for the human and natural condition but instead freedom from an obligation to come up with the data or arguments to support somebody else's questions and preconceived answers.

Life 2: As Preserver and Transmission Belt

The college also has assumed the role of a preserver of man's heritage. In the journey from his beginnings man has seen and done many things, and he has searched for understanding of what he has seen and done. The story of his experiences through thirty-five thousand years of time is told in the libraries, museums and classrooms of the college. The tales and chronicles of the rise and fall of civilizations, of the growth of the plastic and performing arts, of the discoveries about natural and human phenomena, of the birth of inventions, of the change of life styles, of the record of man's reflections about himself and nature are part of what the college attempts to pass on from generation to generation. With a proper mixing of appreciation and candor, the college attempts to facilitate familiarity with the glory and the horror of man's past: what man has accomplished and what he has bungled; how he has developed and how he has remained the same; and when he has soared to the heights of beauty and creativity or plunged into the depths of ugliness and degradation. Those of the college seem to feel that college must not only be a repository of as much of this story as possible but that it also must actively encourage those who pass through its doors to develop a better understanding of themselves and contemporary society by gaining a perspective of the past. Moreover, it is hoped that the college graduate will realize that he has a legacy from the past which is to be held in trust for the future. Trees, a book, a poem, a painting, a bay, an atmosphere for health are all part of this legacy and the college is a place for pointing this out.

In a related, less historical sense, the college has taken on the burdens of preservation, it has become one of the places in society for recruiting the active agitants in the battle to preserve this heritage—natural, historical, and human—from the depredations and insensitivities of the today people. Indeed, rising on the intellectual horizon is the field of human ecology through which the colleges and others hope to help man understand that he lives in symbiotic relationship to his environment and that now, with the press of population growth and run-away urbanization, careful and systematic planning is absolutely necessary if man is to continue to survive on this planet.

Devotion to the causes of preservation is not without its controversial elements. The telling of the story of the past can easily be misinterpreted as blanket, unthinking approval of the past. Indeed, those who tell the story of the past may well count among their numbers those who have a preference for the past. Whether it be in the field of music, literature or politics, the study of the past and the presentation of the results of that study may often carry with them a sense of legitimacy and approbation not accorded to contemporary efforts in the same areas. With increasing frequency, students are questioning the relevance of spending all that time on certain traditionally taught aspects of the past.

Why not focus more on interpersonal experiences and the pressing problems and exciting developments of today from new perspectives and with new people? Beatles not Beethoven; Carmichael not Comte; Fanon not Weber; Warhol not Rubens; encounter groups and sensitivity training not Freud and Jung. In the either-or world of the young, there is disenchantment with the past and a protective support of their own brand of contemporaneity. As a place where the past is important, the college thus finds itself in continuing tension with the now generation. Whether the college can win or maintain the serious attention and enthusiasm of this student generation for preservative excursions into the past is a sharper question than ever before. Significant numbers of students are still attentive to the need for learning and preserving the story of the past. But the drive for student power and the rise of experimental colleges may force the college to pay more attention to how it lives the life of preserver.

Life 3: As Processor and Quality Controller

The college is also a factory turning out semifinished products for the world of work. A strong and persistent vocationalism captured the American college from its earliest days. From its first task of training preachers it has expanded to training teachers, doctors, lawyers, dentists, businessmen, accountants, psychologists, economists, veterinarians, nurses, astronomers, writers, engineers, policemen, chemists, biologists, archeologists, musicians, coaches, artists, botanists, journalists, homemakers, farmers, disk jockeys, physicists, social workers, criminologists, warriors, secretaries, and dozens of others.

In part, students go to college to learn a genteel or prestigious trade, or at least gain access to one. And the college has almost responded willy-nilly to this desire for a trade by seeming to offer enormous variety of occupational opportunities to the incoming freshman.

Like the British empire, the empires of the college seem to have expanded in fits of absence of mind. But suddenly there they are all in place, vested interest upon vested interest.

Where there is variety there is usually complexity, and where there is empire building there is usually conflict. In a sense, the college factory today can be characterized as a congeries of vocational and disciplinary shops linked together by ribbons of administrative red tape and a few cords of common concern and mutual interest. The master craftsmen in these shops—with their ever-shifting constituencies and natural alliances—are constantly struggling, scheming and proselytizing so that they can fulfill their productive missions and feather their nests. Although the struggle sometimes threatens to exceed the bounds of good sense and logic, it is probably based on the rational knowledge that to do a thorough job of training for vocation the shop not only needs to gain plentiful resources but also must have more of the trainee's time than is really available in the short time he is there.

The latter is a particularly acute problem because, unlike many factories, the product to be turned out by the undergraduate shop is worked upon and shaped by other nonvocational shops whose purposes may even be antithetical (at least in terms of time spent) to the primary vocational thrust. Furthermore, in the college factory there is no carefully orchestrated production line with the product moving from one intermeshing stage to another. Instead, there is a cafeteria line where the product-to-be is forced and encouraged to sample one shaping delicacy after another. This means that intensive vocational efforts are continually frustrated and stymied at the undergraduate level and that a powerful pressure for extending true professional training to the graduate level bursts forth. Yet the recruiting ground for graduate trainees remains at the undergraduate level and vocationalism often masquerades under the guise of liberal arts and general education. Moreover, so strong is the claim of vocationalism that even legitimate undergraduate liberal arts and general education take on a semivocational cast. Students are required to have majors and the majors that do not obviously have a trade connection are often open to the cynical question "What are you going to do with it?" or the statement "With that major and fifteen cents you can buy a cup of coffee." It seems that the student needs to justify somehow or other that the undergraduate training he is receiving will pay off at the vocational box-office.

As one reflects on this confusing situation, it becomes apparent that, with the possible exception of the traditional postgraduate professional schools, there may have been far too little effort to differentiate the functions of the college in some rational manner. In their undergraduate days are students really in college to learn to think better, criticize more effectively, and appreciate more thoroughly? Or are they there to learn the rudiments of a trade? Or can they do both as undergraduates? In trying to answer yes to both questions many colleges may have been further entrapping themselves in a sort of institutional schizophrenia. In the *Academic Revolution,*[1] professors Jencks and Riesman point out that the trend in American higher education has been toward professionalization of the undergraduate curriculum. Students are expected to make an early choice about their disciplinary and career interests even though they cannot be full professionals until they have completed their studies in graduate schools.

Are there reasons for interrupting this trend toward undergraduate specialization? Should the undergraduate colleges be vocational at all? Is it really wise or efficient to prepare undergraduate students to take their places in business, teaching, government, and other complex professions? Should not the undergraduate days be days of maximum freedom to explore, to think, to reflect, and to feel? Questions and considerations such as these are not new, but they appear to be no less pressing in this time and place.

The college as a processor is under challenge as never before. More and more people are becoming concerned with the product both within and outside the institution and with the intellectual and societal impact our particular brand of processing and evaluating portends. It is ironic that those of us within the college have been so concerned about processing and its handmaiden, quality control—in terms of our curriculum structuring, grading system, and distribution of rewards—that we may have lost sight of what we are trying to do. Yet the irony may be more apparent than real because we have become a willing, often enthusiastic part of the system that purports to train people and recommend them in accordance with the evaluative standards that we have established. We justify this processing and comparative evaluation partially on the grounds of needed motivation but

[1] C. Jencks and D. Riesman, *Academic Revolution* (New York: Doubleday, 1968).

also importantly on grounds that we have a responsibility to the graduate school, the employer, and the public to help them make their recruitment judgments or to make certain that the recipients of an expensive educational opportunity are not loafing. Again, do we need
to do this? Is our job really quality control? Are we deceptively im-
posing our will on students and thus denying freedom? What is the
relationship between our quality control and the living product in the
workaday world? Does this quality control produce people who are
particularly creative and wise? Do they remain alive to the excitement
of learning and the life of the mind? If the answer is yes, is the control
still justified in light of the possibility that those much larger numbers
down farther on the quality scale may have been forever alienated
from efforts at reflection, creativity, and an independent search for
meaning? Would the absence of quality control at the undergraduate
level improve the overall quality of the product? Would more real
education be accomplished? Should not the keepers to the keys of employment or further training operate their own quality controls by
administering standardized and open-ended tests and interviews at the
time of entry and by operating their own internships? Would we not
get brighter, more enthusiastic, less frustrated and anxious and more
creative "products" if the college teacher were permitted to shed his
role of making quality control judgments and to focus exclusively on
helping the student to learn?

Life 4: As Quasi-Home

Despite the product orientation of a significant part of a college
life with all of its impersonality and anxiety, the college has also tried
to live another life. In loco parentis, in place of the parent, is the
phrase that is used to denote this role for the college. During most of
the period of the rise of mass higher education and particularly with
the influx of a large number of women into higher education, the college has been expected by parents and by society to operate as a home
away from home. Off to college meant that the young student was
leaving the protection of the home, but was going to a place where
some of the home functions would be performed. The parents were
placing their offspring in the trustful custody of the college, which
was to bring the youth through the next four years with an improved
mind and an unsullied character. The colleges accepted this role and
proceeded to provide rules of proper conduct, house mothers, dormi-

tory proctors, and deans of students. Chastity, sobriety, and propriety were the early watchwords of the college as parent. From the great state universities to the small denominational colleges zealous efforts were made by college authorities to control "improper" conduct. Girls were not to be out after hours; drinking was often grounds for expulsion or milder disciplinary action; even smoking was prohibited at times; first floor visitation rights in dormitories and other housing units were carefully supervised, and room visitation by the opposite sex was proscribed. The college tried to provide proper study conditions, to feed the students a balanced diet, to maintain their health by establishing student health services, and to nurture their psyches by providing extensive counseling services.

For the parents who were not yet ready to cut the control strings, the performance of these functions was a boon. For the students, much of it was a drag. However, as the twentieth century approached its sixth decade, it became increasingly apparent that a significant contradiction was at hand in the relationship between college as parent and parent as parent. Significant numbers of real parents had moved away from the rigid, authoritarian patterns of child raising and were more flexible, permissive (although rarely as permissive as some critics now maintain), and considerate when it came to respecting the capacity of their children to assume responsibility for their own behavior. The colleges began to reconsider the role in loco parentis, perhaps under the impression that the parents themselves were passively, if not actively, supportive and surely with the knowledge that many students felt that the rules were unnecessarily repressive, undemocratic, and insulting. In loco parentis is dying, if not already dead.

In a broader context, anyone who views the intents and purposes of a higher education at midcentury may well raise questions about the value and justice of many of the restrictive rules that the colleges have attempted to enforce. For example, should the college intervene on questions of sexual behavior? Should the college have more restrictive rules of conduct than the society at large on matters that are basically interpersonal and unconnected to the educational mission of the college? What is the effect, if any, of the college attempting to play often contradictory roles of disciplinarian and educator? Should there be a separate independent judicial arm of the college to administer justice? Who in the college community shall administer justice for students?

Perhaps it is time to redefine what kind of quasi-home the college should become. Rather than the nuclear family model with father at the head, is it possible that an extended family or community model could take its place? The young person moving into the college environment needs some of the comforts of home, but these are probably not the comforts of discipline. Instead, what the college student may need is that aspect of home that was supportive, loving, guiding, sharing, and personally concerned. To a certain extent, the American college has attempted to provide this kind of familial concern in its counseling and advising programs, in its housing units, and in its extracurricular and cocurricular efforts. The curse of bigness seems to have overtaken the college community so that it is no longer, if it ever was, proper to speak of the college as a true community. Membership in many of the college institutions today provides little of the sense of belonging and involvement that a true community promises. While the college has its natural groupings in the disciplinary majors, these have rarely provided the focus for the growth of community, except perhaps on some graduate levels and in some performing disciplines like creative arts and athletics. The difficulties in establishing a sense of community—particularly with a highly mobile and transient student population—are enormous. These problems are compounded by the increased professionalization of the faculty with its consequent diminution in contact with students, by the superior-inferior and evaluator-evaluated relationship between faculty and students, and by the lack of effective student voice in critical decisions affecting their lives.

Indeed, a case can be made that the student entering the American college is looked upon and treated more as a client than as a fledgling member of a community. He is purchasing an education with his time and money, and "buyer beware" may be appropriate to the situation more frequently than we would like to admit. Study after study shows us that we do not have a viable community of faculty and students at many colleges in this country, and that the disenchantment, alienation, and disgust are in part manifestations of this void. This suggests that the real questions for the college are not primarily questions of fatherly discipline at all, but rather questions of how the college can develop and sustain a community of hope, support, creativity, social commitment, and intellectual excitement among all of its members. Perhaps only when it does will alma mater mean anything significant.

Life 5: As Tribal Rite

It may be instructive to view the college as an anthropologist might view a foreign culture. In this light, the American tribe with all of its subtribes seems generally agreed that one of the important rites of passage into privileged positions in the adult world is the rite of passage through college. In college, some of the adult members of the tribe establish and conduct various tests of skill and learning and initiate the candidate into the special secrets and customs of the tribe. Since this is a complicated technocratic culture, the rites are believed to require at least four years attendance in the advanced school. Although other routes to membership are increasingly available, the elders of the tribe still demand that candidates for the full rewards of the group must have their college degrees. All cultures have symbols of status, and the college degree seems to have become one of our major status symbols. It has a social significance that should not be underrated, and it now has a job significance of major importance.

If the American tribe now insists upon the rite of college commencement as desirable for attaining status and position, then it seems to many only fair and just that all youth of the tribe have an opportunity to pass through the initiation ceremony. More specifically, it is argued that no youth in the tribe should be kept from college commencement because he lacks money or other types of support. This is particularly true of our ethnic minorities who find so many other obstacles in their paths. As long as the tribe holds to a democratic ethos, it cannot be true to itself if access to an honored or influential position is blocked to offspring of even the lowliest members of the tribe simply because of their deprived situation.

The American tribe, through custom and usage, has also designated the college as a hunting ground for mates and as a place for carrying on the rite of courtship. The growth of the coeducational college has been a rapid one in this country. Even in the traditional citadels of separate education for men and women, the walls of sex separation are beginning to crumble. The effect is somewhat obvious. The massing of large numbers of unattached young men and women on the college campus has meant that an important part of college

life is involved in rituals of mate-search and courtship. This has also
been true in the non-coeducational colleges, which always seemed to
be near other collegiate sources of dating supply. On occasion, this
activity seems to take on such importance that it threatens to overshadow all others. The frustrations, uncertainties, and excitements involved in the highly complex dating-mating game add great pressures
to the college student's environment. Moreover, a significant number
of students have been taking on the joys and sorrows of marriage and
family. When the uncertainties and doubts of courtship or early marriage and family are augmented by the pressures for grades and graduation, it is small wonder that most observers characterize college life
as anxiety-filled years in which many students attempt cleverly to beat
the academic game and search long and sometimes desperately for
satisfying human relationships with other youthful members of the
tribe. Suicide, dropping out, underachieving, interpersonal aggression,
and serious personality problems are among the consequences of this
tension-torn college life.

Tension or not, the rituals of mate-search and courtship are
not likely to disappear from the college scene. The college must find
ways to relieve the tensions and to provide a more pleasant and inviting environment for the search. Dramatic improvement on both counts
is needed on many of the college campuses in our country. To search
for beauty where there is ugliness, to look for freedom where there is
depressing crowding and unreasonable restriction, and to seek knowledge of self and world where there is form rather than substance is to
find a shadow of what might be.

Life 6: As Critic

In its ideal state, the college community leads the life of critic.
Throughout the whole range of subject matter, faculty and students
hopefully are involved in focusing critically on the conventional wisdom and the orthodoxies of past and present. Whatever the discipline
or subject matter, wherever the place in the curriculum, and whenever
the opportunity occurs, criticism is an order of the college day. The
college attempts to insure that no person will emerge from four years
of study without understanding that the search for truth, beauty, and
justice must go on throughout life if college is to be more than memo-
rization and regurgitation of dogma and orthodoxy. The instrument
of the search is the critical attitude of the faculty and students alike.

From this perspective, college life is often subversive—not usually in the violent revolutionary sense but in the sense that, at its best, the college asks all who enter to come with inquiring and critical minds, willing to examine all assumptions and to question the values of man. Men of scholarship recognize the impermanency of truth, the shifting perceptions of beauty and the contextual character of justice, and they attempt to make this recognition known and appreciated by all members of the college community. The physics of Newton is not the physics of Einstein; the painting of Raphael is not the painting of Picasso; and the justice of the preindustrial age is not the justice of the post-industrial era. The college must preserve the critical marketplace of ideas, where error can be challenged in the glare of rational argument rather than in the heat of violent conflict. When John Stuart Mill contended that all mankind has no right to silence one dissenter and that people should be convinced, not coerced, he was providing not only the rationale for a free society, but also an eloquent statement upon which stands the case for the college as critic.

In this context, an unsettling uncertainty about college life and a danger of misunderstanding and suppression prevail. The intellect that is programmed to the thought of "seek and ye shall find" may be disconcerted by the substitution of the critical spirit for the promise of answers and may tend toward cynicism. Students and even some faculty may reject this aspect of college life. Yet the college that is not guided by critical analysis is a static museum exhibiting its discoveries to the uninvolved, glancing parade. The college must discern how to defend its need to give free play to this role of critic against the rise of the possibility of cynicism and rejection within the institution. It must also worry about the growth of efforts to repress this role by those outside the institution who either misunderstand its crucial necessity or wish to suppress any significant challenge to the status quo.

Of the two aspects of the problem, the danger of outside misunderstanding and suppression is probably the greater in the present climate in the United States. The college, its faculty, and students—through action as well as argument—have become more visible critics of the social system and decisions made within that system. Today in a period of unusual uncertainty about standards and ways of organizing life, the American college is receiving more attention as the social criticisms from faculty and particularly by students mount. Whether American society will be tolerant and sophisticated enough to permit basic criticism to live with any vibrancy on its publicly subsidized campuses is not clear. Certainly, questions about the limits of criticism will occupy the public dialogue concerning colleges for many years to come.

Life 7: As Change Agent

The college as critic has raised the concerned attention of the public. The college as change agent has plunged the college into deep controversy. Although the defenders of the status quo (and they probably constitute a smashing majority in the United States) may be willing to countenance an institutional role that leads to criticism of life styles, knowledge, and social systems, there appears to be less willingness to support the college role of direct change agent. But even here the picture is clouded because the colleges have long been instrumental in initiating and promoting change in various aspects of the life of society. Indeed, public support seems to have come in part because the colleges were agents of change. The range of areas in which the college has been expected to promote change is great. Some of the very beginnings of mass public higher education were connected to the desires of the agricultural interests for help from the college in changing methods of farming. The colleges have also been supported (sometimes grudgingly) in initiating major changes that make us what we are today in public health, public law, the application of new scientific techniques in business and industry, civil rights, social welfare, national defense. These change activities were supported by society or segments of it. But support was not constant, and some of the changes growing out of the campus were accomplished against major opposition from many important people in the society. Nonetheless, and despite occasional set backs, the promotion of change has been a part of the role of the college. However, in controversial areas the college community has rarely spoken as an institution. Rather it has been individual scholars and groups of scholars who led the way.

Not only were the members of the college community directly involved in change, but, in a more indirect manner, the college community has also had an impact by influencing students who have gone out to assume places of importance in the society. Although one should not overestimate the magnitude of the college-induced changes in attitude, it should be remembered that great societal changes can come about as the result of small shifts in attitude and belief on the part of large numbers of people. It is interesting to note that in most public opinion polls, the college-educated generally register as more liberal, more oriented to change than other groups singled out.

Notwithstanding the fact that the college has clearly played a significant role in the changes that our society has gone through, it probably cannot accurately be characterized as a launching pad for direct, immediate social change. In a sense American colleges have been very much a part of the change-resistant mainstream of American life. Even today when the cases for departure from Vietnam, for urgency in solving problems of race and poverty, for a stepped-up attack on the problems of conservation and crime, and for adjustment of our national priorities seem almost beyond debate, the majority of the college community is probably not overwhelmingly different from many other attentive publics in pressing for change. Many members of the college community—faculty, students, and administrators—have a stake in things pretty much as they are and see very little need for a radical uprooting of the major institutions of American life. This does not mean that many college people are not working hard at seeking change in many areas of the social system, from Vietnam to poverty. They surely are, but many seem to be opting for nonrevolutionary change which would leave the basic socioeconomic institutions intact.

One of the major problems for the colleges, particularly for the faculty members who wish to nurture the life of the campus as change agent, is that scholarly, academic debate, careful analysis, peaceful persuasion, and patient work through channels has come under blistering attack from significant numbers of our brightest students and some faculty. Discouraged by what they consider to be the inability of society to be reformed rapidly enough and disenchanted with the traditional change styles of the college, they are turning to direct action techniques of civil disobedience, massive confrontation, and even threats and intimidation. Some radical students and faculty have even raised a challenge to the continued existence of the college as it is presently structured.

Ironically, the radical threat comes at just the time when the reactionaries are mounting their attack on the college for almost opposite reasons. There is wide belief in certain circles that the colleges have involved themselves too much in questions of social action and social change. The troubles facing American society are attributed to radical faculty and students who stir up problems and create dissension where none existed before, at least not in such intensity. The college is condemned for both effectiveness and ineffectiveness in its role of critic and change agent. Presently, the critics on the right seem to have become even more stridently obsessed about any action, from poverty picketing to draft resistance, that tends to demonstrate how far from ideals we have wandered. While this obsessive antichange attitude may be hidden in the rhetoric of accusation of un-American activity (for example, "If you don't love America, leave it!"), much of the criticism stems from the fact the college pressure for change threatens established interests and calls for revision of our sense of priority and style of private life. To those in positions of power and influence, this means that their prerogatives may be altered and their life styles threatened. Assessed in these terms, the college becomes a source of great danger which must be carefully watched, thoroughly controlled, and directly circumscribed.

Another related, perhaps more perplexing problem for the college is the possible contradiction between the college as change agent and as a place for the challenge, exploration, and criticism of all orthodoxies. When the college, as an institution, takes a position on the nature or direction a given change should take, does it not run the risk of becoming an orthodoxy itself? Is the college in some ways an institution like any other, or is it expected to play a peculiarly separate role? If a government, a lodge, a church, or a political club can take a position on Vietnam, pornography, or capitalism, why not the college? Why not have the college community vote on its position vis-à-vis this particular political question or that certain social issue? What happens to the college as an arena for continuing debate if it has already taken an institutional position on a subject? Are there not some issues which are so clearly within the educational and human commitment of the college that it must take a position? If the college is to take positions on certain issues, is the style in which it does so of major importance? These questions, perhaps more than any others, dramatize the uneasy dilemmas of the college in an America filled with problems of social change.

Life 8: As Place for Self-Discovery

The American college has been offering the student an invitation to self-discovery. Through encounters with various fields of knowledge while attending college the student is to find himself, to discover and develop his talents, and to join the larger society as a man or woman better equipped than most to deal with the onrushing complexities of life. Whether it ever works precisely that way is doubtful. But it is true that significant numbers of young men and women have found new vistas open to them at college, new worlds to conquer and new satisfactions to be gained. As more and more people flooded into the universities and colleges and the society became more massive and complex, some professors and some students questioned whether the college was really serving as a place of self-discovery or was a diploma mill whose diplomas were necessary to get a better job or a better husband.

Germane to the whole question was the argument raised on a number of college campuses during the fifties over the conception of the college as a personal need-filling institution. Was college to be a place where the student was invited to develop "life adjustment" skills or a place where the student was required to adjust to the demanding task of acquiring knowledge in the various complex subject fields? Battles were fought, scars were received, and the victories in many places seemed to have gone—though rarely in a clear fashion—to those who insisted upon "all power to the disciplines." In retrospect, these victories may now seem pyrrhic in light of the rising tide of student discontent with college as they experienced it in the sixties. Certainly the outbreak of free universities and experimental colleges suggests that significant numbers of students are questioning whether colleges have much to do with their lives and their felt needs.

Students increasingly raise questions of relevance about the college curriculum. Do college courses and programs really prepare them to meet the confusing challenges of postindustrial America at either the interpersonal or the social level? Where are the utopias of the professional men and women of the college? Some have argued that the increasing secularization of American life has made it imperative that the college assume a role of moral leadership and become a place of conscience as well as a place of knowledge. Many feel that the ethical neutrality they find as they enter college provides few satisfying life models for a person searching for a meaning to life and for ways to cope with the self-destructive potentials of modern society. The question of whether the college can or should lead to the discovery of attractive alternatives to opting out of society either by apathetic alienation or by departure into the other worlds of psychodelia or primitive communalism may be deeper than we like to admit.

Life 9: As Corporation

The final life necessary to complete our sketch of the current college is the life the college leads as a corporation. Even a casual glance at the organizational structure of most of the colleges in America reveals that the institutional models in the business and industrial worlds have their close counterparts in the world of education. Boards of directors (trustees), chairmen of the board, chief administrative officers—whether they be presidents, chancellors, deans, department chairmen or directors—have become ubiquitous parts of our college structure. From our beginning days as a nation to the present, many of our colleges have been organized and run in part like a business corporation. Today many believe that the colleges, whether public or private, are nonprofit corporations in which the faculty are employees. The rightness of hierarchical authority seems so thoroughly accepted that the thought of discarding or revising this model seriously distresses certain of the attentive publics.

Is the corporate model appropriate at this time and place? Encompassed in this general question are many more specific questions relating to the role of the college and its governance. Does the corporate model provide the most efficient and effective framework for development of scholarship and inspired teaching? In an institution where freedom of inquiry is essential, are hierarchical decision-making lines facilitative or repressive? Can the faculty member be reasonably certain of obtaining impartial justice as he questions the conventional wisdom of the day? Do the boards of governors or trustees have sufficient knowledge of the educational product to involve themselves actively in the management of the corporation? Are the boards of the public colleges and universities truly representative of the public, or are they skewed badly in the direction of vested wealth and conservatism? Are the mechanisms of governance such that boards are encouraged to play an advocate and explaining role as enthusiastically as some play the governing role? These and many more questions are raised by the role of the college as a corporation.

The corporate model runs headlong into the quasi-independent, self-governing community model which so many faculty and now students hold as the proper structure for handling the affairs of the academy. And that conflict provides some of the underlying reasons for the continual conflict between faculty and the administration of the corporation. Many faculty, like other professionals, clearly feel that they should be masters in their own academic houses, and that those who nose around in an unfriendly, domineering manner are intruders to be resisted and turned out. As we write these words it is difficult to tell what, if any, bases for compromise and change remain during our present time of trouble. But men and women of good will must tackle this problem if the colleges are not to be severely damaged by dramatic pressures in the new falls and springs of our discontent.

A mere enumeration of nine lives (or is it ten or eleven?) of the college points to its complexity and its contradictions. Instrument of change, yet vehicle for preservation. A quasi-home, yet a semi-factory. A critic, yet a defender. An explorer, yet a conserver. An arena for romance, yet a place for serious study. A portal to opportunity, yet a gate of selectivity and quality control. A way for freedom and originality, yet a channel for deception and conformity. The college is an institution with so much diversity and from which so much is expected—in terms of training, preparing, questioning and problem-solving—that to picture it as a place of quiet harmony and pristine reflection removed from the world is to distort what the college is or can be. It is a place of conflict and contradiction or it is nothing. Like the church, it is a part of the world, but also apart from it. Also like the church, it has its own traffic in evil and its own inconsistencies. The men and women of the college can destroy it by attempting to force it to choose one life at the expense of all others or by failing to appreciate the complexity of its charge and the elegance of its mission. They may find that its destruction is the destruction of hope. For a college is one of the few nurturing places of the collective conscience of mankind.

The chapters that follow dramatize the very deep difficulty in which the lives of the college are now enmeshed. As we attempt to analyze the confusing nature of this difficulty, time and again we find the several lives we have been discussing under severe attack and searching question. For a college one of the consequences of crisis is exposure of its weaknesses and its strengths as it receives challenge after challenge. Challenge from within the institution by students and faculty and challenge from outside the institution by trustees, chancellor, legislators, and patron public necessitate a reexamination of the several lives we lead. Out of this educational arena comes a cry of concern about the life styles of the college and a developing demand for action. It is in the spirit of concern and with a commitment to suggest lines of action that we attack the issues in the remainder of the book.

TWO

Student Initiative
for Radical Reform

To the public, San Francisco State appears as a place of occasional strife, riot, and rebellion. Much attention has focused on the politics of confrontation and disruption, to the neglect of the exciting, fledgling effort at reform that had been underway for several years prior to the troubles. Much of this effort at reform used the regular channels of the institution and was student initiated. This chapter attempts to delineate the theory and practices of these reform efforts and comments briefly on what went wrong. The next chapter explores in some detail the formulation of the radical and extreme patterns of ideology, which came to overshadow the ideology of reform.

One pervasive panacea that crops up whenever people consider the problems caused by youthful dissent over the issues of poverty, racism or education states that "we should treat the disease, not the symptoms." In terms of action strategies for college and university policy makers, this advice indicates that these authorities should not waste their energies attempting to repress student rebellions or punish the dissenters, but rather should seek out the causes of this disease—and then give first priority to eliminating them.

Viewed from this perspective, the two year turmoil at San Francisco State, climaxed by the four month student-faculty strike, is difficult to understand. Goaded by an informed, dedicated, aggressive student body, leadership at State had moved faster and further than most colleges in the nation in making its curriculum relevant, in enlarging the student power base, and in responding to the desires of its ethnic students. Journalists, educators, and foundation executives designated the college as liberal, progressive, and academically distinguished.

Possibly another cliche—"too little, too late"—explains the failure of this treatment to prevent widespread confrontations. It may also be that academic distinction accompanied by the realistic possibility of liberal reform and change has inherent dangers. The Commission on Campus Government and Student Dissent of the American Bar Association comments: "It is ironic that many of the disruptive disturbances have taken place in institutions least deficient in their sensitivity to student concerns. Indeed, the commission believes that the very excellence of a given university and its lack of repressive policies may be conditions conducive to unrest." This irony of disruptions despite sensitivity and excellence may be explained by a theory about rebellion and revolution propounded by James C. Davies:

> The J-curve is this: revolution is most likely to take place when a prolonged period of rising expectations and gratifications is followed by a short period of reversal, during which the gap between expectations and gratifications quickly widens and becomes intolerable. The frustration that develops, when it is intense and widespread in the society, seeks outlets in violent action.

> This is an assertion about the state of mind of individual people in a society who are likely to revolt. It says their state of mind, their mood, is one of high tension and rather generalized hostility, derived from the widening of the gap between what they want and what they get. They fear not just that things will not get better but—even more crucially—that ground will be lost that they have already gained. The mood of rather generalized hostility directed generally outward begins to turn toward government. People so frustrated not only fight with other members of their families and neighbors, they also jostle one another in crowds and increase their aggressiveness as pedestrians, bus passengers, and drivers of cars. When events and news media and writers and speakers encourage the direction of hostilities toward the government, the dispersed and mutual hostility becomes focused on a common target. The hostility among individuals diminishes. The dissonant energy becomes a resonant, very powerful force that heads like a great tidal wave or forest fire toward the established government, which it may engulf.[1]

[1] H. Graham and T. Gurr, *Violence in America* (New York: Signet, 1969), pp. 671–672.

Students at San Francisco State—black, white, radical, liberal—certainly went through a period of rising expectations between 1964 and 1967. During the summer and fall of 1968, student proponents of educational and social reform faced growing limitations on needed resources and facilities as well as resistance within the college administration and the trustees to their plans and their autonomy.

The rueful truth is that, during the five years prior to the 1968 rebellion, at San Francisco State various student groups had considered most of the major issues of American higher education identified in Chapter One. In that process they developed campus and community programs of instruction and service. They organized pressure to influence college and community policy in relation to issues of concern to them. From the early sixties, reform minded student leaders worked hard to identify faculty members and administrators who were willing to support novel programs and assist students in influencing the college bureaucracy, faculty who could restrain themselves from coopting the student initiated programs.

By spring 1968, the major programs developed through such efforts were loosely associated in the student directed Center for Innovative Education, financed in large part by student body funds and assisted by the assignment of about twenty Educational Opportunity Program people. The major programs, involving perhaps two thousand students, included the Experimental College, the tutorial program, the work study program (Community Services Institute), and black studies.

The programs also gained unprecedented support during the summer of 1968 through a fifty thousand dollar grant from the Carnegie Corporation, with the expectation that the grant would be renewed in the fall of 1968. (In fact, approval for a one hundred thousand dollar renewal was obtained in November 1968, contingent on stabilizing the campus. The campus was not stabilized. The funds were not released by the foundation.) The programs as well as the student leadership rapidly gained national attention among educational leaders seeking reform in higher education. Programs such as the Experimental College and black studies at San Francisco State helped set the pace in other colleges and universities. For example, the Experimental College, launched during the 1965–1966 academic year, was the first in the California state college system. By August 1968, there were nine experimental colleges in the eighteen member college system.

Harold Taylor, who had followed closely the innovative developments at San Francisco State for a number of years, wrote in 1967:

> These students were without doubt leaders in educational reform on the campus, but they thought of themselves as persons actively engaged in carrying on education itself rather than trying to develop a new system of education for teachers or even for students in the context of the college as a whole. I believe that the contribution they have made at San Francisco State, not merely to the enrichment of the intellectual and social environment of San Francisco State, but to the development of projects similar to their own on other campuses is a serious and important one. It is the basis for one set of answers to the drastic need for reform of undergraduate teaching and the education of teachers.[2]

Three semesters later, the student led programs were in serious disarray or had been largely wiped out, funds to sustain them had been withdrawn or impounded by the attorney general of the state, and the prospects for redevelopment had been dimmed by President S. I. Hayakawa's reduction of the student body fee from ten dollars per semester to one dollar. Further, action by the California state college trustees had drastically revised the relationship to the college of auxiliary corporations, including the Associated Students, providing for much tighter program and policy control by the president and the trustees. Black and ethnic studies had moved into the regularly financed college curriculum through the organization of a new School of Ethnic Studies. The patterns of student initiative and institutional response combined again at San Francisco State to smash the efforts of young adults to work within the system to revitalize it in line with their diagnosis of its ills and their ideas of needed changes.

The span of time—September 1965 to September 1969—considered in this analysis is short in the perspective of the development of a college. It represents, however, a generation of students shaped by the civil rights and other youth led struggles of the early sixties. Five of the six student body presidents serving from September 1963 to June 1969 were actively involved with innovative educational and community action programs. The single exception, Phil Garlington

---

[2] H. Taylor, *The World and the American Teacher* (Washington, D.C.: The American Association of Teacher Education, 1968), p. 197.

during 1967–1968, is credited in the Orrick Report[3] on the San Francisco State College crisis with contributing to the student frustrations leading up to the student strike in the fall of 1968.

The leaders in this prolonged attempt to use the resources of the student government to give a new direction to the college were both articulate and prolific in their statements of purpose. And so there exists a wide range of student literature that speaks to these basic student concerns. Some statements stress the learning styles, some focus on the humanistic purposes, and some address themselves to the larger goals of institutional and social change. One of the most comprehensive documents is a seventy-four page report by Mike Vozick entitled "The College and the Community." The most distinctive feature of the many programs that were developed over this six year period was the emphasis upon community involvement as a way of both facilitating social change and making learning relevant and personal. In September 1965, student body president Terry McGann sent a copy of Vozick's report to a number of faculty and administrators, urging a critical response. The tone and content of McGann's covering letter contrasts sharply with the strike support attitudes of the Associated Students officers and the program people expressed three years later in November 1968. His letter states in part:

> Over the past few years, students, faculty, and administrators have moved toward working relationships of a sort which few colleges enjoy. We at the Associated Students are proud of our part in this movement. . . . We believe it is important to think before we act in the community; and that it is important to *act* on the most serious problems, as a part of coming to know the world. We want any program which emerges to be an all-out college effort and we specifically want your support. . . . We do know that a program with any real meaning will take time to develop. We also know that we must start, now.

The Vozick report asserts that students live in the world and are concerned about it.[4] They do not see the college experience as isolated from the problems of the world or the community. "The core of the feeling is a sense of isolation, of powerlessness, a sense that one is merely

[3] W. H. Orrick, *Shut It Down! A College in Crisis: A Report of the National Commission on the Causes and Prevention of Violence* (Washington, D.C.: U. S. Government Printing Office, 1969), p. 106.

[4] The subsequent quotations and content derive from Vozick's effort to summarize the range of ideas student reformists were working on in 1965.

a spectator of the decisions and processes that determine one's life." The thrust of the student generated programs was to be an intensification of efforts already underway to relate higher education to life, with the perceptions of students determining the quality and style of that relationship. The assumption was, further, that sympathetic faculty and administrators would support such efforts on campus and would back up off-campus projects with professional support and ideological commitment, but on the students' own terms.

Vozick's analysis, along with the rationale developed to guide the tutorial programs, the Experimental College, and the other major student directed enterprises, including the projected plans for a new student union, provided both a critique of the status quo in higher education and a projection of the directions in which concerned students were planning to move. The ideas and projected directions give something of the flavor of new left thought on the San Francisco State campus at that time. The hope shines through that students, faculty, and administrators could work to build better communities both on campus and off. "Our survival requires it."

This process was to be based on the "recognition that the mark of an educated man is the critical judgment he brings to bear on himself, on his society, and on his government, rather than his passive acceptance of authority or his submission to social pressures." The revolution in knowledge offers the choice of meeting the physical needs of man in ways that "would have seemed incredible . . . . when the college was founded" or of "ending those needs in a . . . . holocaust." New means must be devised by each generation to manage the transmission of existing knowledge and the creation of new knowledge.

The college was to help those in the larger community assess pertinent new knowledge and function creatively as well. "Men must be kept alert to the continual uncovering of vital new understandings, no matter how much this knowledge challenges popular modes of living or is for other reasons controversial or unpopular." But this responsibility also requires sensitivity to underlying community needs so that knowledge is used to enhance "the possibility of the sense of community fulfilling its potentiality of liberating mankind." The students assumed that "the more the involvement of this college in its community deepens, the more the people in the college can hope to affect the direction in which the community develops. The more involved the

community feels in the college, the more it will support the college."
(This assumption bears testing.)

This student analysis of the nature of the college and the city
stresses the breakdown of communication, the rise of alienation and
conflict, the festering racial tensions in the city, the endemic poverty
amid affluence, and the pervasive sense of powerlessness, uselessness,
and exclusion from decision making. The analysis was a conscious attempt to raise "the hardest questions about community and conflict
which any serious program of the college in the community must sooner
or later face up to. . . . To work for a world with less alienation
seems to be a fair description of a proper job for the educational
process." The best knowledge must be brought to bear on the deepest
community problems, and students have as deep a responsibility to
find ways of doing so as have other citizens.

> A program of the college in the community can be thought of as
> a loom, where threads of ideas and commitment to learning are
> woven into those of experience and commitment to action to pro-
> duce a flowing social fabric. To conduct this sort of program
> requires that some people at the college do not fear to become
> generalists concerned with integrating the intellectual work of
> others and outlining areas where new knowledge is needed. It
> means we must be willing to face the real problems and seek to
> create knowledge and transmit that knowledge to where it is
> needed. Research in the community is useful when it helps reveal
> a new need that was not perceived earlier, aids in strengthening
> an existing program by effectively evaluating the problems of that
> program, or when it succeeds in directly creating a new activity
> that meets a felt need in the community. It is plain that we need
> to develop greater facility at balancing feelings and formality in
> the institutions which emerge, relating the college to the com-
> munity. Ways must be found to avoid emphasis solely on knowl-
> edge or solely on action; the classroom and experience in the com-
> munity must come to complement each other especially when the
> relation we are seeking between them is one of creative conflict.

Repeatedly, in student discussions and in their speaking and
writing, the theme recurs that high quality education results from
casting direct experience against the canons and content of formal
knowledge in a search for deeper meanings, with the students and instructors committed to doing something significant about a need or a
problem. The concept predates the Christian era but is often buried
under the load of traditional, academic instruction limited to intellectual and verbal exercises. What is new is the increasing numbers of

students who perceive it as a general model of learning and embrace it so intensely that they are impelled to do the extensive analysis and organizing characteristic of the late sixties.

Basic to the perception of the emerging student leadership was a classification of organizations and institutions as those which emphasize "feelingful, human adaptive qualities of which one might say that the people are more important than the organization" and those "which emphasize formal, rational, structural qualities in which organization is of greatest importance." Although the two types of institutions were not seen as mutually exclusive, the reform movement wanted to stake its commitments on the former in shaping its programs, in seeking liaison with other organizations, and in pressing formal, structurally stable organizations in the direction of "adaptation to human feelings in a mass culture."

The involvement of many of the students in the middle and late sixties reflected crucial, earlier periods of personal testing and growth in civil rights activities, the Peace Corps, and community involvement. In their long deliberations they were able to pool perceptions of social, political, and educational problems from a variety of direct experiences. Efforts were made to glean helpful knowledge and methodologies from their formal education. Their deliberations showed a conscious determination to shape the issues and determine the needs to which their efforts were directed, needs which education and social organizations should serve. The students acknowledged the difficulties of attempting to promote social change as a part of education and personal development and accepted conflict as a necessary corollary.

The students' independent efforts to conceive and plan a program of education and community action were paralleled in the activities of several schools and a number of departments and individuals at State. Professors in humanities and other areas volunteered to try to work with the youth in trouble in the Haight Ashbury. A faculty member gave free service as a psychological consultant to the medical center (in the same neighborhood) that was operated on a shoestring with dedicated volunteers. A professor of education developed a college-student-teacher-community centered teacher preparation program tied in with curriculum development and in-service teacher preparation. In 1968 this program won a national award as one of five significant programs in teacher preparation.

The exchange of artists between the campus and the Bay Area

extended to students through the Poetry Center and through the development of neighborhood arts projects. The program of urban studies was launched, and plans were formulated for an ambitious Urban Teaching Center to be open to scholars and students around the world. This program was aborted, largely because Congress failed to fund the International Education Act of 1965. In December 1965, some faculty in the School of Education were pushing to involve the college as a key contractor for neighborhood and community development in model programs focused on a complex of schools but drawing together the full range of educational and social services in coordinated efforts to improve community life. At the same time the resources of the college and community were to be made available to students so that they could both learn and teach. Somewhat parallel proposals came from professors in interdisciplinary studies in social sciences and in political science.

The students were not working in a vacuum. The ferment in the college made a broad base for growing success in gaining foundation and federal grants for research, development, and training projects. The college was far ahead of many other institutions in the system in operating development programs in the ghettoes, and in socially disorganized areas in West Africa and Latin America.

Permeating these conceptions for involving the students with their own education and for involving students and the institution with the community and its concerns was a carefully reasoned theory of institutional change. It was assumed that as students began to take charge of their own lives and education, they would become a decisive force within the college for modifying its operation to give more power to students. It was assumed that as students had experience with meaningful educational activities, they would insist on formulating a curriculum and a teaching style that spoke to their real needs. And it was assumed that as the community became enmeshed with the college, it would press for new power relationships that would ensure a strong community voice in institutional decision making. But the expectation, probably equally important with these assumptions, was that, as faculty and administrators participated in these student-initiated plans for educational reform, they would become convinced of the validity of the plans and would encourage changes in the operation of the college so that these new roles and styles could become incorporated in the on-going institution. Facilitating alternative models for institutional operation was preferred at this time to confrontation or revolution as a way to social change.

Few faculty or administrators perceived this long-range strategy or the deep seriousness of the student leaders. Some encouraged student developed programs as an indication of the basic liberality of the college. Minor adaptations of college policy reflected the view that student-led programs were parallel or auxiliary to the main concerns of the college.

The explicit student prescriptions for treating the societal and college disease rather than expending energy on the symptoms are here delineated in three of the Associated Student programs that developed during this period: the Experimental College, the student developed program for evaluating faculty (MAX), and the Community Services Institute. (A fourth, the black studies effort, is discussed in Chapter Four.) The next section describes these programs in some detail.

Experimental College

The growing ideas about personal development, concern for social service, and needed social change as a base for revitalized education were taking shape in the fall of 1965 and were reflected in the Experimental College. Three student initiated seminars in education provided a beginning. The following semester saw twenty-three student organized seminars. By spring 1968, some 1,500 students were registered in Experimental College courses, and nine different patterns of experimental colleges were under way in the eighteen college system. The July 1968 meeting of the state college trustees concentrated its attention on a testy hearing and evaluation of the experimental colleges, with special attention to the daddy of them all at San Francisco State. By January 1969, the Experimental College at State had been destroyed. Some of its remaining fragments attempted to function as pseudo-underground activities, while others such as black or ethnic studies were incorporated into the formally approved curriculum of the college, where the struggle for autonomy continues. For a brief period the Experimental College and the student developed programs associated with it captured national attention among foundations, colleges and universities, and officials in higher education associations and in the United States Office of Education. *Newsweek* (November 7, 1966) referred to it as "Do It Yourself U" and the "most promising attempt at student initiated reform."

The central purpose of the Experimental College was to encourage students, faculty, and community persons to organize instructional activities in areas not adequately treated in the existing college curriculum. The basic premise was "that students can and should take an active responsibility in their education." The sixty page proposed schedule for fall 1966 included a rationale for the yearling college and course descriptions in the following areas, each coordinated by one or more students: advising, communication and the arts, social change, black culture and arts, urban communities and change, arts and letters, styles of thought, interpersonal communications, and a scattering of independent courses. The rationale provided in the 1966 course schedule by Mike Vozick and Jim Nixon follows:

> *The Experimental College: What Is It?*   In the fall of last year, it was three student initiated seminars and it had no name. At the beginning of the spring semester, it was twenty-three student organized seminars, a visiting professor, and a name (The Special Section) that didn't stick. Then it came to be 350 students studying and working together, in learning groups for which they shared responsibility, with twenty-five student organizers and thirty faculty advisers: The Experimental College. The Academic Senate and the Council of Academic Deans liked it, and sixty-six students who wanted academic credit were able to get that through special study and other arrangements. The kinds of things studied included social change, personal development, avant-garde art, education, and the ordering of knowledge. Perhaps because it so simply got at the problem of freeing students to learn in their own way, it received national recognition as a new model for innovation in American higher education.

> *What Is The Idea Behind It?*   The idea is that students ought to take responsibility for their own education. The assertion is that you can start learning anywhere, as long as you really care about the problem that you tackle and how well you tackle it. The method is one which asks you to learn how you learn, so you can set the highest conceptual standards of accomplishment for yourself. The assumption is that you are capable of making an open-ended contract with yourself to do some learning and capable of playing a major role in evaluating your own performance. The claim is that if people, students, faculty, and administrators work with each other in these ways, that the finest quality education will occur. The Experimental College was built to develop a new style of learning and teaching, to serve as a model for the direction in which San Francisco State College might grow. The experiment has no single experimenter. Each person who participates joins in setting the conditions for his or her own learning,

and each organizer is free to set a different context for participants.

How Is It Run?   Anyone can try to organize a course on
anything. The only requirement is that he accurately describe
what he is trying to do. The students make the final decision about
whether a proposal becomes a course by signing up to attend or
not. The organizer has the responsibility for setting up the plan
for the way the course will run and for talking with any student
who wants to join. Entering a course means making an agreement
with an organizer about what each expects of the other. Credit
can be arranged only through agreements between students and
faculty, using one of the regular college procedures. Organizers
will work with each other in different ways. Some are joined into
areas; some of these areas have formed staff organizations which
will have regular meetings. These areas are not disciplines or
departments; they are characterized by the particular people associated with them, and the philosophy and style of working
which emerges from those people. Representatives from each area
come together to provide overall coordination, administrative services, and planning. Everyone participating in the Experimental
College is invited to regularly scheduled Experimental College
town meetings, which will consider current problems and seek to
set a direction for the work of existing or proposed new areas. If
problems of particular difficulty arise, special conferences to deal
with them will be called.

How Do You Get Into It?   You can sign up for a course
by coming to the Gallery Lounge and talking with the organizer.
If necessary, this discussion can take place at the first session of
the class, but you should be signed up in advance to protect your
place. You can design a course and work to organize it. This
means writing a description, talking to people who might be interested in learning with you, and making arrangements with the
Experimental College office to have your course listed. It is also a
good idea to seek out some faculty members to consult with about
some of the problems you may have to face. You can join one of
the area staff organizations or the office administrative staff if you
want to do any of the support jobs that are needed. Participate
in "The Quiet Revolution."

The sense grew among student activists that they must have a
major share in setting their educational goals, in selecting educational
experiences and evaluating for themselves the worth of such efforts.
The proposed thrust into the community and the development of the
Experimental College were examples of student action to propose
alternate programs within the framework of the college. The students
sought assistance where they could find it inside the college, as long
as it could be gained largely on their own terms. Elbow room to ex-

periment was crucial; pressure on the conventional functions of the college and its personnel was equally important. This flavor is sharply illustrated in the description set forth in the 1966 schedule of the Experimental College advising program organized by Lew Engle. (Engle was a graduate student in psychology and the architect of MAX, the faculty evaluation program discussed later in this chapter.) To some the description below may sound subversive, to others it may appear to deal with content every student has a right to know.

> The purpose of the advising office is to supplement the regular advising program by providing a place where students can find out how to use the regular institution to their best advantage. When a person first comes to college, he can begin to make the familiar fundamental decisions which determine his life. He need not allow educators to decide what he should know, advertisers to decide what he should buy, and politicians to decide how he should live and die. For the person who feels that the standard programs do not meet his needs, the advising office can tell him how existing college regulations permit him to: write his own major, substitute courses he wants for required G. E. and major courses, organize his own course, get credit for individual work in which he is interested, obtain a waiver for almost any college rule or regulation. The advising office will also maintain a file of student descriptions of courses offered by the regular college.

The 1966 Experimental College fall schedule described a course organized by Russell Bass,[5] The Possibilities for Magazine and Newspapers:

> It will work toward a theory of the meaning of format. We will probe such questions as: how the various aspects of a publication order and reflect its editorial policy; how does a publication order reflect the environment it serves; how, as a culture force, might a publication act to increase and decrease people's expectations of what they can do as individuals.

Resource people were used, and each student worked with an on- or off-campus publication. The fact that the growing underground press provided experience had additional significance. Most existed because they were antiestablishment. Thus, students could arrange credit for learning heretical approaches to reporting.

Courses were offered in critical assessment of disc jockeys, "new

[5] Russell Bass was elected president of the Associated Students in the spring of 1968 and served in that role during the hectic 1968–1969 academic year.

wave" films, and theater. A course in involvement theater organized by Loren Means is described, in part, as follows: "This course is an attempt to create a genre of theater in which the audience is involved to the greatest extent possible—perplexed, threatened, and ultimately seduced into total intellectual, emotional [involvement]." Participants were to explore plays and theater games reflecting the above approach as well as new plays written and directed by students.

Within the framework of the Experimental College, four student organizers founded The Institute for Social Change. One of the four, Jim Nixon, was president of the Associated Students at that time. The description says,

> The Institute rests its existence on the belief that meaningful social change is possible when those seeking change know what they want, of whom they want it, and why they want it. Among the basic problems which the Institute is attempting to address is the myth that men are essentially alone and powerless, that they can neither fight nor provide alternatives to established institutions. The Institute hopes to change these doubts and fears—not by arguing, but by helping small groups work effectively to bring about change. The Institute will act as a research and experimental center which helps groups know what they want and which helps them evaluate, report on, and give context to their work.

The student organizers assumed that institutions exist to fulfill needs. Those needs must be identified and considered if the institution is to be sensibly changed or abolished. "Consequently, if the institution of war were to be eliminated, it would have to be replaced with a substitute that fulfilled the same function." The institute sought to make explicit a theory for accomplishing social change, to develop a "mutually held but tentative world view for evaluating organizational purposes and methods," to test the functioning of organizations in light of their own assumptions and in light of the tentative world view, and to "consider the differences between the two sets of criteria and develop a final set." The students stubbornly searched for ways of evaluating and adapting or changing the world around them in keeping with their own pattern of premises at a given time. At the same time, their frame of reference, their world view, was being changed largely through their efforts to act and derive meaning from assessment of such experience.

One of the most troublesome aspects of the student program approaches is precisely the determination of the students to act on real problems—including institutional arrangements from cafeteria prices to the grading system and the hiring and evaluation of personnel. The stylish leisurely approaches to change in a college are thrown into disarray by the introduction of new variables that arise outside the established patterns. What students view as "creative conflict," deliberately generated, is seen by college officials, faculty, and trustees as presumptuous disruption of their roles or prerogatives. The most prevalent traditional model for teaching and learning casts the students in passive, recipient roles, under continuous supervision.

The notion that students can or should strike out on their own in search of priorities arising from their definition of needs is not new. Current rhetoric in education says that learning is a lifelong process and that a major function of education is to teach students to assume responsibility for their continuing education. A decade of elementary and secondary school ferment and reform has raised to the level of cliches terms such as *discovery learning,* self-directed *independent study, inquiry training,* and *self-assessment.* But students are not supposed to cut loose on their own until our final stamp of institutional approval has been placed on them, a degree or a credential. And then they are expected to go it alone somewhere else so that, if they stub their toes, they will not embarrass their alma mater. For students to seize the initiative and then move to act on their own in the community and the college in serious efforts to effect changes is upsetting. Resistance results from the blithe intrusion of students into areas considered complex and sensitive and from the use of the college as a base of operations. Post-Sputnik education has succeeded beyond the intention of the college and community elders.

MAX: Maximizing Your Educational Possibilities

Student efforts to revamp their educational experiences were not confined to developing community action and work programs and alternative course patterns within the Experimental College. It was always a major part of their intent to have both a direct and indirect impact on the curriculum and on the teaching-learning processes of the whole college. The search for faculty sponsorship, for both independent study and experimental course credit, was one such effort.

The development of MAX was another. This student designed project evaluates regularly employed faculty on a five point scale over eight criteria. The results were published on campus to guide students in the choice of instructors, insofar as choices were available. MAX began as an Experimental College seminar for credit titled The Professor Evaluation Seminar. During the fall of 1967, questionnaires were distributed to and collected from about one thousand San Francisco State College students. The following description of MAX is from the spring 1968 Experimental College bulletin.

> The first edition, . . . containing evaluations of 213 professors, was published in time for spring registration, 1967. One thousand copies were printed. They were sold out in three days. In MAX San Francisco State College appears to have one of the best professor evaluations in the country. Recently its director, Lewis Engle, was asked to the U.S. National Students Association Annual Congress to address representatives on the techniques that went into MAX. The spring publication is the second edition and is available now.

The development of MAX was subsidized by the Associated Students. The disorders of 1968–1969 plus the impounding of student body funds interrupted the further development of MAX. It reappeared in the fall of 1970.

All faculty members are encouraged to cooperate in making the questionnaire available to their classes, enabling students to evaluate professors of the previous semester. The criteria reflect the MAX students' perception of a good professor. They provide a feedback system from students that enables them to help develop the criteria as the project continues from year to year. After professors are rated on the eight criteria, the rater is asked to rate the importance to him of each criterion, and to describe the good and bad points of the professor as accurately as possible. Analysis of patterns of response can assure development of evaluative criteria that are important to significant numbers of students.

It is axiomatic that criteria for evaluating instructional activities reflect a conception of excellent teaching. All eight criteria listed below are readily subsumed within conventional educational theory appropriate at all age levels: This professor motivated me to work on my own. This professor and I had excellent rapport. This professor allowed student participation in deciding the direction of the course. This professor graded fairly. This professor impressed me as having great knowledge of his subject. This professor was able to explain the material clearly. This professor was able to make this course relevant to contemporary life. This professor helped me learn to think for myself. The criteria are significant for what they do not include: adherence to rigid standards, expectation of subject mastery by students, concentration on achieving breadth or depth in the subject matter. The bias of the MAX criteria complements the educational ideology of the Experimental College and community program thrusts toward student autonomy. A premium is placed on self-direction and a qualitatively different relationship in the academic community based on empathy and colleague relationship rather than formality and paternalistic or autocratic models of faculty-student interaction. These criteria prize professors who know their stuff, can be lucid about it, and can help relate it to student life. MAX is the kind of thing a profession may well do for itself if its own deadwood is a serious concern to its members.

Community Services Institute: A Work/Study Program

The 1966 Experimental College bulletin carries a description of the program to be developed in work studies in the area of urban communities and change, organized by students Sharon Gold and Donna Mickelson. Their brief critique of existing approaches to community study and the teaching-learning processes sets initial guidelines for what became the Work/Study Program, renamed the Community Services Institute in spring 1968. A thirty unit bachelor of arts degree in community services was proposed in the spring of 1968, with five variant patterns. A description of the institute at that time listed forty students on the Work/Study staff, twenty-nine cooperating professors, and one dean—the dean of undergraduate studies. The 1966 statement says:

> College teachers and students purporting to study urban communities have tended to regard them as laboratories in which their theories could be tested or social experimentation could be performed. Writing and research were aimed at other academicians and students or at the heads of agencies. Thus people became either cannon fodder in internecine academic battles or—especially in poor neighborhoods—rationales and guidelines for those who held the power to direct, propel, or inhibit change. All of this was far removed from those to be affected and worked to perpetuate a passivity which was then termed "apathy" and used as an excuse to formulate more theories on which agencies could base policy. This area of the Experimental College is an attempt to find a third and more creative alternative based on a few basic assumptions: that students can learn most about communities by making them the environment of learning; that knowledge can

and ought to be gathered in response to needs of people actually living in communities and desiring to actively influence and control the decisions that direct their lives; that teaching and learning are mutual processes (the public housing resident is just as much an expert on public housing as the student of pressure legislative politics may be an expert. The bugbear of submissiveness to authority has all too long been frighteningly real in the way people have bowed before science and "expertise" regardless of the sort or amount of relevance they had to a given situation[6]); that the single most profound change that could take place—in urban renewal or welfare policy or developing recreation programs or whatever you choose—would be to transform the process of decision making to dispel impotence and decentralize power so that people can become active participants rather than passive recipients of policy.

None of the ideas were new. Using as research subjects people who do not benefit from the research has plagued modern behavioral sciences for decades. San Francisco State College has coordinated a variety of work/study experiences as an integral part of professional programs since 1950. One in professional education has involved up to one thousand college students with as many as one hundred community agencies in a single year. John Dewey stated much of the theory and the perplexing issues of practice in his *Experience and Education*[7] in 1938. The notion that students can select and guide their own work experience has steadily gained ground in higher education.

While the ideas were not new and some of the principles were already in practice in various sectors of the college, they did not often involve the same students or the same faculty. In fact a review of the ferment within the college in the mid-sixties reveals that many of the laudable faculty projects extending themselves into the community did little to involve significant numbers of motivated students.

This is not intended to disparage the determined and creative efforts of the work/study student leadership and a number of faculty. The program was new in emphasis and highly innovative. The student impetus was in problem determination and program design, with the asserted objective of emphasizing the *work experience* for liberal arts students; the prime focus was on training students to "make institu-

[6] See P. Meyer, "If Hitler Asked You to Electrocute a Stranger, Would You?" *Esquire*, 1970, 74 (2), 72ff. Stanley Milgram's experiments at Yale on conformity in the face of an authority figure.

[7] J. Dewey, *Experience and Education* (New York: Crowell, Collier & Macmillan, 1963).

tional changes on the campus" and to develop leadership in community groups so that these groups could make changes themselves. This point is driven home in a further statement: "All of our community-based programs have the explicit purpose of developing the resources of the community participants in the programs." The emphasis on fostering change and providing the resources for change through student involvement was new. Most college-sponsored work experience and community involvement programs have traditionally viewed students as trainees expected to work within the structure of community organizations. Promoting change has not been the student's role. This new emphasis became a crucial issue in the relations between higher education and other jurisdictions in the communities and the state. And it began to stimulate resistance.

During 1967–1968, Sharon Gold and other work/study students made an impressive presentation to a class in the sociology of education. A similar presentation to faculty teaching in that area included a request for one or two sections of a multisection course to be used by the Community Services Institute in the coming fall semester. According to the student rationale, such an arrangement would enable experienced work/study students to get academic credit for their work, would provide a framework for making sense out of their experience and contributing relevant knowledge to it, and would enable them to proceed three units toward a teaching credential.

There were several sticky aspects of the proposal. One was the stubborn insistence that the course, as offered, had to be prepared to give way completely to the institute students' conception of what it was to accomplish; another was that any faculty assigned responsibility for the course had to accept it in the spirit of a colearner, foregoing any claims to authority; a third aspect was that the courses were to be reserved for work/study students exclusively. There was deep student skepticism that any faculty were really up-to-date in "how it is" in the urban community, though many faculty had been and were continuously involved in tight urban situations. The experienced student leadership cadre of the several programs had accepted the concept that they were, in fact, professionals in innovative programs on and off campus and merited autonomy and participatory status on a level with full-time faculty. In analysis and argument about their programs, they were quite able to think with the faculty about the issues. The students often appeared to have the edge in acuity if only because of the intensity of their preparation when cast against faculty senate and committee members for whom the issues were often marginal. Their associations and antiestablishment stance made these students more akin to the aggressive radicals and revolutionaries among students and faculty than to the official administrative and faculty leadership of the college. This affinity was later to lead to their downfall. During the campus disruptions of May 1968 and November-December 1968, most program people faded into the ranks of the strike supporters.

Further review of the Experimental College course offerings from the fall of 1966 through the spring of 1968 reveals two things of significance. First, although the total course offerings were slightly expanded, the number of courses focused on peace and nonviolence dropped from seven to one. This shift may be an index of fading interest in nonviolence as an approach to power. Second, interest in encounter groups, sensitivity training, self-awareness, the search for identity, and new patterns of interpersonal relations (including sexual relations) continued and expanded. In 1966, ten of seventy courses stressed the self-understanding themes. In 1968, fifteen of seventy-six fell in this area of interest. Further, by 1968 the number of courses exploring both Eastern and Western religions increased from four to eight.

The journey to selfhood in a tumultuous period of change is a rugged one for the thinking young. Colleges and universities have made their adaptations more to the knowledge explosion than to the existential issues facing young adults. Thus the curriculum has tended to be elaborated in particular and specialized aspects of subject fields, while students want to ask the broad humanistic questions of what life is all about, anyway. The stated purpose in developing the Experimental College was to explore areas of learning and experience not adequately provided for in the existing curriculum.

One of the central theses of the community programs and the Experimental College curriculum, noted earlier, is that students badly need to involve all of themselves in the learning process and that the root of the process is real experience—an engagement with the central issues of society and life as the students perceive them. Further, this learning process involves thought, inquiry, risk, and conflict. Ideas and methods must be tried out in settings in which the stakes are for keeps. Whether the effort is in communications, tutorial work, neighborhood drama activities, legal aid for juveniles, or tenant unions, the intent is to transfer the control of processes from the bureaucracies and the guardians of the establishment to the students and to the people in the community who represent the "disestablishment." The purpose of such a transfer is to enable the students and community people to learn to function more effectively *for themselves*. Instance after instance on the campus reflected the effectiveness of such learning.

These theses, shared by perhaps a third of the faculty, are central to American democratic thought. The colonies were settled by the disestablishments of Europe. The West was settled by those who had defected from the communities of the East, or who had been thrust into the role of outsiders. There is no place for the young Ahabs of today to run. Whales are almost extinct, most mountains have been climbed. The last physical frontiers have been occupied and are smog-ridden—and often are right wing political preserves. Even the arctic slope of Alaska has fallen to the establishment. The urban black and brown ghettos provide a new kind of frontier, as do the white ghettos of the suburbs. This frontier is the frontier of the quality of the life of the powerless. The thing that is more difficult than it was for Ahab or John C. Fremont or the outcasts of Poker Flat is that the struggle of these earlier explorers for redemption through achievement went on in a setting in which the umpire, Nature, was tough but relatively neutral. The outcome seemed open and up to them.

Today youth cannot get away from the establishment. Even the astronauts read the Bible and chatted with the President in flight. Campus activists work under surveillance of the "blue meanies" wired to take orders from the governor's office. If it is true that the Experimental College and the community programs that caught the imagination of many across the nation are in fact dead at San Francisco State, what can we learn? That the classical myth of Phaethon is still alive? That the young must not be permitted to drive the chariot toward the sun lest they burn the world?

The program students and their scattering of faculty associates were rich in ideas about the kind of education they wanted and the kind of world they hoped to build and about how to realize these aspirations. Inwardly uncertain and self-questioning, yet they projected a dogmatic, aggressive facade to those outside the movement. This posture reflected both rejection of the status quo along with the people who are identified with it and a fear of cooption or seduction into the pit of convention.

In 1938, Dewey stated many of the basic problems involved in moving from tradition bound education to an experimental, experience based approach. As though he were describing the Experimental College and its linkage with community programs, he said that the progressive schools of his day reflected some common principles among the variety they represented.

> To imposition from above is opposed expression and cultivation of individuality; to external discipline is opposed free activity; to learning from texts and teachers, learning from experience; to acquisition of isolated skills and techniques by drill is opposed acquisition of them as means of attaining ends which make direct vital appeal; to preparation for a more or less remote future is opposed making the most of the opportunities of present life; to static aims and materials is opposed acquaintance with a changing world.[8]

Dewey made two further points that have a direct bearing on student thrusts for reform over the short span of five years at San Francisco State. A vision of new principles on the basis of which the old education is rejected leaves the reformers not with a *new education* but with a new set of complex problems related to practice. Abstract principles such as those stated above must still be translated into programs and experiences. The tendency, Dewey says, is to falter in practice because "in rejecting the aims and methods of that which it would supplant, it may develop its principles negatively rather than positively and constructively. Then it takes its clue in practice from that which is rejected instead of from the constructive development of its own philosophy." A new movement "will tend to suppose that because the old education was based on ready made organization, therefore, it suffices to reject the principle of organization in toto, instead of striving to discover what it means and how it is to be attained on the basis of experience."[9]

Examples of the problems projected by Dewey in effecting educational reform were rife during the developmental phase of the Experimental College. A sharp break with tradition imposes burdens on the reformers even if they do not have to withstand the counterassaults of those threatened by change. During the first year of the Experi-

---

[8] Dewey, *Experience and Education.*
[9] Ibid., p. 20.

mental College the students struggled with the problems of administration, supervision, and coordination. They seemed to say, "The college is stultifyingly bureaucratic, we will have no bureaucracy. Supervisors and administrators inhibit creativity. We shall depend on every teacher to do an effective job. If he does not, students will drop his course. The qualifications held for college professors are mostly irrelevant: degrees, research, publications, teaching experience. Anyone can teach who wants to teach, can describe his course, draw students, and keep them. If our instructors are not qualified, students will know it and leave their classes. Admission requirements for students are skewed and restrictive. Anyone in the college and the community can attend Experimental College classes."

The ordinary penchant of reformers for falling into the trap of transvaluing the status quo by contradicting its premises and practices point by point was intensified in the student and faculty reform movements of the mid-sixties by the aura of simmering revolt which permeated the college. Perhaps equally significant were the developing theses of existentialism and anarchism that have stoked the fires of dissent among the young.

The radical individualism of the students exceeded by far the individualism of the ideology, which for Dewey was pragmatic, experimental, and democratic in its temper. The students, already widely distributed over the metropolitan area in tutorial programs and social agencies, continued to define projects to provoke direct change. In so doing they crossed jurisdictions with unconcern. Where they saw a need they helped the powerless to organize, to challenge their particular establishment: a youth agency head was pressured to resign by dissatisfied parents and youth; student demands were made on a school principal; draft counseling programs were developed to enable youth to challenge local draft boards.

This campus based movement by active students crisscrossed the infinitely fragmented jurisdictions of city and community organizations, making more enemies than friends among those in middle- and upper-level leadership roles. The students were charged with outrageous presumption. In the conventional wisdom, change must be introduced from the top through deliberately planned policy, and then program implementation follows only when resources are available. Change introduced from below, or generated by outsiders, tends to be resisted. The projects of college students may grow up within existing agencies, as alternate services to an agency that students believe is malfunctioning, or to provide needed services not otherwise afforded. If successful, projects offer either direct or indirect challenges to establishments, and the college is involved if only on a de facto basis.

Some of the consequences remind one of a western wagon train scenario in which a group of families, in their eagerness to get to the gold fields, refuses to accept community discipline, believing they can move faster on their own. But with limited discipline among themselves they make both stragglers and forerunners vulnerable to attack by marauders. In the end, attacked from both the right and the left, they refuse to draw their wagons into a circle and wait for the main party to draw up with them. They are decimated.

By summer 1968, the leadership of the Experimental College and the community programs showed a growing awareness that the operations (movement might be a better term) could be jeopardized by too great a diffusion of responsibility and by lack of limits. The college officials—not formally committed to student off-campus programs, embarrassed by counterpressure from the community and trustees, and aware of alleged excesses—aided the retrenchment. In July 1968, a state college trustee inquiry into the whole Experimental College movement raised a series of issues at the state level. Some should have been settled on the campus as the programs developed. However, during that short period, 1965–1968, the college had three different presidents. Almost all key administrative personnel in academic affairs changed at least once. Five of seven school deans changed. The only continuity in the college administrative structure was in the area of student personnel and student activities. Caught between the increasingly radical student rhetoric and action and the growing resistance among conservative faculty and trustees, the student personnel staff became less and less effective. The dual role of supporter of student programs and dispenser of justice became difficult if not impossible as conflict grew. The Academic Senate Committee on Student Affairs remained largely inoperative.

The student programs and the Experimental College grew under the leadership of the Associated Students and were financed largely from the three to four hundred thousand dollar student body budget. These programs had begun as significant shifts in the direction of student activities on campus within the jurisdiction of the dean of students. The successful push for cooperative faculty staffing and for academic credit through independent study or experimental courses quickly involved the academic affairs area, from the departmental level to that of the academic vice-president. Leasing of off-campus centers, payment of student program coordinators, and increased pressure for expanded use of campus facilities rapidly challenged the already overworked and understaffed business affairs area. In each of the three areas (finance, instruction, and student personnel), individuals sympathetic to student efforts lent a hand now and then, but the policy issues and the questions of ultimate responsibility for such operations below the level of the president had not been faced.

The serious debate among students over anarchy as a route to creativity and innovation continued and left them subject to provocateurs, calculating disruptors, self-professed revolutionaries, and the irresponsible. The rapid growth in numbers of students, faculty, and community people involved also posed problems both for student leaders and college officials. The problems involved in the Experimental College and community programs alone would have taxed an experienced administrative staff noted for both toughness and flexibility. For a dozen or so student leaders—skeptical of administrative roles—and a handful of activity counselors it was a close race between creative disorder and chaos. All this occurred on a tightly scheduled, drastically overused campus in which there was less and less room for informal, ad hoc activities of any kind. Yet these activities were an integral part of the programs that students were intent on developing.

Colleges and universities have little successful experience as yet with large scale movements by students to shift the direction of their own education through programs initiated by students. When such programs incorporate deep commitments to community service and action programs, the problems mount for both students and college supervisory personnel. As noted earlier, new, overlapping jurisdictional conflicts abound. Students move into the socially disorganized areas of large cities and attempt to cope directly with the human wreckage so ill served by the urban bureaucracies in education, welfare, justice, public health, and employment. Students then absorb the stuff of which radicalism is made. They have firsthand experience with the failure of established agencies. They see evidence which convinces them that agencies, or personnel within agencies, contribute to furthering the social disorganization and personal defeats of youth and their families. Their burning concerns are marginal to most faculty and most programs. Their commitments to direct action as a route to social change nursed in the bosom of a college or university provide a major dilemma for colleges rooted in traditions of distinct detachment from the centers of social conflict.

The bureaucracy and the movement, operating from such diverse conceptions of organization and function, developed a host of minor and some major frictions before John Summerskill's departure in May 1968. School deans, responsible for buildings and equipment in their areas, felt increased pressure in an already difficult situation. Supervision and janitorial costs and equipment loss or damage mounted against tightly fixed budgets and staff. Miniconfrontations were common.

The problem of space and facilities became acute. The urgency felt on campus to begin construction of the long planned student union was closely related to the problem of how to house a variety of programs and student instructional activities on a campus already used about 25 per cent beyond established state standards. Activities outside the formal curriculum had second priority at best. Most were thus squeezed into the late afternoon and evening hours—beyond the conventional day—compounding problems of general supervision of the campus. Part of the reputation of the Council of Academic Deans as a conservative, obstructionist body grew from having to resolve the dilemmas of overlapping programs and overlapping demands on the same resources. Physical education and creative arts, because of their specialized facilities and equipment in the area of communications and activities, became focal points of tension. Significantly, the Associated Students budget attempted to withdraw all financial support from activities in those two areas in June 1968.

Pressure for academic credit for courses taught by students, some only nominally supervised by faculty members, began to build. A general accreditation visit, the first in a decade, was scheduled for the fall of 1968. This prospect added to the nervousness on campus. Horrible examples began to circulate, marring the well-deserved aura of serious intellectual and academic ferment surrounding many of the student initiated programs. For example, one fifth-year student registered for thirty-six units in one semester, more than double the conventional amount for a graduate student. He argued he should be permitted to complete his Master of Arts requirements during that semester, although he had not yet received his A.B. degree. The units were completed with a B average.

A group of students in an experimental course in black studies attempted to pressure the cooperating professor, who is white, into dropping out of the course. He insisted on staying, eventually winning a measure of acceptance. Two professors of higher education agreed to the roles of consultants to a cooperatively designed seminar to be managed by and for the student leaders of the Experimental College. One professor, distressed by a series of nonclasses, refused to continue with the seminar. The other carried through on his agreement but judged the course a destructive waste of time. Student leaders of the course argued that they had at least three units coming to them because they were busy doing the creative work of college reform that was neglected by the faculty and administration.

In addition to such questionable enterprises, reports mounted of lost or stolen audiovisual equipment, some drawn from the college on signatures that could not be traced. By spring 1968, a pattern of response to such incidents was underway.

In late summer 1968, the School of Creative Arts, working with the business manager, formulated a new schedule of fees to be levied against student programs for use of facilities, equipment, and technical personnel. It was an effort to reduce the overuse of resources and to conserve operating budgets, already badly underfinanced. Audiovisual services began to move in the same direction. The issue was placed on the agenda of the Council of Academic Deans. Students and activities counselors began to protest immediately.

This proposal followed hard on the heels of the aggressive trustee inquiry into the Experimental College in July and release of the initial information of the chancellor's intent to tighten control over student body budgets and programs. By September, when the trustees refused approval of the Student Union building, student leaders were sure they saw the handwriting on the wall. Their programs and aspirations had been expanding rapidly as had their national recognition. With the aid of the fifty thousand dollar Carnegie grant, student program leaders had spent much of the summer projecting additional projects to provide involvement for more students. Their funds were threatened, their access to facilities and course credit seemed in the process of being curbed, and their student financed building had been disallowed.

Trustee intervention in the George Murray affair in late September further inflamed the program student leaders. Murray had been one of them for several semesters, and he was being picked off at the pleasure of the trustees. By September it was also clear that a $750,000 fund raising campaign, precariously launched by John Summerskill and Mayor Joseph L. Alioto in May, was dying without a whimper, leaving three hundred special admission students in trouble all the way.

Several administrators and faculty leaders grasped the relationship between impending campus disorder and the almost random acts that disappointed and frustrated each of a growing spectrum of unstable crowds on the campus. Repeated efforts to get special help from the chancellor and the trustees were blocked. The college staff could not convince the chancellor that they were dealing with a fabric of interrelated problems requiring additional resources rather than a series of issues isolated from each other.

Abuses within the programs did take place. Friction between the student leaders and the college administration did develop as the new ventures upset the conventional style of the college. Support was certainly not provided by a suspicious chancellor's office. Yet the failure of this student-initiated educational reform to reduce college tensions sufficiently to avoid large-scale confrontations cannot be attributed simply to these abuses, these frictions, or this lack of support.

In looking for an answer to this paradox of reputed liberal reform yet consequent chaos, we again go back to Davies' theory quoted at the beginning of this chapter. For the previous five years student expectations that the college would become transformed by their efforts to serve their needs had risen in a steep gradient. On the surface the institution seemed to be responding. Compared to the situation in times past or to the conditions at other colleges progress had certainly been made. But compared with the emerging urgency of the demands for change, the sense of "now!" the institutional pace had indeed been slow. Although many of the participating students believed their work in Experimental College courses had much more influence on their behavior and attitudes than did conventional courses, little of this work was granted college credit. The styles of teaching, the general education requirements, the composition of departmental majors—all these had remained essentially unchanged. Student representation in the college power structure was still merely token. Much student labor had gone into a work/study program, yet the program, while authorized, had not been included in the college curriculum. A student who struggled with the program year after year could be graduated before the program had materialized, and his participation thus was eliminated. A projected major and an M.A. program in community studies had not eventuated.

Although much of the academic world seemed intrigued with the student efforts at San Francisco State, little concrete financial support had been offered by the national foundations or by the California educational establishment. Work/study programs were floundering for lack of resources and lack of skill. And MAX, for all its ingenuity and effort, had seldom influenced student choices of faculty during a hectic registration process in which student options were severely limited. Departmental retention and promotion policies remained largely beyond student reach. In short, student expectations had skyrocketed but institutional behavior remained oriented toward the status quo coated with a patina of liberality.

Thus did the program people fail to achieve their Camelot. The tragedy was that ideas that generated such enthusiastic concern and hope among students and some faculty were viewed with much suspicion and distrust by most of the faculty, the administration, the trustees, and the chancellor. And so those ideas were probably doomed from the start. Few were willing to grant that out of the supposed naivete, confusion, and inexperience of the reformers could come educational ideas more potent, effective, and relevant than many of the efforts of the traditional educational establishment. The student reformers were not the first to find that attempting to turn an institution with established traditions in a different direction is a gargantuan task. Yet they may have been some of the first to discover how close one can come when undergirded by a sophisticated assessment of the problems and a reservoir of committed energy. The onrush of events dramatized that there was neither world enough nor time for the reformers to make their case. Ironically the *nowness* which is so much a part of the ethic of this student generation, reformer and revolutionary alike, made deep efforts at reform seem inconsequential and thus discredited efforts among potential constituencies.

The reformers were working with many concepts and processes which were more deeply rooted in current knowledge of human development and learning than were many of the traditional academic programs. The faculty and administrators failed to take into account the degree to which the student directed programs were to become a lusty countercollege, urgently concerned with challenging the academic status quo. So, the entrenched ways in which established institutions behave played directly into the hands of those who waved the banners of violent revolution or alienation.

The more promising the programs became in exploring and modifying basic assumptions, the more resistance grew. As student programs moved away from strictly academic problems toward direct action, problems of budget, propriety, the role of the university and the place of students in the scheme of things came sharply into view. Reaction from both left and right, inside and outside the institution, put this promising movement to rest. One is tempted to write the experiment off as merely another demonstration of the inflexibility of our institutions when faced with the need for significant change. Yet, San Francisco State can never again be the same. Out of the plaguing ferment of the reformers' years may still come something that is important. We cannot draw easy conclusions about how to adapt higher education to students who insist on major social and educational reforms. But in the next chapter, we peer into the ideological abyss that beckons beyond the outer margins of reform.

THREE

Radical Ideology and Strategies

Growing rejection of things as they are (or are perceived to be) has led to withdrawal of youth and young adults from the dominant society into loosely affiliated enclaves, into a world of interpersonal experimentation and self-scrutiny aided by psychedelic experiences and meditation. The movement toward passive or active rejection of convention is helped along by drugs, literature, music, art, and existential styles of thought and action. A mood and an attitudinal set difficult to capture in words is a part of it. Self-destruction beckons some; some discover novel patterns of self-fulfilment on the margin of the society.[1] Others rejoin the square society after a period of experimentation.

The more publicized patterns of rejection, however, are those that issue direct challenges to the schools and colleges, the cradles of the existing power centers of the community and the nation. Campus rebellions marked by concerted action to control or force abrupt changes in the colleges reflect a growing trend toward active rather than passive revolt. At San Francisco State College, during the period 1967–1969 there was rapid movement toward extreme styles of thought and behavior when measured against traditional conceptions of academic life in an urban college of liberal reputation. Struggles for power and for the levers of power, by individuals and groups who felt powerless and manipulated, were in dead earnest. Proponents of radi-

---

[1] In *Essay on Liberation* (Boston: Beacon Press, 1969), Herbert Marcuse describes such movements as "the great refusal."

52

cal alternatives to the status quo on the campus and in the society have made it explicitly clear that the campus is only the first objective. The larger society is also marked for assault. As these theses were projected beyond the campus, they provoked sharp reactions.

In the mid-sixties students and faculty sought opportunities for *dialogue* with colleagues, administrators, and trustees. *Encounter* quickly became a more cherished term. During the years 1967 and 1968, *confrontation* better described the intent and tactics of campus activists. Confrontations merged into disruptive sit-ins and scattered assaults on persons and property coupled with trenchant verbal attacks on selected individuals. In November of 1968, the student strike at San Francisco State was called by the Black Students Union and joined by the Third World Liberation Front. "Flea attacks" and various adaptations of the tactics of guerrilla warfare were introduced on campus in a purported effort to gain fifteen nonnegotiable demands for Black and Third World students. Subtle patterns of sabotage of institutional functions also grew.

The description and analysis of ideological ferment that follows is intended to be illustrative rather than exhaustive. It is an effort to direct the attention of those involved in campus confrontations both on and off campus to the ideological content and emotional dynamics at work in campus disruption.

Returning to campus for the fall semester in 1967, one was struck by a shift in the militancy of the rhetoric, by the tone and appearance of campus life. There were testiness and a hard-nosed questioning that had not been apparent only a year earlier among many undergraduate and graduate students. The area in front of the commons and the temporary units had changed markedly. More litter accumulated each day. More groups at tables were purveying radical and revolutionary literature. The rhetoric from the speakers platform was more trenchant than before and its content more aggressively revolutionary. Faculty and administrative colleagues seemed depressed and anxious, uncertain of John Summerskill's leadership as president. Some spoke of early retirement. They talked of a savage summer attack on the Black Students Union and the president by conservative forces both on and off campus. Summerskill's opening speech to the faculty in September of 1967 reflected a man shaken by his first year's experience in the college yet determined to struggle in behalf of the college and the aspirations of its students and faculty. It seemed clear that in the academic year ahead testing of limits in a variety of directions would be stepped up. It was. Ideological ferment, once under way on a campus, has great potential for shaking up and changing an educational institution. Potential for deep disruption of education and institutions is also found in the sharp responses from the threatened defenders of the status quo, both on and off campus.

Ideological heresy expressed in word or action by individuals or small groups is often tolerated by defenders of the system, who dismiss such dissenters as interesting kooks. Heresies that begin to gain the strength of a movement capable of seriously challenging an institutional or community structure are something else. Such heresies breed disgust, anxiety, fear, and retaliation. California's citizens and political leaders have been pushed to something approaching a frenzy by college and community disorders and by the ideological overtones projected.

Our intent in this chapter is to identify themes of thought, perception, and action that emerged at San Francisco State College during the 1960s, and particularly since 1966. When taken together, these themes provide an umbrella of ideological elements that arise out of dissent and come to serve as guides to further efforts of dissatisfied students, faculty members, and a few administrators to reshape the college and the society more to their liking. The significance for higher education is great, if not yet clearly perceived, but the impact goes well beyond this and other campuses experiencing similar stresses. As the ideological theses become clarified, they form a framework—for those who accept them—that is broadly applicable to issues in the wider society, the nation, and the world. They significantly shape the life style of individuals and subgroups within the college community. The subgroups include those who accept the ideologies and others who feel the impact of actions arising from persons acting on the emerging beliefs.

In attempting to identify ideological elements and illustrate their impact on the college and its operation, we are interested in the common themes expressed by those who most deeply reject the status quo and the assumptions on which the status quo, as viewed by its bluntest critics, allegedly rests. At the close of the chapter an effort will be made to summarize the major ideological preconceptions we have extracted from a cauldron of ferment.

Ideology as a Guiding System

Daniel Bell, writing in 1960,[2] concluded that the social ideologies of the nineteenth and early twentieth century had largely lost their potency to direct or control social change. A decade later, ideological ferment among young adults is a powerful force to be taken into account. The power of existing ideologies to command belief, passion, and action was at a low ebb, perhaps marking the closing of an era. Bell surmised that the ideological ferment rising in Asia, Cuba, and the emerging nations of Africa would test the end of this ideological era. The title of Bell's work, *The End of Ideology,* was misleading, reflecting his restricted use of the term. We may well be into an era of ideological renaissance. Bell thought that the new generation was producing a "new left" with "few memories of the past," with "passion and energy, but little definition of the future." The new search for freedom and self-determination, Bell feared, was rooted in a too careless thesis that demeaning means could achieve utopian ends. Bell was aware, however, that "for the ideologue, truth arises in action, and meaning is given to experience by the 'transforming moment.' He comes alive not in contemplation, but in the 'deed.' One might say, in fact, that the most important, latent function of ideology is to tap emotion."[3] Our nation has not attended closely the nature and functions of social and political ideology. The term ideology has long been suspect in the United States, gaining currency slowly since World War II. Colleges and universities have had little experience in dealing with aggressive popular movements that challenge the institutions directly and from inside.

A fully developed ideology provides individuals and groups with a frame of reference that includes assumptions, projected ideals, and expected patterns of behavior and processes. It carries a plausibility that commands faith, impels action, and can generate passion, commitment, and sacrifice. When analyzed by a skeptic from outside the belief system, fact and myth appear to be wondrously interwoven. An ideology is a system for simplifying the infinite complexity of living and interpreting experience. It provides a pattern of selective percep-

[2] D. Bell, *The End of Ideology* (rev. ed.), (New York: Crowell, Collier & Macmillan, 1962).
[3] Ibid., p. 400.

tion that operates below the level of awareness for individuals or groups. Some view a social ideology as a secular religion. Mature ideologies include assumptions about: (1) the nature of the universe and man's relation to it; (2) the nature of man and his relation to his fellows; (3) the purpose of institutions and their relationships to individuals and groups; (4) ideal goals and purposes of individuals to be nurtured by institutions and society; and (5) appropriate processes and acceptable behavior providing the means suggested by (1) through (4) above.

The ebb and flow of campus tumult, including sharp conflict among dissidents, reminds us that it is not an easy task to project coherent ideological systems from the disorder of widespread dissent. Such projections are made even more difficult in a society of massive complexity beset by rapid change and deepening conflict. During the decade of the sixties, the major sources of ideological ferment in the United States, other than in the arts, have been the campuses, the ghettoes, and the colonies of young adult dropouts such as Telegraph Avenue, Haight-Ashbury, and similar enclaves in other cities and rural areas of this land and the world. Dissenters from those several bases interact with and complement each other's challenges to the conventional wisdom in a variety of ways. Ideological notions are grown and spread through the overlapping membership and by means of mobility of those identifying themselves with the "movement" or the "revolution." Much of the noise, movement, and probing in a time of drastic change harbors a deadly serious search for identity to assuage confusion and anxiety that are heightened as old patterns erode and dissolve.

Plans for action to express alienation, dissent, aggression, and need for reform or revolution require justification as part of the build up for confrontation. Such justifications require simple appealing rationales—elements of ideology. Once an action has run its course, a period of assessment, sharing of experiences, and analysis of gains and losses follows. The emotional intensity of the experience provides reinforcement for the projections made before the event and for the conclusions following it. Thus the parts of an ideological orientation are forged in three phases: a sharpened bill of particulars justifying rejection of the status quo; an accretion of ideological theses that have found favor through testing in intense action settings and through an imaginative, creative projection of additional theses to be tested later; and the growth of a mood or frame of mind infused with emotion that causes despair when viewing the tenets of the status quo and exaltation and hope when viewing countertheses.

The challenges to the status quo by students at San Francisco State College during 1966, 1967, and 1968 mounted steadily in intensity, as did the breadth of things challenged and the means used to push them forward. The proportion of the student body involved also grew. Much of the buildup toward the naked struggle for power that characterized the academic year 1968–1969 went on beyond the perception of most of the faculty and administrators. By the close of that academic year such was no longer the case! Five months of sustained disorder and more months of corrosive aftermath caught the attention of most of the campus community and of most of the citizens of California. The membrane of indifference which hides the meaning of significant emerging events around us was partially torn away. The membrane's name is business-as-usual.

The November 1967 College Convocation on the Vietnam War Crisis provided the first large-scale opportunity in the history of San Francisco State College for students, faculty, administrators, and staff to state their views about the war, the nation, and the relation of the college to the war, to the society, and to the students. Concurrent confrontation arising from the aggressive behavior of the black students and the staff of *Open Process* also broadened the arena of debate and direct action beyond the week long convocation. The context of controversy was broadened, too, by related events in the Bay Area: Oakland antidraft demonstrations; disorders at University of California, Berkeley; and demonstrations at San Jose State College. Rhetoric flowing from the convocation, the December 1967 campus demonstrations, and the Hyde Park type speakers' platform on the San Francisco State campus was studded with blunt ideological theses and demands for action that challenged the college's neutrality.

Liberal positions were attacked even more trenchantly than were those of conservatives or the radical right. Throughout the convocation and the subsequent platform discussions, Summerskill (then president) served as one focal point of trenchant attacks by all groups seeking immediate solutions to complex problems. In a revealing statement, John Gerassi challenged Summerskill to join the anti-Vietnam protest and "go down with the rest of us."

The November 1967 Vietnam War Convocation was sponsored by the academic senate and the Associated Students. It was an effort to accommodate severe antiwar pressures on the campus, which some felt were building toward violence. The planning committee was chaired by an outspoken liberal professor of international relations, Marshall Windmiller, who frankly opposed the war in Vietnam, the continuation of AFROTC on campus, and military recruitment. He was also deeply committed to the freest possible discussion of all views of a problem. Each of the issues was discussed and debated at length. The overriding concern, however, was whether the college *as an institution* should take a clear stand in opposition to the war in Vietnam, thus departing from the traditional position of institutional neutrality in the face of deep conflicts within the body politic. Windmiller stayed with the conference but by the end was shaken by the intensity of the attacks on him made by those who were unable to force the outcomes they wished and disenchanted by the low level of support and participation among faculty. The convocation ran for five days, two or three hours a day parallel to the class schedule. It used the gym and the main auditorium, augmented by closed circuit television to accommodate the crowds of students varying from perhaps seven hundred to three thousand during the talk marathon. Twenty-seven propositions were developed during the five days of speeches, discussion, and allied activities at the school and department level. The following week those propositions were submitted to vote by students, staff, and faculty.

As faculty members and students drifted in and out of the convocation, it became clear that the radical left—the Students for a Democratic Society, the Progressive Labor Party, the Young Socialist Alliance, and a sprinkling of leftist faculty—intended to keep the initiative. Two floor microphones were used alternately, one by the anti-establishment speakers and one by all other comers. At times there would be as many as thirty-five speakers lined up at the anti-war microphone with no more than one or two at the alternate station. Few faculty bothered to participate actively. The handful of active faculty participants urged many of their colleagues to attend and participate, to little effect. Most recoiled from the rhetoric, which they believed bizarre. Most did not know how to discuss issues of ideology, nor did they believe they had any obligation to lay their dignity on the line, "to roll on the floor in a brawl," as one faculty member put it. The few faculty who stayed with the convocation took their turns at the microphone, attempting to keep liberal and moderate theses alive. Three liberal faculty followed the results of the convocation into the student-faculty-staff resolutions committee and argued the thing through with the "militant" left in a continuous eight-hour session. The efforts of the radical left to control the issues to be submitted to referendum, and the wording of each, were unceasing. The moderates, however, won consistently. Moderates who wished to withdraw in the face of the conflict and go home to their families were cudgeled into staying by a few committed colleagues. It was apparent that much of the acrimonious, lengthy discussion was designed by the true believers to drive out the moderates thus tipping the vote in the direction of only those issues of sharp concern to the militants' programs.

Both during the convocation and within the resolutions committee, it became clear that the intent of the most militant was to turn the student-faculty-staff vote on the resolutions from a formal expression of campus opinion to instant policy binding on the college through a "one man, one vote process" *if they won.* In this, they were unsuccessful. When challenged directly as to whether the issues that had *lost* would then be considered *settled,* the militants said anyone accepting such a position clearly did not grasp the meaning of struggle.

What we were seeing was the growing split between the traditionally and experimentally oriented liberals and the new more doctrinaire left and militant nationalists of the racial and ethnic minorities, although few of the latter participated. The tendency of the liberal-moderate-conservative faculty and students to default in situations marked by ideological conflict was clear. Radical spokesmen of the convocation began to lose their audience support by the fourth day not as much because of the effectiveness of the countering rhetoric as because sympathy for liberals as underdogs seemed to grow. The left became tiresome and committed the error of overkill still possible in those relatively innocent days.

From informal discussion around the edges of the convocation, there was much evidence that most students who attended were genuinely disturbed about the issues surrounding the war in Vietnam, failures in the area of civil rights, and the functions they felt education and the college should serve in their lives and in the society. Significant numbers of faculty were unable to see such an event as a potentially powerful educational experience. Many saw it as nothing more than an interruption of the instructional program, or as an effort to placate radical dissent, or as a boondoggle. This attitude helped skew the proceedings toward the militant left.

As stated earlier, trenchant attacks on President John Summerskill were launched by the militant left. Summerskill had forthrightly stated that he was liberal, a dove, anxious to support the drive of minority groups for equality and justice and the drive to eliminate poverty—goals espoused by the student dissenters. He supported proposals for academic reform, defended the rights of dissent and a broader sharing of responsibility for decision making within the college. He differed with the radical students, as he clearly stated, about the need to keep the campus open to the widest possible range of views and activities in keeping with the functions and traditions of the college, its regulations, and the law. He stated his willingness to seek change in college modes of operation when proposed innovations were arrived at by responsible processes involving interested parties including students. Summerskill's actions during the sixteen months of his administration suggested an intent to follow his liberal beliefs in his role as president, even in the face of a reactionary state administration. This stance committed to progressive reform suited neither the campus militants nor the more conservative of the trustees.

Anxious legislators and citizens, disgusted and frightened both by campus turbulence and disorderly incidents and by the sharp questioning of national policy and values, demanded drastic action following the December 1967 disorders led by Gerassi, the SDS, and the BSU. Summerskill's job was suddenly threatened by the conservative chancellor, Glenn Dumke, as the "fire the coach!" syndrome so prevalent in American life came into play. The speaker of the assembly, the superintendent of public education, the governor and miscellaneous politicians, including the assemblyman from the writer's own district, joined the hue and cry. The trustees acted precipitously, and the Assembly Education Committee launched hearings. The militants operating on campus countered by accusing Summerskill of racism and politically motivated acts of discipline and administrative behavior.

During Summerskill's administration the pattern of delegitimizing and destroying the president's role in campus crises was well set. Radical students charge that the president is a racist and puppet. Trustees and politicians charge that he is weak, irresponsible, and subject to fits of bad administrative judgment. Faculty defect from support of his administration, and finally his chief lieutenants and deans break ranks. The press and other media amplify the progression toward disorder at the top. During this now often repeated process, the president himself may contribute to the deterioration of his role through fatigue, personal problems intensified under stress, overload on the decision-making structure, or mismanagement of a particular problem.

The silent middle—the moderates—lose because the radical dissenters score a victory by picking off the top man and adding to the confusion. The trustees think they win because they have their scapegoat. One of the key tasks in nurturing an alternate ideology is to neutralize or destroy the symbol of the controlling or operative ideology.

John Gardner, after lauding Kenneth Pitzer of Stanford in an inaugural address in June of 1969 at the close of Pitzer's first semester as president, reflected on the growing plight of university presidents.

> I call to your attention, with some sorrow, that a number of fine university presidents have had their careers destroyed by the conflict that has raged on our campuses. Looking back at those incidents, I do not think they reflect credit on any of us—the faculty, the students, trustees, or alumni. We have now proved beyond argument that a university community can make life unlivable for a president. We can make him the scapegoat for every failure of the institution, every failure of society. We can use him as a target for all of the hostility so that he is clawed to ribbons in the process. We have yet to provide the kind of atmosphere in which a good man can survive.

At State the process was repeated four times in five years. During the twelve month period beginning May 1968, the eighteen California State Colleges lost presidents on six campuses, only one of whom retired. By the summer of 1970, Pitzer had resigned.

In the Summerskill affair, the California right, the new left, and the black students clamored for their pound of flesh. The faculty, substantial numbers of whom had already written Summerskill off on previous accounts, suddenly rallied around the president, threatening a strike if he were summarily fired. The faculty perceived too late the stark trend of events. Summerskill's role had already been destroyed in the crush of forces building both on and off campus, and Summerskill was smart enough to recognize it.

When adamant revolutionists or counterrevolutionists launch

programs of disruption or retaliation, the liberal or moderate administrator tends to look shabby and weak if he refuses to reject his values and his commitment to orderly processes in favor of arbitrary initiative or retaliatory action. Demands pile up that he suspend democratic procedures, including due process, that he arbitrarily meet demands, or that he "clean up the mess." If efforts to push him off base are successful, he is then subject to charges of violating his own procedures—procedures to which his antagonists among the students, faculty, and trustees often hold no allegiance and which they themselves violate at will when it serves their purposes to do so.

Reform Is Not Enough

Theses of the left at State included a melange of existentialist ideology—neo-Marxist concepts in the styles of Franz Fanon, Regis Debray, Fidel Castro, Ché Guevara, and occasional ideas from Mao Tse-tung. Mao, Ho Chi Min and Marcuse had apparently not yet "arrived." The sweeping indictment against the college and the society was cast largely in the alleged betrayal of our democratic ideals and the presumed hypocrisy with which we assert one thing while blatantly contradicting ourselves in action as a nation, a college and as individuals.

As noted earlier, the major effort of the liberal left and leftist students and faculty was to cudgel the college community into taking forthright stands against the war in Vietnam, against military and war related industrial and government recruiting, and against AFROTC on campus. The traditional posture of institutional neutrality in the face of explosive public and political issues was labeled as immoral. It was argued in response that the stance of most publicly supported colleges and universities is to protect the campus as a market place of diverse ideas and unceasing search of defensible positions with corollary efforts to protect the right of individuals to inquire and to express themselves freely. Dissenters from this position argued that institutional neutrality and openness made the college complicit in an unjust, imperialist policy fostered by the military-industrial complex. The college and its faculty and students were, therefore, helping to kill Vietnamese children, defoliate their crops, and destroy their nation. It was argued that Vietnamese are not Caucasian, thus our unconcern had a racist basis. It was argued that, in fact, we willingly sanctioned racial genocide both by decimating the Vietnamese and by sending a much higher proportion of black and other minority citizens to their death in Vietnam.

Military and industrial recruiting on campus were portrayed not as a service providing broader and freer choices to our students but as proof of the college's conscious subservience to the military-industrial complex. It was thus argued that the college's neutral position made it part and parcel of a militaristic, imperialistic, oppressive government, of a national policy of neo-colonialism usurping the resources of other nations and suppressing the rights of self-determination of other peoples. The arena of duplicity was expanded in the discussion to include our operations in Latin America, Africa, and other nations in Asia.

The concept of neo-colonialism was also turned inward to the domestic front alleging that minority groups, the poor, and large segments of students in the United States are the victims of a sophisticated pattern of colonial suppression directed against our own people. The military-industrial-education complex, controlled by an exploitive privileged elite, systematically deprives these groups of economic independence and self-determination. The curriculum and the teaching at the college are designed to perpetuate this vicious pattern and to suppress dissent. Students and faculty have an obligation to struggle increasingly, unto the death if necessary, to gain their own right to self-determination and to cast their lot with other oppressed peoples both at home and abroad. To do this, it is necessary as a first step to seize power in the college. The college must not remain neutral. It must become an agent of drastic reform or revolution. Because of its complicity in a corrupt society, the authority of the college and of the administrators and faculty are illegitimate. Through whatever means necessary, the college must be made to serve the purposes of its students and the oppressed groups in the ghettoes and other areas of the society. Otherwise the college must be ground to a halt or destroyed. Free speech and academic freedom were attacked repeatedly as covers for inaction, as sophisticated ploys defending the status quo. The post-convocation poll, registering some 4,600 votes, showed 1,800 of the campus community unwilling to rule out force and coercion as a means of making changes in the college.

The thesis that the nation and the college were serving an economic and political system benefiting an elite was stated repeatedly. Concessions and reform, then, could not be the goals of radical dissent.

Structural changes are necessary. Capitalism, bureaucracy, and the white middle class were three prime targets for such change. All are portrayed as exploitive and dehumanizing. Student obligations were to attack this ugly complex wherever its tentacles were exposed. Draft proceedings collaborated in by the college, ROTC, and military recruiting were cited as key targets.

Nathan Glazer,[4] writing in 1969 about the progression of student dissent since the Berkeley Free Speech upheaval in 1964, ruefully noted, "Our gravest mistake [in 1964–1965] was that we did not see what strength and plausibility would soon be attached to the argument that this country was ruled by a cruel and selfish oligarchy devoted to the extension of the power and privileges of the few and denying liberty and even life to the many; and to the further assertion that the university was an integral part of the evil system." Glazer recognized that, for many students and faculty, the subsequent massive expansion of our involvement in Vietnam in 1965 gave credence to the above charges. Further, the same events hastened the split between the liberals and radicals.

The slogan "All Power to the People" graced handbills, appeared in graffiti, and became an amen to platform flights of rhetoric. During the following year the ideology of the movements was extended and elaborated by both the white left and the Third World leadership. The concept of *struggle,* borrowed from Marxist revolutionary theory, was touted as a highly moral approach to social change "by any means necessary." Those out of power, students, minority members, the poor, and the workers are the vanguard of a new regenerative, just society. Those in power are corrupt overseers of a corrupt establishment. They contaminate what they touch. They are powerful and resourceful, but must be challenged. Hence the struggle for "absolute autonomy" for the Experimental College and for black studies. Hence the experimentation with coalitions and fronts involving several groups with distinctive programs and patterns of action. The December 1967 demonstration, during which Gerassi and the white left stormed the administration building, also included a BSU operation an hour or so later that brought young off-campus Negroes to campus and led to beatings and destruction of property. Those operations were parallel but complementary. Jointly, they greatly intensified the chal-

[4] See N. Glazer, "The Campus Crucible: Student Politics and the University." *Atlantic Monthly,* July 1969, 43–53.

lenge to the college and in fact made it more difficult to hold the actors accountable for the disorder and destruction because of a swirling anonymity in a crowd setting.

Search for Power and Leverage

Experienced activists are convinced that going through channels in a bureaucratic system is playing the opposition's game. Through such due process, good causes get redefined, bled to death bit by bit, or pigeon-holed. Popular support cannot be maintained. The issues cannot be held in sharp focus. Even if a group is successful in running a bureaucratic maze, the time lag is too great. A bureaucracy is by nature resistant to change and hostile to those who press for change. Activists argue that energy spent in gaining official sanction and support can better be used in operating programs. Thus the fait accompli becomes an important element of change.

The essential functions of demonstration and confrontation tactics are three: to wring a quick concession from a torpid institution made nervous by threat of greater disorder; to reveal the centers of strength and weakness of the institution through the response of those in decision and policy making roles as they work under stress; and to implicate and gain commitment from those who join in the confrontation. Membership in a movement will grow if direct action leads to serious mistakes in institutional response or if deep individual investment in the action occurs—such as individual acts of courage, daring, or persuasion lauded by the crowd, or martyrdom because of arrest, beatings, or disciplinary procedures. Membership also grows if quick victories are won.

In both the May 1968 and the November 1968 demonstrations, the lists of demands included programs already sanctioned by the college, but the demonstrators claimed those programs as victories. This tactic assures in advance at least a partial victory from a planned confrontation. It is equally important to include in a list of demands some that cannot be conceded. Another common tactic is to add to the demands as a demonstration progresses. This tactic helps prolong a given struggle and may recruit other groups with specific grievances to the fray. It also confuses any efforts to achieve any settlement that may be already under way. Robert Searles has noted that those who are experienced in the strategy of confrontation wait for emotionally provocative mistakes by the officials attempting to cope with the confrontation and seize upon those mistakes to raise the "holy issues." Racism, repression of freedom of speech, police brutality, violation of due process, and suppression of self-determination are examples. In an inflamed situation interlaced with a measure of hysteria, both the unconscionable demand that is rejected and the leap to the "holy issues" gain plausibility among wavering dissidents and lay the groundwork for continuing struggle.

Grievances, converted into specific issues and then into demands, are often real and sometimes long standing. They may or may not be viewed sympathetically by faculty and administrators. More often than not there is contention about the merits or the priority with which such demands are viewed against other unmet priorities. There is growing evidence that, among the young adults most deeply alienated from the college and universities, the specific issues—however real—serve an important function as vehicles in a drive for power and for a broader base of support. Power to the powerless is the crucial aim.

The concept of *struggle* means a no holds barred contest over time. "My father died in chains, I may die, but my young brothers and sisters and my children must be free!" Such aspirations involve longer range goals, short range objectives, strategy and tactics, aspects of an ideology. A defeat must be viewed as only an episode in a long struggle. A defeat, just as a victory, provides a learning situation.

Nathan Hare, in an analysis of the 1968–1969 student strike, argues that the quick take-over of buildings and the massive confrontation dissipates energies quickly and seldom produces lasting change.

> At San Francisco State we seek to supplant such symbolic behavior and the notion of instant victory with a concept of protracted struggle, cemented by the strategy of uncompromising nonnegotiability. We may compromise on tactics but never on principles. This added a do-or-die kind of spirit to our struggle, and, though it presented some problems of its own . . . it nevertheless held us together in this strike longer than we otherwise might have been. It was necessary time and again to gag would-be upstart negotiators who would have divided the ranks between those who wanted to negotiate at a given time and those who wanted to hang on longer.[5]

One of the most difficult tasks for the officials of the college,

[5] M. Thelwell and N. Hare, "From San Francisco State and Cornell: Two Black Radicals Report on Their Campus Struggles." *Ramparts,* July 1969, 58, 59.

however, is to recognize and cope with the 40 to 50 per cent of the students and perhaps the 15 to 25 per cent of the faculty who, while intrigued at the prospect of some transfer of power, really may come to believe the specific demands are the total sum of the problem, that they are just and must be met. They seem not to be aware that the structural changes—major objectives of the most radical dissenters—go far beyond the specific demands in ways that often contradict the larger group's own academic and institutional commitments. In large scale campus disturbances invoked over a slate of adamant demands, the propaganda dimension of the struggle is crucial both on and off campus.

The argument was frequently advanced both by the students and faculty that it was the "spirit of the demands" that was crucial, and that they should be granted in that light. Stokely Carmichael made that issue explicitly clear at a prestrike meeting of the BSU on campus on November 5, 1968. He argued lucidly that it is crucial for black students seeking self-determination to have real power to hire and fire faculty. To demand that a white person be removed and replaced by a black person is not enough. Attitude and political ideology are more important than specific competence. Black students must have the "real power" to hire so that the person hired will "do what we want." Without that power, if the change in personnel is made but the person hired by the college does not possess black consciousness, the fight begins over again. The specific demand is subordinate to the general principle, power to hire and fire.

Departmental faculties have struggled hard for the right to hire under their own criteria and in keeping with their program needs. The same issue is being pressed by militant students. The implicit transfer of power must be examined critically, both in the specific instance and as it relates to general policy. It should be obvious that unilateral student control or specific vested interest control over personnel strikes at the heart of academic freedom. If it can be established as a principle in black studies, it can be established in any other sector of the college.

Polarization and Isolation as a Strategy?

During the academic year 1968–1969, there were repeated efforts to accompany confrontation techniques with the thesis that you are either for us or against us: there is no middle ground; there is no third alternative. The thesis was advanced by true believers among students and faculty, the chancellor, and a number of trustees. They argued that in a moral crisis, failure to choose, to make a total commitment, is cowardly or malicious. Smith tried while president to resist this strategy stubbornly, to blunt the naked struggle for power which must ensue when polarization takes place over emotionally charged issues. His resignation statement of November 1968 was criticized by several people of different persuasions because it did not level a dramatic blast at one or another of the contending groups—trustees, politicians, students, or faculty. In those criticisms, the proposed target of such a blast depended on the critic's own devil theory. During a period of ideological struggle, there is little acceptance of conciliatory approaches designed to leave the contestants' dignity intact.

The militants continually experiment with the tactic of discrediting and isolating subordinates in the administrative hierarchy. The thesis is "we must talk directly to the president." The vice president or dean is portrayed as unsympathetic, prejudiced, incompetent, or without power. Another strategy is to seek appointments with more than one administrator and then press them serially on a request or demand, not informing the others of that fact. The search for ad hoc approval or potential conflict can be exploited later. Conversely, if the president deals directly with militant students or faculty, he isolates himself from his staff. The process of polarization and isolation of individuals is evident in student affairs. Student body elections have shifted to the formulation of coalition slates that almost eliminate the unaffiliated leader. Ideological differences determine the slate: the radical-anarchist students in liaison with the TWLF vs. the moderates and conservatives. A parallel dichotomy has developed steadily in faculty affairs. The result is excessive caucusing and block voting on candidates and issues. Some departments become so sharply split that the vote on a variety of issues can be closely predicted in advance.[6]

Students involved in the press for student power have contributed remarkably to the polarization process as a part of the ideology-action pattern. During the past several years they have developed the tactic of applauding and groaning appropriately in large meetings as discussion on major issues ebbs and flows. The faculty has come to exercise little restraint in the same matter. All but the boldest or the

[6] See *By Any Means Necessary*, pp. 317–350.

most deeply committed avoid exposing themselves to such embarrassment. Antagonists, then, carry the discussion.

Black Students Union leaders and militant black faculty demand that all black faculty and staff commit themselves to a militant separatist position. You are for our program or radical action, or you are for "whitey." If you won't join with the brothers, you are no longer just an Uncle Tom, you are a *traitor*. A memorandum dated October 31, 1968, from Nathan Hare to all black instructors and administrators, says, "The trustees and the administration are trying to destroy us. . . . The Black Student Union and the Black Faculty Union take responsibility for the welfare of all black people on the campus (workers, students, administrators, faculty)." This intent to act for all black personnel was viewed by some as both a demand for conformity and a threat.

A long meeting of the President's Committee of Ten on campus race tensions provides another such example. The Committee met with a number of the BSU leaders to seek their suggestions. Most of the two hour meeting was taken up by punishing, threatening student attacks on the Negro faculty members of the committee, demanding their commitments to BSU programs. White members were dismissed as irrelevant. After the meeting adjourned, the discussion continued with some of the students. They were demanding Committee support to lift suspensions arising from the *Gater* incident. One black student said to a Committee member, "As we see it, our lives are at stake, and whether you know it or not, so is yours." The frequency of such incidents suggests a deliberate tactic to force conformity within a militant group and capitulation to its demands.

An essay by Jon McKinney in the February 20, 1968, issue of *Open Process* attempts to sum up the ideological implications of the war convocation. He sets student radicalism and the SDS critique of the state and the college on one side and all other views together on the other. McKinney argues that the "right wing" is a "monster myth." He claims that Marshall Windmiller, Ronald Reagan, Lyndon Johnson, Barry Goldwater, the Communist Party, and the Neo-Trotskyite movement are all of the same "liberal" package. As viewed by SDS, they are in a tradition that views "the state as a weapon that a dominant and predatory ruling minority wields against uncounted victims." Humanitarian ends are served only when such efforts benefit the rulers. He closes with:

> If these are, at least in part, the assumptions underlying student radicalism, then the political views which SDS expounded over the last eighteen months on this campus have more justice than our critics care to admit. The questions of class ranking, college cooperation with draft boards, campus recruiters for the "military-industrial complex," ROTC (whether voluntary or not), and "liberal racism" all dissolve into the single question of the function of the university, and the view that the university is just as much an instrument of corporate oligarchic rule as the army, and that its effect is often more penetrating and invidious than armed force. Finally we add to this simple ethical assumption, which we all understand well, that failure to struggle against evil is itself evil; and that to achieve victory in this struggle justifies *any methods which are sufficient for such achievement.* (Italics inserted.)

Even this bold attempt to lump all opposing positions together is more promising than seems possible in an intensely emotional setting of campus crisis. Dissenters then muster themselves as the "good guys" and all faculty and administrative leaders become the "bad guys" unless they defect to the position of the militants.

Such efforts to achieve polarization suggest that no viewpoints, even those only nominally within the establishment, are worth salvaging. Such a projected view appears romantic, obtuse, or cynical and provides a rough measure of the ideological distance of militants from the middle of the road. Extremists find it difficult to discriminate among viewpoints other than their own irrespective of the range of the spectrum of alternative positions. This perceptual phenomenon appears in the literature both of socioeconomic class and interethnic relations. Those at the bottom as well as those at the top of a status hierarchy have little capacity for distinguishing differences among a range of subgroups whose views differ progressively from their own. Yet, if a society or an institution is to survive and change within limits short of violent revolution, the *distinctions within* the fringe of adamant extremes must provide the elbowroom for adjustment as circumstances change. Those who can lump together all other views and boldly reject them while marking them for destruction really lie in deadly wait for other fanatics who will challenge them. If those of more moderate and critical temper go carelessly on with business as usual they may be the first casualties. The rage and hostility of the extremists must be defused and absorbed. Liberals and conservatives often show no broader span of ideological perception as they lump each other with the appropriate extremes, thus paralyzing their capacity to act jointly to restrain aggressive fanatics of whatever orientation.

Search for Antiestablishment Allies

Where shall the radical left gain the allies needed for the struggle if so many must be classified as beyond the pale? The argument runs thus. The powerless and the exploited far outnumber the powerful and affluent. All available means must be used to educate and radicalize students, faculty, ethnic minority groups both on and off campus, high school students, the working class, artists, and intellectuals. Liaison must be maintained with students around the world and with people of color in the Third World. The whites, who maintain the exploitive system in the world, are a small minority. The struggle will continue through time until all people are free. As Glazer noted, the syndrome sounds like an echo from the nineteen thirties. That is no reason for dismissing the challenge today. The questions are: how many of the earth's population are wretched, and can their anger be mobilized? Many of the basic theses identified above are subscribed to by the most aggressive young militants among both blacks and Chicanos as well as growing numbers of other minority groups.

John Levin, Progressive Labor Party (PLP) student organizer in the Bay Area, had been in the forefront of radical campus strategies. He argued[7] that students are "taught by rote to produce isolated bits of information for sale to industry and the government." "Their work is not used to solve people's problems," but for maximizing profits and "expanding all forms of exploitation." Levin asks, "Who are our allies?" Not the liberal faculty, they hide from the need for basic change. Students who organize free universities and experimental colleges are misled because that activity drains off energies that should be used to disrupt the college or university and permits the corrupt operations of the institutions to continue unchallenged. The leaders of the Experimental College, the Tutorial Program, the Community Involvement Institute and other student directed operations joined the 1968–1969 strike. By the end of the strike those programs were in shambles. By joining in attacks on the college, those working for radical reform within the college framework were co-opted by those determined to block reform to set the stage for more massive dissent aimed to destroy the institu-

[7] J. Levin. "Power in the University." *Progressive Labor*, November–December 1967, 35.

tion. Levin criticized the cry for student power as a dead end. The drive must be for power for all who were out of power. The need is to make common cause with the workers. The aim must be workers' power over the government. The core of his thesis follows: "By raising the university as the main enemy, the key question of who holds state power is obscured. The fight against the administration is not seen as part and parcel of the revolutionary struggle between the working class and the bourgeoisie for control of the state. But it is precisely the question of the state and how to gain control of it which is the key to power."

Levin thought the time was ripe to forge an alliance with workers. "If we are going to stop the napalm from going to Vietnam we had better get our ass down to Boeing or Douglas. . . . We need to start talking to the workers who have the strength to do it." The aim is "real power" based on a "dictatorship of the working class as opposed to the present imperialist dictatorship." Many of the specific concepts set forth by Levin in the 1967 article are repeated in the political and historical analysis of the 1968–1969 Strike Committee pamphlet published early in 1969. This publication precedes the split in SDS both nationally and on our campus between those committed to the Progressive Labor Party position and the Joe Hill caucus and the later emergence of the Weathermen.

Levin inserted himself into the first meeting with the leaders of the TWLF two days after Smith's appointment as president. It was obvious he and a colleague had seized a role in the meeting requested by the Third World students and they were uncomfortable. The May demonstrations had just ended. It was a week before graduation. The Third World people wanted to talk about amnesty. It was made clear to them the college administration would not intervene with the courts or campus processes for those apprehended during the disorders.

During the 1968–1969 academic year, the PLP and other student allies involved themselves in an oil workers' strike in Richmond and a Bay Area bus drivers' strike in the search for working class allies. These activities were complemented by the summer work-ins sponsored by SDS. The pattern of ideological projection-action-review of response and further projection is again evident. The authors' independent inquiry into the results of the Richmond effort, widely publicized on campus as a partial success, may have turned up a different result. One local union almost withdrew from the AFL-CIO because officials of the Central Labor Council didn't protect the union from "those dirty, hippie kooks" from the campus. But remember, the ideology says a specific defeat is a learning experience in a continuing struggle.

In the search for a broader base of militants, black and Third World students reach for the ghetto residents, high school students, and the militant minority community leadership. At the same time they aim to neutralize or convert the moderate and integrationist inclinations of minority group members. Increasingly separatist, they accept assistance and support from white activists—*but only on their own terms.* Prior to the November 1969 BSU student strike, the SDS appeared intimidated by the BSU, awaiting their marching orders. In one confrontation with SDS, Smith had planned, sourly, to ask them if there was anything that he as president could do to protect invasion of their civil rights by the BSU. His lines were discarded. He was surrounded by BSU members armed with a competing bullhorn and in no mood to be provoked.

From the perspective of revolutionary potential, the drive for black power has the same built-in limitation as has the narrowly conceived drive for student power criticized by John Levin. Both appeal to relatively powerless minority groups in the society. Viewed coldly, a fanatical approach to separatist black power in this violence ridden nation is a long step toward the self-fulfilling prophecy of increasing numbers of Negroes—genocide. It is possible for a frightened, aggressive majority to decimate a minority perceived as a threat. Twentieth-century models have been provided by Russia, Germany, Indonesia, Nigeria, and others. Recently, militant black spokesmen are including progressive whites in their public statements, and some are arguing that black studies must be open to white students. The close coalition during the strike between the BSU and the other groups of the TWLF are examples of the search for allies.

Black militants accept most of the negative assessments of the status quo, applicable both to the nation and the colleges, developed above. Their preemption of radical campus activities during the 1968–1969 academic year probably reflected a greater urgency than that infecting white radicals and a longer history of struggle and frustration. The academic year 1968–69 was marked by greatly increased numbers of campus disruptions led by black and other Third World students. The student strike of the Black Students Union at San Francisco State

College from November to March caught the attention of the nation.

The growing struggles of racial and ethnic groups of color on campuses have paralleled the rise of militancy in black and other minority communities. Campus movements have produced much of the nation's young, sharply militant leadership from this generation rising to fill the place of the murdered Martin Luther King with a more aggressive militancy. These are young men in their twenties, including Stokely Carmichael, Charles Hamilton, and Jimmy Garrett. At San Francisco State, the process of forging a revolutionary black ideology was carried forward by Garrett and his colleagues in the BSU including Jack Alexis, Nesbit Crutchfield, Leroy Goodman, Bennie Stewart, Jerry Varnado, and George Murray. The SDS and the emerging Third World contributed to the process. Ideas and stratagems were freely borrowed among dissenting activist groups and tested for fit in the calico pattern of evolving ideologies.

The Marxist oriented critique of alleged capitalist-imperialist exploitation is interlaced in the rhetoric of individuals of the several action oriented groups. College and university complicity is a corollary proposition. Activists work persistently to spell out new definitions of power relationship among militant groups and between such groups and existing institutions, including colleges and government. For example, since the SNCC separation of black-white leadership in the mid-1960s, a number of SDS leaders—some of whom are veterans of the southern civil rights programs—have come to support the separatist drive of militant racial and ethnic groups. For them, too, integration is a dead issue, but collaboration is important.

During a question and answer period at a "Black Today" conference, held at San Francisco State College May 23–June 1, 1968, Charles V. Hamilton—coauthor of *Black Power* with Carmichael—spoke to this point. Hamilton referred to the alliance of the Black Panther Party with the Peace and Freedom people as "ephemeral, temporary," eliminating the chance of co-option. Hamilton continued, "I think that political sophistication calls for an end to permanent alliances. You never enter into permanent alliances. If you enter alliances you devise means of punishing any 'cop-outs.' " And further, "if we start from an independent power base, with sophisticated leadership, then I am not afraid at all of the potential of having our alliance in danger."

Those involved in radical revolutionary dissent project an unbending rejection of the society as it is and of the control mechanisms it employs. Spokesmen press for self-determination and absolute autonomy while projecting a sense of messianic mission demanding internal discipline and cohesion among the in-group. Thus forced into a minority position hostile to existing centers of power, coalitions and occasional alliances are sought in efforts to seize power. It is an old game played in a new arena. Efforts to transform powerless minorities into the elite vanguard for a long difficult struggle for control over their own destiny and the domination of the destiny of others are clearly there. Common to militant group ideologies on our campus is the any means to the end thesis. This premise repeatedly crops up as well among the hard line proponents of "law and order."

Violence as a Means

BSU spokesmen and the SDS spent little time even in 1967 debating the issue of violence as a justifiable means of pressing for change. The more pertinent questions are when and for what purposes is violence *appropriate?* What level of intensity and what kind of violence? The rhetoric of violence employed by Murray and others reflects the following themes: White racist institutions and societies making up the United States are violence ridden, willing to kill to suppress people of color—willing to practice genocide where necessary. Violence is necessary for self-defense; in fact it is a matter of counter violence. In many circumstances, violence is the only means of forcing the establishment to respond. Violence must be used in a disciplined, functional way to achieve specific goals; turning to violence out of rage, impulse, or for catharsis is understandable but incorrect. If desired changes can be forced without violence, violence should not be used.

Militants believe that the concept of institutionalized violence, like institutionalized racism, goes well beyond conventional concepts of specific acts of assault against property or persons. This society and its institutions are charged as perpetrators of violence against the powerless through the whole fabric of its culture. Social, political, and institutional arrangements that inhibit growth and development of individuals are expressive of violence. Acts of discrimination and deprecation of people of color are acts of violence against individual dignity. The acculturation process dominated by white middle class ideas and perceptions and imposed on all cultural groups through the schools, the media, and other communications agencies wreak violence on the personalities and self-concepts of persons of color and on groups seeking to express divergent cultural patterns. Violence becomes necessary as a counter measure of defense as does violence in the service of a program or a dissenting movement.

"*A new mood* has sprung up among Negroes, particularly among the young, in which self-esteem and enhanced racial pride are replacing apathy and submission to the system." Their drift toward violence as a necessary means has not grown in a vacuum. The Kerner Report notes, "A climate that tends toward approval and encouragement of violence as a form of protest has been created by white terrorism directed against nonviolent protest; by the open defiance of law and federal authority by state and local officials resisting desegregation; and by some protest groups engaging in civil disobedience who turn their backs on nonviolence, go beyond the constitutionally protected rights of petition and free assembly, and resort to violence to attempt to compel alteration of laws and policies with which they disagree."[8]

Jimmy Garrett, then a key strategist of the San Francisco State BSU, delivered a paper at the Black Today conference in 1968. Some of the diffidence on the part of the colleges about rushing into Black Studies on the impetus of Black Nationalists may arise from statements such as the following from Garrett's speech to that conference.

> One part of our work is to build our own schools, but I think that comes as we are building our own nation. In the meanwhile, a great deal of the information that passes between the student and the teacher will be whispered in alleys. . . . in basements and street corners. And the lesson plan will include in chemistry, what is the proper mixture of KNO_3 and S needed to make a good thermite bomb. And in mathematics, calculate the distance between the police station which will be dynamited and the nearest fire station. In English, how can we use Black English as a code to pass information from black to black. Black people are the most skilled, underdeveloped people on earth. And we must use these skills to destroy the enemies of the earth. And then use these skills to create a new world.

At San Francisco State, the inference can be drawn that the white, the black and other Third World militants practiced a measure

[8] O. Kerner et al., *Report,* pp. 10–11.

of restraint in the use of violence during the four months of the strike. Fortunately, there was at that time a gap between the promise of the rhetoric of violence and the operation. The combination, however, of terrorist threats and scattered, illustrative incidents of violence forges a potent weapon. Firearms were in the hands of strikers on campus. Bombs did explode (eight of them). Most were timed for off duty hours, aimed at destruction of property. One appeared to be of an antipersonnel type. Only the explosion that seriously injured BSU member Tim Peebles was clearly demonstrated to be associated with the BSU.[9]

On November 13, a week after the student strike began, an unidentified girl spoke with passion to the crowd after several speakers had insisted that the campus be shut down immediately by any means necessary.

> What I have to say, well, a lot of people are advocating that we use violent means to get teachers to go to our side and support the strike. There are a lot of teachers around who are not violent. And you cannot *speak* to them by violent means. The cops *are* violent. This is what they understand.—I know one of my teachers who was assaulted and now he has turned against you. Before, he didn't know.—Now I can support this strike as long as you use violence against violent people. But for non-violent people, what are you doing? You're turning into what the cops are!

That evening the campus was closed by presidential order as a result of sporadic outbreaks of violence and attendant tension and hysteria.

The White Strike Support Committee offers a revealing account of the efforts to involve students in violence.[10] The pamphlet cites the background strategy applied in several situations to teach students to fight back against police action. It deals obliquely with the use of violence to discourage the students who continued classes late in the strike, as a last resort after a variety of other methods failed.

> After two months of trying to win them over, we made the estimate that the 15 to 20 per cent left were hard core scabs and were beyond education. . . . these scabs had to be dealt with. We discussed this question in the mass meetings, making parallels to labor strikes and how workers deal with strikebreakers. It was pointed out that many could not be won—the "Hayakawa youth,"

[9] See *By Any Means Necessary*, pp. 302, 303.
[10] San Francisco State Strike Committee, "On Strike, Shut It Down!" (undated).

> the rugged individualists—and they would have to pay the price
> for breaking the strike. . . . it was only natural, therefore, that
> changes were going to be made. No one knows from where these
> changes came, as the Strike Committee only "intellectualized" this
> position and discouraged people from engaging in sinister activ-
> ities!!! Yet, from some unknown quarters, things began to happen.

Examples of "things" are cited: two dozen stink bombs; disruption of
the library just before finals; a fire bomb in the Education Building
that melted lockers; harassment of students, who were followed to
classes or cars or had their pictures taken for "future reference." The
analysis continues: "Also, lingering for a moment on the subject, it
seems that Edward Duerr, Hayakawa's right hand man, had his house
fire-bombed and a Professor Bunzel, noted reactionary and opponent
of the strike, found "racist scab" painted on his two cars—in addition
to discovering that he had eight flat tires simultaneously. A meeting,
called by a right-wing group called SMART, to form vigilante committees was broken up by "unknowns"—these occurrences came from
unknown sources—this activity served as an extension of education by
other means." The suggestion that violence is required is coupled with
specific threats of violence that are not carried out. The combination
of terrorist tactics—violence and threat—is designed to pin down "the
enemy" (the college administration and the police). It is designed to
trigger atrocities, also a tactic of ideology builders. If a college is a normally benign institution, it can be trapped into becoming a barracks-
like subculture under persistent threat of violence.

The extreme efforts of black militants to view violence as a
necessary countermeans when employed by them is illustrated by the
public statements of a BSU spokesman when nineteen year old Tim
Peebles was injured. Peebles' hands were maimed and his sight was
impaired when a bomb exploded in his hands in the Creative Arts
Building, allegedly while he was working on the timing device. Statements in his behalf attributed the violence and his injury not to Peebles
but to racist administrators.

Violence runs as a powerful current beneath the surface of the
nation's culture. When black militants adapt to their purposes the patterns of coercion and violence that they have experienced as victims,
the role of their white tutors is forgotten. A black graduate student,
who had been pushed hard by striking students to join the strike but
had refused, stated that the pattern of student control being attempted

by the BSU-Third World strikers was precisely that of the White Citizens Council in the southern town in which he lived.

The interpretation placed on the unfortunate Tim Peebles tragedy will seem bizarre to proponents of law and order, as well as to those who reject violence as a method. But those attempting to build a revolutionary movement and an ideology to support it build folk heroes and martyrs as models from the ranks of the fallen and injured. Ché Guevara, dead in Bolivia, and Regis Debray, young French born ideologist imprisoned in Bolivia, do double duty as heroes for both white and Third World militants. Bobby Hutton, dead at the hands of the Oakland police, and Huey Newton, imprisoned, are important to the Black Panthers as comrades and as charismatic figures who have paid a heavy price in the struggle. Their words are cited as sanctions for ideas and programs, their deeds held up as examples to be emulated by young recruits. Those who have been bold in thought and action have a special place. The degree to which the heroes of a movement are an anathema to public officials tells us the degree to which the ideology of a movement contradicts or transvalues the conventional wisdom and its ideology.

The rising incidence of violence on campuses is paralleled by persistent efforts to build a moral, justifying rationale to support violence as a necessary instrument in achieving educational change and changes in the broader society. This trend is paralleled by a growing willingness among trustees and community and state administrators to bring massive force to bear quickly to put down campus disorder. Thus, the central values and ideals of the academic community are increasingly brushed aside. Violence, long a negative value in democratic ideology, becomes a positive value sanctioned by plausible doctrines of the new ideology, and by those who are challenged.

John Gardner, speaking at Stanford in 1969, commented on trends that threaten to destroy the university and the society. He sees a "swift rise of violence as an instrument of social action."

> I know all the subtle defenses of violence. But I know even better the stark consequences. Violence evokes—I would even say *seeks*— a violent answer. Coercion invites countercoercion. The student with an inclination toward violent or coercive action and the policeman with a taste for brutality are waiting for each other. The politician with a fondness for repressive measures and the ghetto leader with a leaning toward violence are also waiting for

each other. Each reacting to the other, they escalate first the tensions and then the overt acts, and draw increasing numbers of moderates into the deadly interplay. Thus do they weave their own shrouds and ours too.

Racism as Focus

The movement toward separate societies was documented extensively and disturbingly in the Kerner report of 1968. The physical separation of whites continues to progress through "black in-migration and white exodus." "White racism is essentially responsible for the explosive mixture which has been accumulating in our cities since World War II."[11] Among the catalytic factors leading to disorders, the report cites two that are especially germane to the above discussions of the growing rationalization and use of violence in campus disorders.

San Francisco State has been in the vanguard of the developing turmoil cited in the Kerner report as it has been extended to urban campuses. Evidence is accumulating that the development of separate societies, black and white, is gathering energies in California. But the formulation is oversimplified. The emergence of militant ideological commitments on campus among Chicanos, Orientals, American Indians, and other ethnic groups is coupled with the growing support for their programs among white students and faculties. The overwhelming response of public higher education in California to campus disorder has turned on retaliation and repression. This has tended to weld a great diversity of dissenting groups together in a mutual search for militant ideological and action patterns that can sustain dissent in the face of what is viewed by them as monolithic lack of comprehension of "where it's at." We may yet provoke two separate societies, *but cut along different lines* than the Kerner report suggests. The emerging society may become a multiethnic, pluralist coalition united by ideological premises antithetical to white racism, poverty, war, conventional education, and the establishment—a coalition committed to radical action organized within and against unresponsive institutions. "We Must Fight Until Racism Is Destroyed or We Die!"

The struggle against white racism in the United States and around the world has provided a major building block for emerging ideologies of the militants. It was a thesis that pervaded the rhetoric of campus conflict, and grew in prominence during the academic year

[11] O. Kerner et al., *Report.*

1968–1969 as black and brown students seized the initiative in campus confrontations. It has powerful appeal to young adults of all racial and ethnic groups of color, most of whom believe that they have suffered discrimination because of their color. The need to eradicate racism has broad appeal as well among the general population of college students, faculty, and administrative staff, though many smugly assume the problem does not exist in their institution, except, perhaps, in isolated instances or as acts of an occasional bigoted person. The rhetoric of a liberal college does not admit that a broad problem of racism can exist.

President Summerskill referred to the racist nature of San Francisco State College during a conference in the Bay Area in May of 1968. The press reported it. The Council of Academic Deans at the college censured him as did the executive committee of the AAUP campus chapter and their actions were reported to the public. The long, tense discussion with the deans showed the divergent perceptions between the conventional and emerging conceptions of racism in a college. The deans insisted that the college had gone well beyond most colleges and universities in seeking state and federal funds to support programs helpful to Negroes and other minority groups. The institution's publicly stated policies rejected discriminatory practices. The college had launched special admissions programs and special courses to assist minority groups and "dug the resources out of its hide" with no help from the state. It would do more if more support could be obtained. Summerskill insisted that press reports were skewed. He had not singled SFSC out as a nasty example, although he did refer to it as continuing "racist practices" as did other institutions. He was using the term in the sense the term is used by the Kerner report, and by the racial and ethnic militants and others allied with them—to refer to a complex, massive stacking of the decks to produce extra burdens of many kinds on people of color.

Since the 1954 Supreme Court decision on desegregation of schools, the major patterns of racism in the South, and more recently in the North and West, have been so thoroughly documented that they need not be reiterated here. The Kerner report on civil disorders published in 1968 documented in detail the massive racial discrimination in employment, housing, welfare services, education, justice, and police work. Increasing numbers of scholars of various ethnic backgrounds are adding further documentation. The white society has indicted itself. This massive failure to support its own core values—the equal rights to human dignity, opportunity, and freedom of choice—is at once one of the nation's most serious failures and most explosive problems.

Militant students now refer to San Francisco State as a racist institution as a matter of course. Administrators and faculty members who earn their disapproval on any item related to racial and ethnic needs or demands become "racists" in the summary court of campus rhetoric. The term is used as a careless epithet as well as a deadly serious accusation. The young leaders of the separatist ethnic nationalist movement have a vested interest in lumping all white people into the category of racists. It aids the polarization process and becomes a tool for demands that all members of a minority group accept a moral obligation to act together. Some believe all whites are by definition and by commitment racist, denying at the same time the racist nature of their own premise if the term is applied to them. Others say that such a high percentage of whites are racist it is not worth sifting through the debris to find an occasional white person who is not a racist. It is better to assume so and act accordingly. White people on campus are believed racist in another complex sense. They are complicit in racism as employees of a racist institution. "Not to fight evil is to subscribe to evil."

The concept of institutional racism has been expanded dramatically to include elements of the entire range of policies, practices, decision-making patterns, curriculum orientations, content, and instructional methods to which minority members of the college are subject. Those things that inhibit or block the aspiration of individuals or groups other than Caucasians are racist. Even the refusal to promptly and on demand reset other priorities to meet emerging ethnic group aspirations is proof of racism. This trenchant thesis is akin to the demand for indemnity for past injustices. The most impatient and militant on our campus view campus due process in curriculum matters, promotion and hiring, and disciplinary procedures as racist because it slows down change, because it is held to be the work of groups not representative of racial and ethnic aspirations, and because it is maintained by an overwhelmingly white administrative and faculty power structure.

The militant theses are rooted in stubborn drives to establish

the authenticity of the minority cultural pattern and generate the necessary power to claim a full share of what the nation or the college
has to offer. This is coupled to a basic (democratic) premise that
genetic potential for developing intelligence and competence is the
same for all racial and ethnic populations. Until an equal or favor-
able balance of opportunities exists in all dimensions of the college
operation, the institution and its officers must bear the charge of racism. Not only must opportunity for education be there. Racial and
ethnic groups are said to require complete autonomy, so that new
surges toward self-determination are managed by the members of the
group who understand ethnic consciousness. The goal of equality is
exceeded as some militants argue this case. Some demand more than
a currently equal share in the culture, going on to demand reparations
for "two hundred years of abuse." Others project themselves as a culture bearing elite whose responsiblity it is to save all America. They
argue that prima facie evidence of institutional racism is there for all
to see. And it is clear what must be done. If it is not done, and rapidly,
the institution must be halted in its tracks or destroyed. This was central to the ideology of the fifteen nonnegotiable demands and the disruptive strategy of the strike as well as its enduring nature.

Perhaps we can set conventional academic formulations aside
for a moment in an effort to understand some of the perceptual framework of militant ethnic and racial groups, most of whom are severely
underrepresented in higher education. Here is part of what they perceive. San Francisco State College had hired or promoted four black
administrators at the collegewide level during the year preceding the
student strike. As the fall 1968 semester opened, only one of those
black administrators held the rank of dean, the only dean in a position
only temporarily authorized. All other school and staff deans, vice
presidents and the president were white. The entire executive committee of the Academic Senate was white, as were all but two of the
senators. All but a few of the department heads were white. Looking
beyond the college, all eighteen state college presidents were white,
as were all top administrators in the chancellor's office. The twenty-
one member board of trustees included only one Negro, and he carried
a double burden as "the trustee from organized labor." Conventional
wisdom in education says not color but educational leadership is at
issue. A good man, regardless of his reference group, will act even

handedly in the best interests of all students and citizens. The response
of many of today's students to this alleged color blind approach to
leadership is brief and pungent. The argument is: "Bullshit!"

Growing numbers of college students and faculty ally themselves with the drive for self-determination in education which has
been given new impetus by the evolving concepts of black power. Yet
traditional support for a pluralistic society also supports the thesis that
a common general education is appropriate for all cultural and ethnic
groups. Differentiations are planned and supported on the basis of
individual needs, interests, and talents. A man is a man is a man. The
common learnings are supposed to provide the cement that holds a
pluralistic society together. They also provide the bases for racial and
ethnic integration. The quest is for social cohesion with room for maximum individual autonomy and mobility in the occupational and social structure.

This is what the racially and ethnically conscious minority leadership feel they must reject. Controlled by a pervasive white policy
making administrative structure, college becomes a brainwashing process producing whitewashed people of color who are stripped of their
cultural moorings and their identity. They are not accepted in the
white middle class culture and are closed off from their class and their
ethnic origins. They become invisible men, marginal in both cultures.
This, then, is the most insidiously racist aspect of education. Those
youth with deep ties to black culture or other ethnic cultures are apt
to be described as "culturally deprived." Ethnic consciousness demands
that ethnic and cultural groups move intact toward the centers of
power, under their own leadership. No more the running of a futile
lonely race into an eventual dead end!

Further obvious evidence of institutional racism, in the perception of minority leaders and their white allies, is found in admission
policies and the growing imbalance in the racial and ethnic mix of the
student body. Parallel criticisms were also directed at faculty composition. Admission standards in the state college system were raised effective fall 1965, in compliance with the requirements of the master plan
for higher education. That plan requires the colleges to admit students
only from the upper third of the state's high school graduates, as determined by high school grade average and a standardized test. This
policy actually reduced the proportion of black students enrolled and

tended to block admission of other minority students clustered in low socioeconomic status. This is the policy at a time when the majority of students in the lower schools in the cities of San Francisco, Oakland, Berkeley, and Richmond (the Bay Area communities served by San Francisco State College) are other than Caucasian, and their proportion of the population is growing. Thus the most geographically accessible, state-supported A.B. degree granting institution has turned away from the rising aspirations of the inner cities' population for higher education. Supporters of a more restrictive admissions policy believe themselves motivated by respect for higher academic standards and quality education. Those favoring wider access to college argue that, at best, the above approach discriminates against culturally different groups. At worst, it is a clear example of institutional racism. Proponents of black power, black separatism and the concept that black is beautiful are being consistent with their ideology when they press for complete program control over black and ethnic studies. The demand by Stokely Carmichael and the BSU for real power to hire and fire teachers and professors also follows. Demands for major representation in the highest councils of the college and the state college system must be expected.

As a result of the 1968–1969 campus struggle, the four black administrators mentioned above all left the college. The dean of undergraduate studies, associate dean of students, and the director of the Educational Opportunities Program all resigned, with a public blast at President Hayakawa and "a racist college." The Chicano associate director of the EOP joined the group. The acting head of black studies and the professor developing Mexican-American and Latin-American ethnic studies were dropped from the staff. White administrators, almost without exception, continued in roles at the college. One of the gravest outcomes of the strikes and the accompanying disorder was the destruction of the professional roles of minority group administrators who are expected to function within the traditional liberal framework of the college in behalf of the interests of the whole college. College officials are also prone to view those administrators as spokesmen for their ethnic groups on campus. At the same time they are viewed by militants as the specific and loyal agents of the BSU and TWLF student groups, in their jobs because of militant action. Sharp pressure from militants to force such a choice on black admin-

istrators and insist they demonstrate their loyalty in public actions had
been apparent for at least a year before the strike. Perceiving the problem did not assure a solution, as one after another chose against the
administration and cast their lot with student strikers. This coupled
with the hard line of the trustees and Hayakawa left them no way
back.

Black administrators complained bitterly because they were not
in the inner decision-making council of the college administrative faculty group. Initially that was a matter of assigned role and status. As
the conflict deepened, credibility became a major unspoken issue. If
black administrators were agents of the BSU and the BSU was sponsoring violence and disruptive acts that the college officials were trying
to halt, the tendency was strong to view black administrators as potential fifth columnists. Police and students were infiltrating militant
groups to gather information and to attempt to offset extreme militancy. Why bring potential double agents into the college councils to
help with counterinsurgency strategies? The tension was sufficiently high
even before the student strike began to trigger such responses. For example, the dean of students and Joe White, dean of undergraduate
studies, a Negro, caught President Smith in the hall the day before
the strike began to discuss the time and place for a Stokely Carmichael
speech on campus that day. White was carrying the formal clearance.
He had mentioned his prior acquaintance with Carmichael several
weeks before. Carmichael's visit to campus was news to Smith. It was
finally agreed that he could speak at the open air platform or the
football stadium. But Carmichael spoke to a closed meeting of the
BSU in the main auditorium, giving lesson 1-A on how to conceptual-
ize, plan and sustain a strike as part of the black people's struggle. Joe
White did not move closer to the inner circles as a result of that episode.

As long as an urban college functions with a major imbalance
in ethnic composition of its faculty, staff and student body in relation
to its service area, with power roles and with policy-making machinery largely in white hands, the charge of institutional racism will be
with us. The rapid ideological polarizations have come to a focus more
sharply on Bay Area campuses than elsewhere in California, if not in
the nation. Provocative issues of race appear to be a major catalyst to
further struggle and further development of conflicting ideology. They
are perhaps as significant as are the issues of violence.

Disciplined Management of Campus Revolt

Emerging from the experience of two years of campus turmoil is a concept of minority control of campus affairs generated among those out of power. Those who hold roles of authority in the administration, in faculty, and in student government are viewed in the lexicon of revolutionary doctrine as usurpers of the power of the people. A well disciplined minority clique can generate great power in a large bureaucracy inattentive to the potential of organized political power and itself characterized by low pressure enclaves. Further, an urban commute college has large masses of students and large numbers of faculty with low involvement in the college beyond their special academic interests. Their identification with the institution as a community is also low and may actually be negative. A coherent response to an aggressive clique or subgroup is hard to mobilize. Because of these factors, reform comes hard, but disruption is relatively easy to achieve if a determined leadership seeks power and moves with persistence and appropriate strategy. Nathan Hare explains: "Mass behavior is the natural tendency of large collectivities, and is more suited as well to America's myth of majority government. As in all cases of revolutionary action, the strike was launched by a minority of individuals who apparently articulated the latent needs, the powerlessness of persons at large. Black students at San Francisco State College generally shunned ultrademocracy as a guiding principle, substituting 'democratic centralism' instead."[12]

Hare reports that during the strike it was necessary to control the decision-making process tightly to discourage casuals, agents, provocateurs, infiltrating policemen, and those wanting to restore peace and harmony. Yet the strike was planned so that, within policies of the tight central decision-making group, supporters could do their thing. Faculty are also capable of bypassing majority rule as they respond to growing moral and ideological commitments.

In November, John Caffrey was observing a struggle in a large faculty meeting in which the vote was consistently going against the minority of faculty sympathetic to the strike on several issues concerning the format of the proposed convocation. He noted the growing anger in the faces of those losing the issues and observed that they

[12] Thelwell and Hare, *op. cit.*

apparently did not believe the majority should decide the issues before the assembly. Later many of the same faculty members struck to force the college to close and the system to bargain with them on a slate of demands, fully aware that they represented a minority within the faculty. Although only a tiny minority of the faculty within the state college system, they pressed demands affecting all faculty within the system. A poll of full time faculty conducted early in the faculty strike showed 64 per cent of the faculty responding to be opposed to the strike.

After Smith's resignation, a more conservative minority of faculty—the Faculty Renaissance led by Hayakawa—took over the administration of the college, quickly establishing two executive positions in addition of that of president. By year's end the same group elected the chairman of the Academic Senate. The faculty, plagued by contending cliques, increased the disorder in decision making through town hall type meetings.

The faculty moved during the crisis from dependence on its executive committee and Senate to town meeting democracy to factional struggles to virtual elimination as a factor in decision making. The BSU and TWLF moved early and consciously toward democratic centralism. And they were successful in maintaining a tight rein on decision making and a solid public front in support of the strike. Three months later in the strike, their control shattered, the BSU and TWLF were forced to negotiate the nonnegotiable demands. Clarence Thomas, writing in *Black Fire,* explains the concept and process: "The central committee of the Black Students Union at SFSC carries out the practice of democratic centralism; the revolutionary government of the People's Republic of Red China and Cuba also carry out that rule of discipline. It is very important for all of the membership . . . to understand this principle, the importance of it and the reason for it." Thomas explains that freedom requires discipline and that the concepts as developed by the United States and Western thought do not work: "If democracy was practiced anywhere on the face of the earth, issues would never get resolved." Centralism is a correlate of his democracy. He argues that if the proposed strike had been placed before all of the black students for a vote, chaos would have resulted and "The strike and the revolutionary struggle against the trustees, Reagan, Alioto, and Hayakawa would never have been put into action with a democratic vote." The central committee selected by the students, "give(s) directions, leadership and make(s) policies for the students. In the final analysis, it is the people who control it." And further, "The central committee must have discipline, set the correct examples, and all of its members have the same political ideology. We must affirm anew the discipline of the party, namely: (1) the individual is subordinate to the organization; (2) the lower level is subordinate to the higher level; (3) the entire membership is subordinate to the central committee. Whoever violates these articles of discipline disrupts party unity."[13]

The concepts of central control and discipline stated by Thomas are further illustrated in an unsigned four-page set of guidelines, "Organization of the Black High School Student." It calls for a hard core steering committee of five or six trained and disciplined high school students. Their job is to mobilize black students to take over their school. They will destroy the school "only if the administration forces give it no alternative." They are to meet off campus with a Black Panther Party member who provides a link between the campus people and the Black Panther Party. The off-campus group should develop an umbrella organization to include all black students. Existing black organizations should be converted to radical uses, neutralized or destroyed. Slates of black candidates should run for office in as many organizations as possible. Again the concept is developed that power can be achieved in a school or college by a purposeful minority educated to the task, disciplined, bold in action, and directed by a small central committee drawing support from a base outside the school or college. Similar efforts among the right or arch-conservative wing of students are under way, though with less spectacular results. The Young Americans for Freedom (YAF) associated with William Buckley is one example.

The age of political and ideological innocence and low pressure bickering around the broad consensus is fast drawing to a close in urban colleges and universities. The new mood is reflected in struggles for power by determined minorities with new agenda focused on the gravest issues of our times. Much the same pattern of tight central control characterizes the internal operation of the apparently looseknit

[13] The quote from Thomas is a paraphrase of the principles as stated in *Quotations from Chairman Mao Tse-tung: The Red Guard Handbook* (Nashville: International Center of the George Peabody College for Teachers, 1967), p. 255.

Students for a Democratic Society. The writers have observed the overtly looseknit, "one man, one vote" participatory democracy of open planning meetings called by the SDS. The microphone is controlled by one of the trusted inner circle, the agenda is adroitly proposed. The discussion goes on as though all possibilities are open. Yet the central cadre, usually dispersed among the larger group, are practiced in moving in to "stomp" errant ideas and proposals. When decisions have been made "by the whole," responsibilities and work assignment are laid out. Key members easily accrue to themselves the subleadership roles. Likely recruits are welcomed in work roles. Jan Valtin describes the above strategy employed on a much larger scale at the first International Seaman's Congress held near Hamburg in 1932. The delegates from all over the world represented an estimated one million workers. "Only a minority were communists. Yet the majority of noncommunist elements was hopelessly at the mercy of the communist 'fraction' (caucus), which never acknowledged its existence to outsiders, operated to dominate the seemingly democratic procedure of the convention."[14] The CIA manipulation of the National Students Association and the Mayor Daley approach to the 1968 Democratic Convention are other examples of the deliberate ideological strategy of manipulating large memberships from a strategically contrived minority operation. The John Birch Society cadres, operating at the community level, provide similar models.

The ideological premises identified in this chapter are largely rooted in negative perceptions and feelings about the performance of the existing society, its leadership and its institutions. The cycles of analysis, agitation, and direct action at San Francisco State College developed a pattern of interlinked ideas, assumptions, and strategies that helped guide the rebellions and lent strength and endurance to them. Key tenets have been identified as they appeared in their operational context in this chapter. Lifted from that context and stated as the components of a rationale for revolution, their potency should not be dismissed. Key premises of the ideology of radical dissent at San Francisco State College follow.

The nation and the college are organized to rob students and other powerless people of their selfhood. To work within the rules of the system is to be co-opted for other people's purposes. This is

[14] J. Valtin, *Out of the Night* (New York: Alliance Book Corporation, 1941), pp. 313, 314.

slavery. Any who hope to survive and live as whole persons must struggle by any means necessary to change the system radically or to destroy it. Black people and other people of color, although a majority of the world's population, are treated as subhuman and are especially exploited by a racist system controlled by white people. The college is an example. Power over others is never relinquished voluntarily by men. It must be seized and redirected to provide freedom for self-determination. Those now leading the struggle are the vanguard of the new or emerging society which must and will come. All of like color and ideology must join in the struggle for freedom. The fortunate and talented must serve those less fortunate.

The nation clings to a capitalist economy geared to profit for the few rather than to the needs of all people. The economy is geared to a mindless production of material goods unrelated to basic human needs and designed to enhance the affluent classes. It is geared to war waged to protect its desire and power to exploit rather than to serve people both abroad and at home. The college and its leadership are parties to this destructive establishment, the military-industry-education complex. Education must be redirected, from preparing manpower for slots in the establishment to providing a context in which the student can educate himself through a process he controls. A college concerned first about human values must deliberately direct its resources toward eliminating the conditions that strip people of their humanity and establishing a qualitatively humane community on campus and off. The ideology of war must be replaced with an ideology of peace. Elimination of poverty and of education and health deprivation must be a top priority. Pluralism and self-determination mean that distinctive racial, ethnic, and cultural groups must achieve complete control over their institutions, including education. (There is conflict on this point within the many groups engaged in radical dissent. The recent split in SDS is illustrative: Should the wretched of the earth be mobilized on a worldwide class basis or should racial, ethnic and cultural groups mobilize themselves on their own terms, effecting coalitions against the establishment as needed? "All power to the people!" "Black power to black people" states the contradiction nicely.) The process of education must be revolutionized to incorporate at all levels the physical, emotional, intellectual, social, aesthetic, moral, and political-ideological drives of man. The intellectual-verbal approach to specialized, packaged knowledge, so typical of formal education, cripples creative initiative. Knowledge and insight must be constantly tested in action and action must be accepted as the generator of new learning. The malfunctioning colleges in a malfunctioning society must be open to radical experimentation. The powerless must gain control of the centers of power which now serve them so poorly in the systems of education, economics, politics, and communication if they are to achieve self-determination and freedom. The vanguard struggling for power must commit themselves to the death to the needs of the exploited peoples everywhere.

The established system of the nation and the college is closed to radical dissent and proposals for radical change. Ultimately it turns to violence to resist significant change. Bureaucratic organization shaped to maintaining the status quo is the first line of resistance to needs that challenge the system. Established administrative and supervisory roles (as well as faculty roles in a college) are designed to support priorities imposed by the exploitive groups who benefit from the system. Rules and regulations, the administration of justice, the basis of admission and exclusion, and the distribution of privileges and rewards are stacked in favor of a brainwashed conformity and against innovation, creativity, and an extension of opportunity to groups and individuals currently excluded from equitable participation. Thus higher education is viciously politicized in the deepest meaning of the term politics. This system functions from the international level to the local campus and classroom level with the backing of the police and military forces. Unlimited resources are available for containment and repression. Miniscule amounts of resources are devoted to token gestures toward change for the purposes of simulating reform while structures remain unchanged, and a host of human problems accumulate.

Vanguard groups must struggle, to the death if necessary, to reset the priorities of the nation and its institutions and to force structural changes. They must use *any means necessary* to carry forward the struggle. Efforts to work cooperatively within the system for reform means co-option by the system. It may be worthwhile to work nominally within the system on a completely autonomous basis using the resources of the college to build an independent base from which to challenge the status quo. Noncooperation and refusal to live by the conventional rules must be a principle of operation. Sophisticated disruption must become so expensive that the institution capitulates to demands for change and a redistribution of power. Shouts of anger from the establishment charging the politicizing of education are merely a cover screening the existing politics of education. An aroused and self-conscious population (students and faculty) have great power. It is the responsibility of the vanguard to lead in educating the people and mobilizing their power against the establishment. It is also a moral obligation. Agitation, propaganda, confrontations, and guerrilla warfare are examples of educational tactics. The power marshalled against change and against the aspirations of those out of power is formidable. The challenges and attacks must be directed to vulnerable points in the structure. Disruptive flea attacks as a substitution for occupation of a building and submission to arrest are one example. Sustained attacks on the president and the president's alleged role as a puppet are another. Disciplined leadership must operate from bases and constituencies, both on and off campus. Reinforcing liaison must be expanded among centers of dissent at national and international levels. Coercion, intimidation, and violence are necessary means, obviously sanctioned by the establishment *in its own service* and justified even by its own rationale. Their uses should be expensive for the establishment and as conserving as possible of the militants and their resources. Contradictions between the stated purpose of the establishment and its performance are rampant. They must be exposed. Polarization must be fostered to isolate the oppressors and divide them from their nominal supporters and the passive. There are no neutrals in this struggle. All possible means must be used to gain commitments to the movement from those not previously involved. Pressure must be incessant to delegitimize the control structure of the establishment. Overload the administrative structure to force it to malfunction. Precipitate outside interference in the college thus neutralizing the capacity of campus officials to respond to challenge. Sustain the struggle through as many avenues as possible at as high a level as resources permit, encouraging initiative and creativity within the objectives of the movement. A defeat provides a crucial learning experience. A victory is no reason to relax. Continue to add to the demands and negotiate only to consolidate gains.

Implications of Ideological Challenges

The tendency is great to dismiss the pattern of ideological theses described above as the irresponsible ragings of a handful of romantic revolutionaries. The assessment of Nathan Glazer cited earlier may dissuade us from brushing off the problem. John Gardner states that he no longer laughs when a student says, "We can destroy the university." The developing ideology outlined above, coupled with the drive of the radical reformist students and faculty described in an earlier chapter, managed to convulse the San Francisco State campus for four months and helped polarize public opinion in California over the issues of higher education. It left a legacy of repression in the atmosphere which has great potential for fueling a continuing struggle. To a greater or lesser degree, other colleges and universities have experienced growing stress from the same sources, as have the high schools.

Attention should be given to the plausibility of many of the stated goals which point to aspirations that are ideals central to American democracy. Similar indictments of this society and of higher education can be found in the writing of critics within the establishment. Among those who come easily to mind are J. William Fulbright, David Shoup, Ralph Nader, Robert Hutchins, and Harold Taylor—men of diverse views yet all drastic critics of the status quo.

The views described in this chapter focus almost exclusively on the limitations and perceived malfunctions of the society. The plausible leap can then be made to total rejection of the society and those who identify with it, accompanied by a call for revolution aimed at its destruction and the seizure of power. The hell-for-leather advocacy and experimentation with violent and coercive means adds a pretotalitarian cast to much of this counter ideology. The hopeful ends projected—a world at peace with societies reflecting equity of treatment, broad sharing of power, and active commitment to humane values and relationships—may thus be negated before the major struggle is far along.

There are hazards in the ease with which scholars of sophistication in ideology, politics, and social movements dismiss the fumbling ideological projections of today's radicals. It is not enough to conclude that "they are lousy Marxists" or that "they have no sense of history" or that "they are powerless in the face of the establishment." The disorderly openness of today's movements lends them strength when wedded to anger, aspiration, a sense of being up against the wall, and a desire for risk in action. If we wish to avoid dependence on widening suppression, it is crucial that the nation and the colleges move powerfully to project a hopeful future supportive of the traditional ideals and values to which many of today's radicals are committed.

Concurrently, determined and sustained efforts to extend equity and freedom must be clearly apparent, rooted in means appropriate to a democracy. Further drift toward polarization on the radical right and left is especially dangerous to higher education. The rapid shift within many groups toward broader acceptance of authoritarian and totalitarian means is polluting the wellsprings of an open society.

Trenchant counter ideologies are emerging in campus settings and other more seriously ghettoized enclaves of dissent around the world. The SDS, the Black Panthers, the Red Guards, the Palestinian hijackers and the students at the Sorbonne embrace many of the same ideology-action tenets and shout the names of common heroes. They call for the violent destruction of the status quo and those who man and defend it. They shout for the seizure of power in the name of "the People."

In this country, colleges and universities, citadels of ideas, have little experience with militant ideologies in action. Instead of expanding the framework of the society or shifting its orientation in ways that absorb the militants, we attempt to quarantine and repress them. Messianic ideologies are hard to stamp out. In fact repression of the believers usually multiplies their number.

Massive numbers of students, restive and anxious in a conflict-ridden time, are politically naive for the most part. They provide the stuff for disruptive movements and ideological ferment. Faculties—iconoclastic, fragmented, and isolated—have as yet shown little elan in coping with trenchant ideological challenges launched from within the academic community, whether such challenges stem from students or from colleagues. As things stand in the early seventies, police, national guard, and army units often provide the first line of defense for the status quo. Hard line administrators are replacing educators as the second line. More explicit and arbitrary regulations and retaliatory dismissals and firings provide the third line. The fourth line of defense marries the hard line administrator, trustee and political figure with the mass media monitoring the ceremony for the multitude. Fear, anger, and bigotry cloud the ceremony. Further polarization ensues.

In California, this cycle has moved the public sentiment so far to the right that political and financial support for higher education is being withheld, a larger proportion of young adults move toward even deeper dissent, and increasing numbers of students are turned away from the state colleges. Radical ideology, including commitments to

violence and calculated campus disorder, draws suppression. Each
cycle of disruption and suppression breeds adamant proponents. Both
disruption and suppression contribute to the destruction of higher
learning as concurrence and consent are replaced by intimidation and
coercion. Campus stability, when it exists on those campuses that have
experienced disruption, represents a truce rather than peace, a breather
while tactics, strategies, and resources for the next round of struggle
are reviewed. (On the day this was written the fall 1970 offensive of
the revolutionists brought three bombings to the west coast, in Seattle,
San Rafael, and Santa Barbara, an unexploded bomb at University
of California, Berkeley, and a bomb threat to the building in which
this was being written.) The activists and revolutionaries who have
severed connections with the campus and those on academic or court
probation move into the streets for another round of agitating and
organizing among youth. College officials talk of depoliticizing the
campus, while candidates from the local to the national level gamble
their political futures on a hard-line stance on campus dissidence, in
itself a politicizing act. Some academes plead for a return to the life
of the mind. Others disparage the search for relevant education lest
education be equated with the shallowness of the morning newspaper.
With the magic eye of television poised to project both the dramatic
action and the subtle nuances of struggle into millions of homes, few
public figures dare admit to uncertainty, to past errors, or even to a
program aimed at reconciliation.

Ways must be found to absorb within higher education a
wider range of newer styles of perception and stated needs. If this is to
defuse growing conflict, the status quo must change to make room for
some ideals projected by dissidents. We are saying that repression directed at restoring the pre-1964 patterns of higher education ignore
the power of both ideology and of new styles of action to disrupt if
not destroy higher education. If social institutions cannot hold the
loyalty of those they are designed to serve, they have no trustworthy
credentials in a democratc society.

The academic community should move quietly, and without
dramatic recrimination, on every front open to them to curb and hold
accountable those who engage in violence and who act to provoke
crowd violence successfully, regardless of their role on the campus.
They should be excluded from the campus for appropriate periods of
time, and held accountable in courts for criminal acts. Direct threats,

intimidation and coercion must be rejected by all who do not wish to destroy the college or university and who wish it to remain viable enough to change and survive.

Faculty, students, and administrators at San Francsico State College were severely limited during months of recurrent crises in their ability to distinguish from activist reformers those individuals and groups whose avowed objectives were to control or destroy the college by any necessary means, who were in fact intent on blocking reform and any planned efforts to bring about change. The tendency was strong to lump all dissenters and their programs together for support or rejection. All defenders of the status quo and arch-reactionaries tended also to be lumped together. Such obtuse divisions within the campus were also reflected among trustees and in public opinion.

The academic community must make up for a legacy of political and ideological naivete broadly characteristic of the citizenry of this nation. Schools and colleges are a priority locus for such efforts, because they are being paralyzed by ideologically based conflict and because they have sophisticated resources of their own for in-service education—resources largely unused, alas, because they are quarantined within the sterile isolation cells of the departmental structure.

There is great need for in-service education as well as instructional programs dealing with: the emerging counter cultures and the ideologies of the status quo; theories of social change and innovation; and conflict management. Citizenship as well as professional practice in today's academic community demands a great deal more than in the past. The tendency to withdrawal and isolation must give way to willingness to learn new roles and perspectives appropriate for a rougher, more complex game.

The decision-making structures of the region and the state are manned by many whose response to active heresies is suppression and retaliation or, less frequently, their own uncritical conversion. In a region such as the San Francisco Bay Area, with its complex of colleges and universities and dissenting communities, there is a great need beyond a given campus for a think-tank approach to ideologically based institutional and community conflict involving the widest possible spectrum of views. Such an operation should be well financed and so designed that access to its institutes, workshops, training sessions, and materials are available to citizens, public officials, students, college personnel, and emerging groups alike. It must also be designed to gain direct access to the centers of ferment and reaction which shape public policy and program. It should develop patterns for extending its programs throughout the state. It is not enough to shoot up the Black Panther headquarters at 4:30 A.M. or label all campus and community dissenters as radicals and revolutionaries. Nor will the bombing of a campus building bring needed reform. The hard task is to find ways to alleviate agonies that lead to insurrection, to develop a better rationale than revolt. A budget for such an institution equal to that of one of the state's hundred plus colleges and universities, a pittance within the larger effort, should bring rich returns.

FOUR

Problems of
Minority Education

The educational institutions now rest solely in the hands of racist millionaires, poorly dressed pimps with governmental positions as their fronts, and the military compound using its influence to extend its vicious thievery throughout the world. For these sinister and ravenous reasons, this power must be seized by Third World people and be utilized to "determine our own educational destiny." We must also begin to act on the diagnosis to Amerikka's most strangling problem—racism. We'll oppose racism with an active war against it. These are old principles, but we are now a new generation of people and must no longer be deceived by the amount of powerlessness, or the type of racism vented upon Third World but must wage an unyielding struggle for humanity and the principles of our lives.

Leroy Goodwin, Off-Campus Coordinator,
Black Students Union

We want freedom. We want power to determine the destiny of our school. We want full enrollment in the schools for our people. We want an education for our people that teaches us how to survive in the present day society. We want power, enrollment, equipment, education, teachers, justice, and peace.

Ten Point Program of the
Black Students Union

Our ultimate responsibility is to the Black nation in this Babylon called America. Black people cannot commit any crimes against

99

white people. The only crimes that we can commit are crimes against humanity. And white people aren't a part of humanity.

Member of the Black Students Union, quoted by
A. Cooke, *Manchester Guardian Weekly*,
December 28, 1967, p. 7

—that there be a Department of Black Studies which will grant a bachelor's degree in Black Studies; that the Black Studies Department Chairman, faculty and staff have the sole power to hire and fire without interference of the racist administration and the Chancellor.
—that all black students who wish to, be admitted in Fall, 1969.
—that Dr. Helen Bedesem be replaced in the position of Financial Aid Office and that a black person be hired to direct it, and that the Third World people have the power to determine how it will be administered.
—that the California State College Trustees not be allowed to dissolve any black programs on or off the San Francisco State College campus.
—that Schools of Ethnic Studies for the ethnic groups involved in the Third World be set up, with students for each particular organization having the authority and the control of the hiring and retention of any faculty member, director and administrator, as well as the curricula.
—that George Murray and any other faculty member chosen by non-white people as their teacher be retained in their positions.

Fifteen Demands of the Third World
Liberation Front

In addition to revealing the rage and disenchantment of a significant portion of our ethnic minorities, the above sample of statements by some of the most active students raises urgent questions about the content and purpose of higher education. In the first chapter we suggested that higher education in the United States is more than ever faced with important role dilemmas. Several of these dilemmas come into sharp focus when the subject of education for America's depressed minorities is treated. Questions of purpose, relevance, control, access, and community action touch some of the most sensitive nerves of the American educational system.

When members of ethnic minority groups cry that they have been forced to deny their background by the white-dominated educational enterprise, we are taken aback. When some militant students reject integration as a value goal of our education and social strategies, our conventional wisdom is challenged. When black and other ethnic minority students demand power to determine their own educational destinies, even the right to hire and fire faculty, we find our system of values directly threatened. When a yardstick of color or race is to be used to measure the worth and acceptability of faculty members, present and future, we are haunted by the specter of racism in reverse. When all nonwhite students are to be admitted to the college regardless of qualifications or previous record, we discover many of our basic assumptions about the purposes, standards, and directions of our institutions under attack. We tend to be amazed and sometimes angry that such demands, postures, and orientations could almost suddenly spring up to disturb the normal patterns of our educational lives. We feel offended and hurt that our traditions—our concerns for scholarship and the search for truth and our devotion to principles of justice and fairness that are color-blind—should now be rejected in a blatant, sometimes vulgar, and occasionally violent rhetoric. To be read out of humanity because we are white, to be lumped in with racist fools and knaves when we have considered ourselves pure and to become the targets of outrageous charges because we are somehow part of a shadowy establishment is unsettling, provocative and, for some, guilt-raising.

What are we to make of it? What kinds of actions and reactions seem to be open to us? What responses shall we make? If the San Francisco State experience is instructive, many reactions are possible. These reactions range from enthusiastic or frightened acceptance of all charges, proposals, and judgments made by minority militants to utter rejection and righteous denial that there could be any validity to those criticisms, at least as far as the colleges are concerned. In this climate, the tendency toward polarization of attitudes and assessments is great. Lost in the resultant rhetoric may be the chance for worrying our way through a grievous problem. Also lost may be the opportunity to arrive at realistic proposals for change. In this chapter we try to listen beyond the rhetoric, to treat the issues raised in a manner forthright and open, yet compassionate and creative. First, it seems worthwhile to discuss the genesis of the problem briefly. Second, we turn to the rationale and strategies for solution that have been proposed by the militant minority students and faculty, particularly at San Francisco State. Then some tentative comments upon this rationale and these strategies are made. Finally, one man's view of a possible path toward resolution of the difficulties is presented.

It is widely recognized that the most difficult problem facing

American society today is the problem of how to deal with the fact of racism in all of our institutions. That the dominant white majority has not completely accepted the concept of equality between the races is well known and documented. But it might be useful, in the context of this discussion, to remind ourselves of the unsatisfactory progress towards the integration of various ethnic groups in American society. This is dramatized most sharply in our educational institutions where large numbers of children and young adults in both the North and the South still go to school and college in segregated educational systems. Despite a widespread understanding of the enormous integrational task ahead, arguments continue about whether the rate of change toward a truly integrated society has been rapid or slow. These arguments are increasingly irrelevant because many members of the minority communities—with varying degrees of intensity—now perceive the integrationist path towards genuine equality as a blind alley so filled with psychological and practical obstacles that it leads to nowhere.

In the eyes of many, the problems of the minorities, particularly in education, are not the problems of integration. The problems of black and other minority students from kindergarten through college are the problems of relevance, estrangement, identity, and powerlessness. It is argued that the high dropout rate, the low grades, and the general lack of motivation among large numbers of minority students are due not only to a general feeling of separateness but also to a more specific folk belief that education under the control of the white community fails to focus upon subject matter that is germane to the life experiences of the people in the minority community. The charge is that black and other minority students have little opportunity in the traditional curricula to place themselves in a meaningful and satisfying historical and personal context. The literature read, the family studied, the music analyzed, the civilization surveyed, the cultures examined and the psychologies explored are perceived as *white-culture* bound, without basic ability to attract the interest and enthusiasm of the minority student and therefore without any real chance to help him reach his highest human potential. Jimmy Garrett, a former leader of the Black Students Union at the San Francisco State campus, speaks sharply to this point in an unpublished grant proposal submitted to the Council of Academic Deans in the spring of 1967:

> Over the past several years there has been an increasing and growing development in the Black community which has the deep-

est implications for American society. That development expresses itself as a growing self-concern among black people, which has been explicated best by the young people of that community. The explication began probably with the sit-in movement in the South, which was a quest for dignity and asserting for humanity. This concern spread with the freedom rides and community organization in the South, which was a quest for the acknowledgment of presence, a desire for recognition. Black people began wanting to know more about their history, both in the country, in Africa, and in the world. . . . We have begun to say that perhaps colleges and universities as they now exist are, at least, irrelevant, sometimes even destructive, to black students in terms of the recognition of new needs in the black community. We have begun to define the concept which is called, "black consciousness." We have begun to say that perhaps it is the recognition of one's self in terms of one's historical presence. That is, black people did not come from the West, they came from Africa. We came here not as immigrants but as slaves.

When asked to give concrete examples of why he and other minority students perceived the present college curriculum to be inadequate, he wrote:

One black student told us of sitting in an anthropology class for an entire semester and being interested in the class only on two occasions—once when the instructor offered a lecture on the negro in America, and again when there was a lecture on Africa. . . . Few black students are really interested in the western "classical" music which characterized entire departments of music. Black students have no fundamental cultural understanding of the western music. And, since a part of many beginning classes is spent instructing students in only the music of Beethoven, Mozart, Stravinsky, etc., as legitimate music, this is seen as a denial of black students themselves. . . . Black people are not westerners; they are "westernized," made to be western. So, basically, their psychology is Freudian, Adlerian, or Jungian only so far as they have accepted westernization. Students find themselves enchanted by the schools of psychology, but as they probe deeper they find less and less in association with their lives. Other black students pretend that they can relate to western psychology by "becoming Freudian." . . . When black students begin to describe themselves in real situations, they're at times put down. A black woman student wrote a paper on Marxism and alienation in which she said that she could not be alienated from a society of which she had never been a part. She had recently joined the Black Students' Union. The instructor attacked the student's basis of thought and gave her a low grade. She soon afterwards had a nervous collapse and has been out of school for more than a year.

Whatever the wisdom and accuracy of these perceptions, they

are factors to consider in any effort to resolve the educational problems of certain minorities. Black students and intellectuals have been
in the leadership in expressing disenchantment with the directions of
our educational system, and others of our depressed minorities are not
far behind if the San Francisco State experience is an indicator. Signs
of growing interest are already present in the self-styled Chicano-La-
tino groups and in some of the Asian and American Indian groups as
well. There can be little doubt that a movement of major proportions
is upon us. Spawned as it has been by the failures, the hostilities, the
insensitivities, and the inconsistencies of dominant white groups, the
movement has often assumed the form of retributive and even violent
expression. What it holds for the future no one can be certain. But
that men of concern must examine and act with careful consideration
is a certainty. With this in mind, we now examine the strategies for
solutions to the problem as seen by significant numbers in the minority
groups themselves.

Strategies for Solutions

The suggestion that ethnic studies courses should be introduced
into the curriculum has been one of the major proposals for meeting
the problem of relevance and motivation for minorities at the college
level. The first people to agitate for the introduction of courses focusing exclusively on their own ethnic group have been the people of
African descent who now prefer to be known as black. Thus, a cry
for black studies has been raised across the nation, with much of the
original stimulus apparently coming from the black students at San
Francisco State. Since the greatest amount of theorizing and agitating
has come from black groups, we examine the rationale for black studies
in some detail and then turn to the rationale of other groups.

Black Studies—Rationale: To put the rationale for black studies in proper perspective, let us reflect for a moment on the history of
the development of various American groups into a reasonably integrated culture. This story has been very complex, but a single, simple
fact seems germane to the black problems currently before us—most
immigrant groups, with the major exception of the blacks, came to
these shores because they wanted to come.[1] America was thought to

---

[1] Part of this chapter is from D. Pentony, "The Case for Black Studies."
Atlantic Monthly, April 1969. By permission of the publisher.

be the land of opportunity, the land where the rigidities for social mobility would be relaxed, the land where a man could be free. That these expectations were not quickly fulfilled is an ugly part of the political, social, and economic history of the United States, but in retrospect the members of most of these groups now view the story of their ethnic past in the United States as a reasonably successful one. Whether the relatively recent voluntary immigrants of Spanish-speaking and Oriental backgrounds will find the fabled American melting pot something to be found only at the end of the rainbow is not certain. Whether the problems facing the indigenous American Indians can be solved remains uncertain as well. But for the others, there has been an obvious lowering of invidious ethnic, social, and political barriers, symbolized by the election of an Irish-Catholic to the presidency and the selection of men of Greek and Polish backgrounds for vice-presidential roles.

In all of this, the situation of the black man has seemed unique. Brought to this country in chains, torn from their families and tribal past, physically and psychologically enslaved, taught by lash and example to be subservient, forced to suffer indignities to their manhood and womanhood, and instantly categorized by the accident of color, black people have too often found the American dream to be a nightmare. Instead of joining the dominant culture, they have learned to exist in a psychologically bewildering atmosphere, neither slave nor free. That they have survived at all is a tribute to their magnificent resiliency and basic toughness. But it is not surprising that many blacks carry with them a heavy baggage of hate and rage.

In order to understand some of the reasons underlying the demand for black studies, one needs to witness the rise and fall of hope in the story of the black man in America. In the aftermath of the civil war, blacks were told that they were no longer slaves only to find that they were not free—not free to be treated as individuals, not free to eat, or sleep, or live, or go to school, or drink from the same fountain, or choose any spot on the train or bus, or enjoy the same political and economic privileges as people of white skin. And when in the twentieth century their hopes were raised by long overdue court decisions and civil rights legislation finally demanding integration, these hopes were once again shattered as significant segments of white culture too often lagged far behind the basic justice of these acts.

This undoubtedly has led some in the black community to

question whether the call to integration was not just another white trick to preserve the dominance of the whites, but a trick with the dangerous twist that required integration of "unequals." Integration seemed to be merely a device to eliminate the black race, at least in the sense of seducing blacks to give up their black identities and to copy the speech, manner, hair, dress, and style of the whites, and to accept the myths, heroes, and historical judgments of white America without reciprocity and without appreciation of or respect for black experience. Moreover, this estimate has been coupled with a hunch that, in any significant way, only the "talented tenth" of the black community could really hope to overcome the monetary, social, and psychological barrier to true integration with whites. The remaining 90 per cent would therefore be left in poverty and psychological degradation, doomed to an almost motiveless, hopeless existence, forever on the dole, forever caught in hate of self and of others. Thus has been posed a transcendent dilemma for the black man and woman: To succeed is to fail; to overcome the outrageous obstacles thrown in their way by the white society seems partially to deny their black identity; and most significant of all, to integrate on an individual basis in a society that makes this increasingly possible for the fortunate may well mean an exodus of the "talented tenth" from the black community, with a consequent decimation of the ranks of potential leaders whose talented commitment to the whole community could help set their people free.

Seen in this light, the call for black studies is the call for training black Moses to lead black people out of the social and psychological wilderness and to focus this training on the role and circumstance of the black man in the society, now and in the past. The argument is that if there is to be an exodus from the land of psychological bondage, an informed and dedicated leadership is needed to help bring about individual and group pride and a sense of cohesive community. To accomplish this, black people, like all people, need to know that they are not alone. They need to know that their ancestors are not just slaves laboring under the white man's sun, but that their lineage can be traced to important kingdoms and significant civilizations. They need to be familiar with the black man's contributions to the arts and sciences, they need to know of black heroes and of the noble deeds of black men. They need to know that black, too, is beautiful and that under the African sky people are proudly at ease with their blackness.

In historical perspective, they need to know the whole story of white oppression and the struggles of some blacks, and some whites too, to overcome that oppression. They need to find sympathetic help and encouragement to move successfully into the socioeconomic arenas of American life.

To help fulfill all these needs, the contention is, a black studies effort must be launched. At the beginning it must be staffed by black faculty who must have the time and resources to do the massive job of preparing a solid curriculum for college students and the time to reach out into the community to introduce the new knowledge and new perspectives as quickly as possible. In a situation somewhat similar to the massive efforts of adult education in some of the less developed societies, the advocates of black studies press to get on with the urgent tasks.

It seems clear that the advocates of a black studies program for the college see it as a remedy for the white studies programs to which they have been subjected all their lives and as a way to bring pride, dignity, community, and power to black people. They are questioning the relevance of the style and content of education that is designed to meet the needs and expectations of the dominant white culture. Some seem to be suggesting that the life styles and ways of perceiving the world in much of the black community are sufficiently different to justify a new, almost bicultural approach to educating the members of the community who are at once a part of, yet apart from the general American culture. While they hope that this effort will range over the whole educational experience from childhood through adulthood, they seem to view the college or university as the place where talents can be gathered and resources mobilized to provide intellectual leadership and academic respectability to their efforts. The college is to be the place for writing books, providing information, and the training of students to help with the critical tasks.

The advocates of black studies also see such programs, in part, as a community organization tool with which the masses of people in the black communities across the nation can be given a sense of direction, a feeling of involvement and importance, and a heightened awareness of the need to make their presence known and felt by the power structures of the present and future. They feel that this is particularly needed now, because too many black people have been politically apathetic and insufficiently concerned about group solidarity.

Thus black studies are to provide the ideological underpinning for the revitalization of the black community and also to provide an increasing flow of trained workers into the community. This latter aspect will be discussed below within the context of community action.

Other Ethnic Studies—Rationale: What about other minority groups who do not yet see themselves as part of the American mainstream? Is the rationale for their drive for ethnic studies roughly the same? At San Francisco State the answer appears to be "yes." Listen to Roger Alvarado, a nonblack leader of the Third World Liberation Front at San Francisco State:

> Look, most of the nonblack Third World people were involved in what we loosely called the movement. Some for as long as five years, mostly working with the black community. About the time that black consciousness became a pretty solid concept. . . . a lot of black literature was circulated and dug by everyone concerned. Those of us in the Third World who are not black, we had to turn around and orient our thinking to what was happening in our own communities.[2]

Although the students and other intellectuals from the Third World Liberation Front (including students from the Latin-American Students Organization, the Mexican-American Student Confederation, the Intercollegiate Council for Social Action, the Philippine-American Collegiate Endeavor, and the Asian-American Political Alliance) have not written and spoken as widely about the underlying rationale of their desires for an ethnic studies program as have the blacks, there can be little doubt that they subscribe to much of the analysis of American society that has been made by the blacks. They, too, see themselves as excluded from and oppressed by the dominant groups in American society. While it is true that Third World students and intellectuals, or their parents or grandparents, came here because they chose to do so, they nonetheless find their ethnic community in much the same situation as do the blacks. The dominant white groups still discriminate against them because of their different appearances or their different ways of speaking and acting. For example, they contend that in the San Francisco Bay area their employment and housing opportunities continue to be diminished by the fact of their ethnic background. They find themselves ghettoized and believe themselves eco-

---

[2] W. Orrick, *Shut It Down!* p. 100.

nomically exploited. They would like to puncture the myth that only
the black community suffers from the orientation and attitude of the
white groups. Mason Wong, chairman of the Intercollegiate Council
for Social Action at San Francisco State, puts it succinctly:

> The fiction is that the Chinese have never suffered as much as,
> say, the black or brown communities in this country. . . . Rather,
> the Chinese community has the same basic problems as all other
> nonwhite communities. The only thing different is that it has
> some neon-lights and a few tourist restaurants, which is all that
> white people want to know about our community. Yet these res-
> taurants are staffed by illiterate Chinese who work fourteen hours
> per day, six days per week, for starvation wages. The only way to
> survive in our community is exploit each other, hence the myth
> of the successful Chinese businessman. This exploitation is per-
> petuated at the expense of Chinese immigrants who can only find
> work in the sweatshops, laundries and restaurants in Chinatown.[3]

Consequently, one of the remedies that they see is to have the colleges
focus on their particular communities by presenting various ethnic
course offerings in much the same fashion as the blacks are requesting.

James Hirabayashi, one of the most articulate and capable
nonblack faculty members associated with the ethnic studies movement at San Francisco State, has argued that it is "not racism per se
that gives us the rationale for Third World Studies; it only gives us
the reason for the development of the rationale." He goes on to point
out that "recognition of the legitimacy of Third World Studies rests
not merely upon assertions of emotional need on the part of certain
groups. . . . [but] it rests upon an assessment of the American society
as a pluralistic society." The argument is that there is more than one
way of looking at societal goals for nonwhite, ethnic groups in American society. One way is to contend that the goal should be to assimilate
them as rapidly as possible into the dominant middle-class culture. A
second way is to propose that the goal should be a mixing of the cultural traits and practices of the new groups with those of the old,
thereby achieving a cultural synthesis that is neither the new nor the
old. And a third way is to support an essentially pluralistic goal, which
ideally would encourage the preservation of major portions of the
minority ethnic culture in the context of a plural American society.

It is pointed out that American mythology has usually glorified
the second possibility, but at the same time American practice has de-

[3] Ibid., p 104.

manded the first, even though society has frequently thrown enormous obstacles in the way of meeting the demand. The third alternative has perhaps achieved only cursory intellectual examination until now except in the separatist rationale of certain religious groups, notably the Roman Catholics and the Lutherans. But practice seems to have structured the social situation so that large groups in addition to the Negro have experienced a version of this third alternative without the needed recognition of basic equality. Despite the dissatisfaction with this segregationist version of their past experience, significant numbers of people from black and other minority ethnic groups apparently find that the third, separatist, alternative is the most attractive at the moment. Yet it is separation with a critical difference. Separation is to be a free choice by the ethnic communities themselves rather than something forced upon them by the intransigent, dominant groups. It is seen as freedom to decide how they shall relate to the dominant groups in American society in terms of preserving their ethnic heritage instead of apologetically shuffling it all off as rapidly as talent and society permit.

Moreover, in psychological terms, the ethnic studies effort, grounded on this pluralistic view of American society, is to be an effort in self-discovery. Advocates of ethnic studies argue that there is a more satisfying and productive way for members of a minority ethnic group to achieve social and personal development. That is by the individual identifying with his immediate primary ethnic group rather than rejecting it totally in favor of attempting to fit into a society that is psychologically distant. By developing pride and understanding of his cultural roots through ethnic studies, it is hoped that the minority person will be able to place himself in some more satisfying perspective and also to relate to other individuals and groups without the relationship-destroying baggage of inferiority, self-hate, and hate for others. In this fashion, the human ideal of interacting with one another in peace and harmony is to be approached. Proponents of ethnic studies see the current system of educating the members of ethnic minority communities as, in part, a demand that they deny themselves and their roots. A member of the Latin-American students' organization at San Francisco State put it this way:

> I spoke Spanish until I was five years old. When I went to kindergarten I wasn't allowed to speak Spanish, I had to speak English, and so I was forced to forget Spanish. . . . Throughout

school I was never once introduced to a piece of Latin-American writing. I was never once shown a piece of art from either the Indian culture or from the real Spanish colonial period. . . . See, the educational system is no accident. . . . it's not simply a matter of not including what our culture is about. . . . it's a process of miseducation. . . . It has a purpose . . . one is to teach us not how to change our community or even live in it, but how to escape it by denying that we are a part of it.[4]

Students like this one contend that this miseducation will continue until there is a reorientation in thinking about strategies of American education and about productive models for interrelationships among diverse groups in our society.

Control of Ethnic Studies: If ethnic studies of black, brown, yellow, and reddish hue are to be one of the hopes of a better tomorrow for our ethnic minorities, then faculty, books, materials, a well-planned curriculum, and other resources must be put in place, ready to go. At this point important issues arise. Perhaps the most important is the question of who is to control the hiring of faculty and administrators, the planning of the curriculum, the selection of books and articles, and the day-to-day content of the courses. The concerned students (and some faculty as well) who have been in the leadership of the ethnic studies movement contend that the ethnic communities themselves must be in control, and indeed some contend that the *students* of minority ethnic backgrounds must be in control. The former contention is discussed first, and the student control contention is then treated as a special case of the former.

The argument is that if ethnic studies are to be offered under the control of the people who currently run the educational establishment, such studies will be little more than the same old product dressed up in a new package. So imbued is the establishment likely to be with the assimilationist model that they will be neither able nor willing to permit ethnic studies to be offered from the perspective of the ethnic community. Moreover, they will not be sympathetic to the pluralist model of American society and will constantly seek to spread the doctrine of integration of the subordinate minorities into the superior majority or mainstream. They will also be so unsympathetic to the pluralist model of American society, now found attractive by certain elements of the ethnic minorities, that they will constantly seek ways to subvert

[4] Ibid., p. 104.

and undercut the basic pluralist thrust of the ethnic studies movement. "Uncle Tom" or "Tio Tomás" professors will be hired for polka-dot courses. Thus, a brief focus on nonwhites will be added to the present white-oriented courses, and the active community aspects of the courses which were to be a major part of the new directions will be suppressed on the ground that this is not the proper role of the college. The advocates of ethnic studies contend that all of this adds up to the absolute necessity for the ethnic community to control the process if there is to be a chance to solve the problems of relevance, motivation, identity and powerlessness.

As can be ascertained from the portion of the fifteen demands cited above, some ethnic studies advocates are demanding not only that the ethnic communities themselves control the programs but also that *students* have the "authority and the control of the hiring and retention of any faculty member, director, and administrator, as well as the curricula." By connecting their desires for ethnic power with the current broader demands for student power in all areas of the college, those advocates strike at still another problem that is bothering this student generation. They seem to be arguing that it is impossible to meet their ethnic needs under the current institutional distribution of power and authority, and also that their needs as students cannot be met as long as students are not in control of their own educational destinies. They seem to have adopted the suspicious attitudes symbolized by the phrase that "you can't trust anyone over thirty," and thus apparently feel that the nurturing of ethnic programs can only be done safely by students who will not stand silent while the establishment works to subvert and control ethnic studies. But suspicion is not the only motivation for the demand for control. In addition, advocates of student control feel a proprietary interest in the ethnic studies movement. They know quite well that the pressure, the spadework, the theorizing, the agitating, and the planning have largely been done by students. Few professors were in at the beginning and not an overwhelming number have come forward to help as the momentum picked up. Why should the students not be in control of a program which has been their baby?

Community Action: In the strategy to solve the problems of ethnic minorities in higher education and the related problems of the ethnic communities, perhaps the most unusual element has been the extent to which reliance is placed upon community action. Again, the blacks seem to be leading the way (if the San Francisco State experience is indicative), but the other groups are not far behind. The kind of community action proposed is extensive and complex. The apparent intention is to utilize the talents, enthusiasm, and manpower of students in the ethnic studies program to promote a revolution of attitudes, perspectives, and behaviors in the broader ethnic communities. Grounded on the educational philosophy that students learn best by doing, the tactic is to include a field work component in courses taught in the ethnic studies program.

In Nathan Hare's conceptual proposal for a black studies curriculum, made at San Francisco State in April of 1968, he argues that it is "necessary to inspire and sustain a sense of collective destiny as a people and a consciousness of the value of education in the technological society." He then lays out an almost staggering number of tasks to be performed. Black information centers are to be set up. They are to be supplemented by a community press in which information, news, editorials, and advice relevant to the black community and particularly to the task of creating a sociopolitical awareness would be highlighted. The role of communication in building a sense of community solidarity is not to be neglected. In addition to a press, it is his intention to establish black cultural councils for sponsoring cultural affairs in the plastic and performing arts, with an eye towards bringing the message of the movement to as many people as possible. Black tutorial programs and back-to-school campaigns are to be organized in an effort to impress the members of the ethnic community with the need for education in a technological society. A Bureau of Black Education is proposed to coordinate community educational activities and to stimulate and aid black scholars as they go about their textbook writing, preparations of syllabi, and presentations of lectures. Community action proposals also envisage bringing the college classroom to the community in the form of lectures and other college presentations. Community organizing techniques for gaining various social and political goals are also to be a part of the strategy of the program.

Access to the Colleges: A final significant aspect of the strategies to solve the problem is what might be called the tactic of unlimited access. The tactic is based on the realization that, with the raising of entrance standards and the consequent heightening of competition to get into college, people from minority ethnic backgrounds are finding it increasingly difficult to enter and remain in college. At San Francisco State, minority students cite the dramatic decrease in percentage of students from minority backgrounds in the short period of only five or six years as proof of their contention that the white community is making college entrance less, rather than more, accessible than in the past. The irony of the situation is not lost on them. They find incongruous the contention that "at long last things are looking up in America" for people of minority backgrounds. While they recognize that there is indeed a greater opportunity for the "talented tenth," they believe that the gap in opportunity for the remainder is increasing. So one of their solutions is to demand that the colleges of the land, and the tax-supported colleges in particular, open their doors to any minority members who wish to come. They seem to be saying that as long as a technological America demands college degrees for access to positions of power, influence, prestige, and higher income, then special consideration in higher education must be given to those Americans who have not been accorded equal educational opportunity in the elementary and secondary schools of their oppressed communities. Thus, access to the college becomes a remedy for such inadequacies as lack of support, overcrowding, uninspiring teaching, and irrelevance which have plagued far too many schools attended by students of minority backgrounds.

There is another aspect to the tactic of limited access. Those who demand unlimited access see it as a device to swell the ranks of the believers and provide the manpower for helping to do the jobs that must be done. It is in part a question of power. Those who argue for unlimited access apparently believe that large numbers of minority students will, through the strength of their numbers, make the institutions of higher learning more malleable and more responsive to their needs and desires. The educational and social battles of today and tomorrow cannot be fought without troops, either within the campus or in the outside community. So, as many students as possible must be admitted.

These plans and strategies are ambitious and controversial. They challenge many of the dogmas and conventional wisdoms of our educational apparatus. They bring a part of the college into the arena of direct social change and political action. And they are proposed in the language of absolute necessity. Indeed, the San Francisco State experience indicates that some of the most militant of the proponents of these strategies will push for their acceptance *by any means neces-*

sary, including occasional threats, some intimidation, and even violence. Where it will all lead is difficult to assess.

Comment on Strategies

Ethnic Studies: There can be little doubt that the proposal to inaugurate academic programs with a specific American ethnic focus is revolutionary. While we have long had area studies programs at the college level in many of our colleges and universities, multidisciplinary focus on American ethnic groups has been uncommon except for some concentration on the American Indian. Partially as a result of this uniqueness and also as a result of the concern about its validity and direction as a separate field of study, many questions have arisen about the wisdom of introducing these courses into the curriculum.

First of all, there is a general concern about the probable outcome of this kind of concentration. Will focus on minority ethnic groups, as one of the remedies of white racism and mistreatment, result in an equally virulent ethnic racism, black, brown, red, or yellow? Ethnic nationalism with its glorifying of the ethnic in-group may only have powerful meaning when it focuses on the hate object of whiteness. The dominant white groups have, through their words and deeds over many generations, provided all the bitter evidence needed for building a negative nationalism based on hatred and rage. And so it may be too much to expect that some of the teachers of ethnic studies will resist the temptation to build towering myths of white original sin and nonwhite purity. Indeed, it is likely that in the beginning stages, at the very least, a significant ingredient creeping into most ethnic programs will be an emotional antiwhiteness or at best a consummate desire to highlight the unseemly side of the white experience in America. Whether an institution of higher learning can adjust to such a prospect is a major question.

While a higher academic institution worthy of the name cannot accept a program that features racism of any kind, it can nurture a program that makes an effort to right the historical record and explain the attitudes, values, and world views of people in the ethnic communities. If such a program reflects the bitterness, suspicion, and even hatred, we should not be surprised, but we might be hopeful that the sense of compassion and humanity—which has been a significant stance of the prophets of the movement like Malcolm X and W. E. B. Du Bois—may win out. Instrumentally, it may be useful for everyone to have these unpleasant facts of life out into the intellectual open where we can deal with them. Is it not good for all of us to know that we must exchange emissaries of peace and goodwill among our communities and, in particular, for the whites to know that they must now deal with the ethnic minorities in their own country with a significant degree of diplomatic sensitivity if they expect to win their alliance and friendship? Like people in the colonized lands of Asia, Africa, and Latin America, some members of the minority communities look at their rather systematic exclusion from first-class citizenship in the United States as a close parallel to the exploitation and subjugation perpetrated by those who shouldered the "white man's burden" during the high tide of imperialism. Do not the majority in the United States need to know this if they are going to find a way to relate to the minorities in peace and freedom?

The ethnic studies effort may help. Indeed, it is entirely possible that the emphasis on ethnic studies will provide the dominant groups in American society with new cues of behavior and guides to appropriate responsiveness, so that they can relate to the members of the ethnic minority communities in other than a patronizing and deprecating fashion. Through ethnic studies there may be opportunities for whites to enrich their understanding of the nonwhites and thereby provide better judgments on how to build bridges of mutual respect and obligation. If it is true that the road to this mutuality has in the past been partially blocked by the failure of whites to perceive the inner feelings and world views of other groups, then programs of ethnic studies are desperately needed.

It is foolish not to recognize that the ethnic studies effort in the present climate is a major gamble. It is also a major gamble to stand pat. The outcome in either direction could be a heightening of racial tensions. It may be that group relations in the United States will have to get worse before they can get better. The outcome of ethnic studies might be a color-distorted perspective of the past and the present, a sort of overcorrection that still leaves all of us blind to the truth of the matter. The outcome might even be a color-centered version of truth, beauty and justice that apes the worst features of the white experience from Hitler to the White Citizens' Councils. If any group is to be run out of the human race because of its ethnic identification, then there is very little left but a fight to the finish. Nationalism of this kind has an observed tendency to become fanaticism. The outcome could also be a further politicization or a contest for the soul of the university, with a consequent disappearance of academic freedom as we know it. Which way it will go is a tale to be told by us all. Whether any of us can keep the faith in the face of the tensions and hatreds of our times remains a question writ large.

Questions of scholarship and standards have also been raised by those who ponder the desirability of ethnic studies. These are difficult questions to answer for any new program. The proof of the intellectual pudding is in the digesting over a period of time. We probably can expect some of the same pressures for high scholarly performance and the maintenance of high standards as in any other new program. Just what the response to these pressures will be is not clear at this moment in time. Perhaps all we can fairly do is comment on certain problems that loom on the horizon, but in so doing, we must recognize that all horizontal clouds do not bring rain.

As in so many matters in the affairs of men, there is contradictory evidence about whether those in ethnic studies will assume a no-holds-barred, rigorous attitude of truth searching or will succumb to the silent sound of political indoctrination in its most blatant sense. This whole question needs to be viewed with recognition of the failure of our present institutions, including our academic ones, to live up to their own standards and ideals in the search for truth. It seems hardly fair to measure new programs against a set of ideal standards when many of our existing programs are not judged so rigidly.

On the other hand, there is little question that the advocates of ethnic studies have a powerful incentive and desire to bring the truth of the matter to their students and to the broader community at large. Chinatown is not a quaint running episode in *Flower Drum Song,* but is a place of sweatshops, alienation, poverty, inhumanity, and exploitation of the worst sort. Landlords who discriminate against ethnic minorities are perhaps the most frequent lawbreakers in urban society. These and similar facts will be increasingly brought to our attention. In addition there is some reason to expect that the scholars from the ethnic communities will present the phenomenological aspect of why the members of the ethnic communities behave as they do, what their values are, and how they see the world. And this presentation may be as free of bias as most of our efforts to analyze society. In drama, in poetry, in painting, in music, in literature, and in some social science analysis there is a good deal of evidence of the potentiality for high scholarship on the part of scholars from the ethnic communities.

Moreover, even if an emotive bias creeps in, in the sense of telling it as it is from the ethnic perspective, the ethnic scholars will undoubtedly be performing a service. While this is not the place to entertain the profound philosophical questions of the nature of truth and objectivity, perhaps it is sufficient to recall that the search for truth is an experience-laden thing, that much of a man's knowledge is culture-bound and that we truly live in a Rashomon world. In this respect, the demand for pristine outside objectivity needs careful definition. A distinguished philosopher has argued that a search for intergroup accommodation must be made on what he terms the discovery of the respective normative inner orders of societies, that is, the values, assumptions, and world views or images of societies and groups in potential conflict. It may be that one of the most important roles that an ethnic scholar can play is to share in the discovery and articulation of this normative inner order in the ethnic subcultures. For that task, he need not review the scene with Olympian detachment—a desire to tell it truthfully and sound professional skill are enough.

On the other hand, there is also evidence that bodes ill for the chances of the scholarly style and scholarship. Stemming from the understandable and commendable desire to provide a scholarly base for the growth of dignity, self-confidence, and group spirit, signs of profound anti-intellectualism in the form of efforts of political indoctrination or blanket rejection of the values of scholarship are unfortunately in evidence. A consequent insistence upon rigid adherence to party lines seems to be emerging at San Francisco State. In the October 15, 1969, issue of *Black Fire,* the official weekly organ of the Black Students Union at San Francisco State, there appeared the following statement under the heading *Classroom Revolution:*

> *Each Black Studies course* has a *teaching assistant* who has been selected by the Central Committee to *politicize* the class and to develop student control over content. Recognizing the need to have student and faculty moving together in the struggle for self-determination on campus as well as in the larger struggle against fascism, capitalism, imperialism, and racism, the teacher's assistant will not be acting as an authoritarian figure indoctrinating the students and perpetuating this education to prepare students to fit rather than change the system. The job of the teaching assistant is: (1) to fully educate the student to the political need for student control over content, which involves developing initiative

and awareness of self-determination; (2) to inform the students of local, state, national, and international news—past, present and future; (3) to organize the students to form collective student power, with the teacher, not to focus on the teacher as the enemy instead of the pig power structure; (4) to inform the students about the Black Panther Party, its functions, how it is meeting the needs and desires of the people; (5) to inform them of the moves of the power structure at State, specifically, Hayakawa; (6) to help the students with the problems they have with the administration at State; (7) to stress the need for the students to work on the different committees: legal defense, public relations, curriculum, administrative, revolutionary arts and culture, and so on; (8) to talk about the strike if necessary—tell how the students got their heads beat in and how they are now facing unjust charges because they were fighting for their beliefs—the troubles they are having in the courts and in jail; (9) to assist the teacher with the administrative duties of the class and to learn the skills from the instructor.

It is possible that in the zeal to bring about a renaissance in a direct and missionary fashion, the scholarly qualities of skepticism, freedom to accept or reject, and devotion to the maintenance of the unintimidated market place of ideas will be discouraged and rejected across the country, as they appear to be in danger of being rejected in at least one of the ethnic programs at San Francisco State. It is also possible that in the effort to present the more positive side of the history and worth of the ethnic people, distortion rivaling that of existing scholarship at its worst will creep in. Would, for example, the black studies historian point out to his students that there were more than four thousand black slave owners in the ante-bellum south? Will the ethnic historian of people of Spanish derivation present the fact of the brutal and inhuman treatment accorded the indigenous people by some of their ancestors? Unfortunately, the answer to these questions is not clear at this time. It remains entirely possible that the ethnic scholars will intentionally cook the data, bias their studies, and create towering myths which bear little resemblance to the shifting realities of human experience.

There are and will be powerful pressures, both internal and external, to have them do so. They may so strongly believe in the cause that they do it on their own. Also, they may go along with a "revolutionary establishment" under the discredited but still attractive assumption that the ends justify the means. Ironically, in doing so they would provide a mirror image of those scholars whom many have heavily criticized as sellouts to the orthodox establishment. Indeed, it will be no easy task to resist the call to party line purity. The goals of revolutionizing the attitudes, self-images, and place in the scheme of things for the members of the ethnic communities may well bring confrontation after confrontation with the consequent pressure for everyone to take sides. At San Francisco State, another extract from *Black Fire,* October 15, 1969, points up the problem:

> In our program, we are asking for the full support of the population of San Francisco State College. We remind you that *'you're either part of the solution or part of the problem'* (italics added). For in dealing with the revolutionary arts and culture, we must remember that the seizure of power by armed force, the settlement of the issue by war, is the central task of the highest form of revolution!

This is not the best climate for the survival of a scholarly style, and academic freedom and scholarly independence may be the first victim in the struggle. Yet the irony may be that without the survival of academic freedom and scholarly independence the revolutionary paths may become a maze leading to nowhere except the center of defeat. To accomplish the task would seem to require the no-nonsense calculations of what the realities and realistic opportunities and paths are. High flowing rhetoric and the assertions of belief in the movement may be necessary to start the march out of the wilderness. But without free, frank, and skeptical measuring of the alternative paths to possible destinations which the unfettered scholar can provide, the danger of taking detours to destruction would seem to increase. In this view, the scholar must preserve the basic independence of judgment and voice while he works in the vineyards of the movement. It is a good trick, and we may be asking too much of the ethnic scholar to expect him to do it. There may be no time for scholarship, only for believership, in the midst of the revolutionary press for social change. Those scholars who wish to see scholarship survive may have a major job cut out for themselves as events push to pinch it out.

Despite some ominous portents, one of the greatest mistakes any of us could make as we attempt to assess the ethnic studies movement is to pronounce a negative judgment too soon. There are bound to be birth pangs in the development of the programs. In measuring potentials both good and bad in the ethnic studies movement, we may inadvertently fulfill our own prophecies of doom if we permit ourselves

to be so alarmed about early departures from scholarship that we crip-
ple the programs by excessively rigid demands. It does not seem fair
to attempt to evaluate the programs definitively before we have really
had a chance to see what is being done in them over a period of time.
Hopefully, the academic community is strong enough and flexible
enough to reserve judgment until some of the fruits of the effort can
be put before us for discussion and debate. More specifically, we need
not panic at the thought that some ethnic professors will profess a certain ideology. After all, some white professors have been professing
certain belief systems for a long time. We need not become overly concerned that professors in the ethnic studies programs will make pre-
scriptive statements about man and society from their own ethnic perspective. We should not even get terribly excited about the ethnic
professor who presents theories and arguments that glorify one group
of people over another. In the great tradition of Milton and Mill, there
is ample time to expose error and arrive at truth as we go about our
academic business. What we do need to worry about and be on careful
guard against, is the departure from the scholarly style of peaceful
argument and the art of gentle persuasion. We need to muster all our
strength and fortitude to see that no point of view is silenced, no professor or student threatened or suppressed because of unpopular views,
that no course is proscribed because of its alleged bias whether pro-
ethnic or anti-ethnic, and that no one is left alone to resist intimidation
by himself, whether it comes from an intervening board of trustees
or from active student groups. What may be at stake is the free market
place of ideas as we move through the troublesome problem of ethnic
studies. But then, that is often at stake when we are dealing with anything of major importance.

     Another question to be considered, when we attempt to make
preliminary estimates about the prospects for ethnic studies in the area
of scholarship and standards, deals specifically with the evaluation of
students. Perhaps all we can safely say is that we should expect the
same ferment over learning, grading, and evaluative practices that we
presently encounter in the rest of the academic curriculum. While arguments about what is proper are likely to continue, we can reasonably
be assured that differential evaluation in order to distinguish the performance of one student from another will remain a part of the academic process in ethnic studies and elsewhere, at least after the shake-
down cruise of ethnic studies. As suggested in another chapter, there

is serious question about the educational worth of our present evalua-
tional standards. It may be that in new programs like ethnic studies,
we will witness a desire to experiment with evaluative practices.

Again, the San Francisco State experience suggests that this
may mean that most of the students in some courses would be given
As and Bs. We would be foolish not to recognize that this practice
might develop, perhaps out of an intensely held desire to prove that
students in ethnic classes have suddenly found the key to high academic performance as a result of their new motivations and new world
views. The real proof of all of this will be in the kind of product turned
out. There are a few signs among the academicians who are pushing
the idea of ethnic studies that they will be content with a half-hearted,
sloppy intellectual effort on the part of their students. The question
remains for them and all of us—is the current grading system the best
means for eliciting high academic performance from ethnic students
or any students? While there may be some efforts to use evaluation
devices to promote orthodoxy, not unknown in our present curriculum, there may well be great pressure to do an instructional job of the
highest character so that out of the ethnic studies experience can come
students who are committed, motivated, socially aware, and equipped
to seek and secure positions of importance in the whole range of human endeavor. Any program that aspires to less or falls far short of
these high aspirations can be expected to fail in the eyes of its most
important constituency, the ethnic community and the students themselves. In the long run, any phoniness in evaluation, any hoodwinking
about abilities, and any sustained efforts to demand conformity would
discredit the whole academic movement for ethnic studies and leave
the students with a mess of educational pottage unusable except at a
political rally.

The question of the legality of ethnic studies programs requires
examination. Like the closely related area studies program, the curriculum would seem to face no legal question from federal or state law.
However, it is in the realm of staffing and student access that the most
serious questions arise. For example, can tests of color or ethnic background be applied when hiring faculty members in the ethnic studies
programs? Posed in this sharp way, the answer to the question is probably no. The equal protection of the laws section of the United States
Constitution and various state legal requirements about nondiscrimi-
nation in employment could very likely be interpreted to preclude the

hiring of faculty simply because they were from a particular ethnic group. However, if the qualifications for hiring are put on a broader experiential basis rather than ethnic background, the questions and answers may change. Factors of ethnic background and experience already play a role in hiring at colleges and universities in the United States. While this is particularly obvious in the hiring of teachers in foreign languages and literature (for example, the number of people teaching the Chinese language and literature who are Chinese), ethnic background has often been considered in other aspects of area studies and in other programs from the Peace Corps to social work.

The question of hiring ethnic faculty is probably not a legal question at all. Rather, the critical point for the ethnic studies program would seem to be on the one hand whether the particular experiences gained from an ethnic background tend to make the faculty member a better teacher and scholar or, on the other hand, whether the ethnic emotional involvement will permit a useful scholarly detachment in the evaluation and presentation of the data. Completely satisfactory answers to this dilemma, probably shared by all area programs if they were to face it, are not likely to be found. Perhaps a short-run solution to the dilemma rests on the ability of an ethnic studies program to attract faculty who have a passion for the truth as well as an emotional identification with ethnic studies, and on the certainty that nonethnic scholars will continue to view, comment on, and analyze the ethnic experience in various parts of the academic community.

In this latter connection, one might hope that enough flexibility and openness exist to permit students majoring in ethnic studies to encounter the views of nonethnic scholars, much as a course on American political thought can be enlivened and improved by examining views of scholars from foreign lands. Similarly, the educational experiences of the rest of the academic community would undoubtedly be enriched by the participation of ethnic studies faculty in the general intellectual life of the college. It would be tragic if the ethnic studies faculty were to be prevented from intellectual interchange on the general questions of man and society by their own preoccupation with or isolation in ethnic studies. Only by channeling the results of their thinking and their analyses into the broader academic arena can they be given the attention and respect that they deserve.

An interchange of ideas and some cooperative efforts are needed if a truly massive attack on our problems of intergroup relationships, and racism in particular, is to be successful. Indeed, it may well be that it is in this broader academic context that proper justification for using ethnic background as a variable in hiring faculty can be found. Surely the infusion of an increasing number of faculty with minority backgrounds into the academic communities is a desirable academic development. The ethnic studies programs would seem to offer one exciting possibility to accomplish this infusion in a more rapid fashion and to provide the communities themselves with the incentives, role models, and opportunities to become a more participant part of the education of youth.

It seems to be true that we are now beginning to recognize that social conflicts cannot be satisfactorily ameliorated unless all ethnic groups have truly equal opportunities to participate in the major institutions and processes of American life. In this context, in the institutions of higher education we cannot rely on narrow legal interpretations and conventional dogmas as trustworthy guidelines to hiring faculty in ethnic studies programs. A sometime country lawyer, Abraham Lincoln, once said: "The dogmas of the quiet past are inadequate to the stormy present. The occasion is piled high with difficulty and we must rise to the occasion. As our case is new, so we must think anew and act anew. We must disenthrall ourselves, and then we shall save the country." Now is the time for higher education to show that it can disenthrall itself and become relevant to the massive problems of social change, highlighted at the moment by the call for ethnic studies.

The second serious question about the legality of the ethnic studies program is the question of student access to it. Can an academic institution deny access to any of its academic programs because of color or ethnic background? The answer is no. Here the legal answer and the moral answer would seem to reinforce one another. If one of the purposes of an ethnic studies program is to "tell it like it is," then that message should go to the students regardless of color, even though it is likely to have a particular additional value to the ethnic students. The college cannot be a place where knowledge is developed and subjects are taught in semisecret. Just as many colleges contracting with the government for secret research would seem to be open to serious charges of violation of the ethics of scholarship, so would any academic program that excludes students solely on the basis of ethnic background raise serious questions of propriety and legality.

However, even in this connection the dilemma remains. As anyone who has participated in area programs and the Peace Corps training effort knows, the things that can be easily said about one's own culture and about another culture tend to be modified when members of both cultures are in attendance. It seems to become more difficult to tell it truthfully, or at least as it truthfully is perceived, when the "outsiders" are in. This is a significant problem that will have to be faced by ethnic studies programs. Perhaps the fortunate thing about many of those who are advocating ethnic studies programs is that they appear to be anxious to tell the truth of the matter to anyone who will listen. They have been shielding their feelings, perceptions, and analyses so long that it will probably be refreshing for them to speak frankly and honestly with nonminority ethnic students as well as students from their own backgrounds. Nonetheless, they may properly feel that the first efforts to get the program established will be so overcome by well-meaning whites anxious to gain new perspectives that ethnic students will not have access to the courses.

In practice, the problems may not be so great, especially since courses about various ethnic communities will continue to be offered in existing departments with, hopefully, an exchange of faculty on occasion. At any rate, the colleges must make every effort within the budgetary limitations imposed upon them to accommodate as many students as possible. No ethnic student who enters the college should be denied the opportunity to take ethnic studies courses; neither, of course, should he be forced to do so. In this connection, the attractiveness of the course offering to whites as well as blacks may be important in the effort to sustain enrollments, after the first blush of newness wears off, and thus help provide the necessary resources which are closely tied to the level of student demand for courses. So the question of student access seems to be not so much a question of legality but of the availability of faculty and other resources. As in so many other areas of higher education, it is up to the society to provide the money if new and creative efforts are to be properly launched.

Control: At the outset the demand that the ethnic communities themselves control all aspects of the ethnic studies programs has come as a shock to many people both in and out of academic life. It has challenged societal myths about the unified nature of American society; it has brought into question the desirability of current integrationist efforts to solve the American dilemma; it has raised the specter of political control over the educational process, thereby seeming to threaten academic freedom; and it has, in its power-to-the-students form, brought into question the whole structure of the American university. Thus, we are not dealing with an insignificant issue, nor is it easy to discuss it adequately in the space allocated here. But some preliminary comments need to be made if we are to gain any perspective on the problems and prospects of the ethnic studies movement.

The desire to give the members of the ethnic communities (inside and outside the universities) control over ethnic programs is reasonable when viewed in the framework of the way we presently control educational institutions. It is a common practice that some sort of community board, linking professional and public, operates as a board of direction and control almost everywhere in our educational system. While these boards vary significantly in their composition and in the manner in which they are selected, the claim has always been that they are representative of the public or community at large. There can be little doubt that many of them are quite unrepresentative in terms of mirroring—even remotely—the makeup of society, but they nonetheless have taken on or been assigned the role of defenders of the public interest in the world of public education. From this perspective, the demand for ethnic control of the ethnic programs by faculty and community can be defended as an effort to remedy the accidental or systematic exclusion of people of ethnic background from the important control points of American education, both from within and without the structure. It can be seen as an effort to break the white chain of authority which minority ethnic students and faculty members know exists as they operate in a system that almost invariably has members of the dominant group as principals, department chairmen, deans, vice-presidents, presidents, trustees, legislators, and governors.

Indeed, it can be seen as a hopeful sign that people of ethnic background are losing their apathy and becoming highly desirous of being more completely involved in the education of the young. Some of our current problems might have been avoided had the avenues for interested participation been easily opened to the ethnic minorities. At the very least, they could now feel a greater responsibility for the education or miseducation of their offspring. At the most, they might have been able to make valuable contributions toward making education more relevant and desirable to their children and those of the dominant groups as well.

It is ironic that in the heat of the debate over the roles and methods of ethnic studies, we seem to forget the rather long experience we have had with pluralist education in religious and otherwise private institutions. From kindergarten through college, several different alternatives—many of them under control of ethnic or religious groups—have been used to educate our young. While there have unquestionably been problems, particularly of an interreligious sort, current evidence seems to show that the dire predictions of disastrous consequences have not materialized nor do they appear to be likely to develop. There are even some indications that by allowing, if not encouraging, pluralist channels for education, intergroup accommodations are easier perhaps because the divisive issue of whether or not they should be permitted is not a point of bitter contention. The folk wisdom in the saying "never argue about religion" may suggest a path for our society in dealing with some of the issues now being pushed by our ethnic minorities on the question of control.

In the recent turmoil at San Francisco State a situation developed which may be instructive. Bishop Mark Hurley, then from the Roman Catholic Archdiocese of San Francisco, was selected as chairman of the Mayor's committee to help solve the crisis. From the observation of many who were close to the settlement scene (one of the co-authors was intimately involved in the settlement process) no single man worked with greater skill and devotion to the task than did Bishop Hurley. The ironies are many and apparent. No one worried about his clerical collar, least of all he, as he jumped in to save a secular arm of the American educational enterprise. One wonders if he could have been as successful, as willing, and as welcome if the issue between parochial and public education had not started to become depoliticized as a result of legislative and judicial decisions in recent years. Is it not possible, indeed probable, that we might have fewer issues to divide us if all the ethnic minority groups, like the minority religious groups, were to have their own piece of the educational action? Must the resolution of intergroup conflict come from a pitched battle with the consequent suppression of the losers and/or their views, or might we be better off to let a "hundred schools of thought contend" in a period of partial pluralism in American education? There should be many paths to a destination of reasonable harmony between groups. Perhaps removing the issue of ethnic control over some part of our educational enterprise from the conflict arena would improve our chances for mutual accommodation and respect.

Any treatment of the idea of ethnic control of a segment of the educational apparatus invariably runs into the knotty problem of what we might term the double standard. Put most sharply, can we as a society fairly permit one segment of our people, the ethnic minorities, to have their own publicly supported yet separate programs while denying the ethnic majorities the same privilege? In other words, are we not forced by the logic of the matter to agree to some of the white majorities' desires to have their own racially pure schools, whether they be under the pretext of neighborhood schools in the north, or publicly funded "private" schools in the south? This is a difficult question for the supporters of ethnic control of ethnic programs to answer, on other than emotional grounds. It is also a difficult question for those who believe that the two routes towards intergroup harmony and ultimate integration—the system as we presently have it and the ethnic program way—should be kept open as viable alternatives. Many in our society would regard a return to full-fledged segregation as a human disaster to be avoided at all costs. So if ethnic control of ethnic programs is going to give aid and comfort to those who would send us further down the path to societal disintegration, it is probably not worth the price.

Fortunately, the logic of pluralism, except in its most extreme forms of separate national political units, does not demand an either-or answer to the question. Within the broader framework of an integrated society, it seems entirely possible to envisage a system of education where people from various ethnic groups are in control of some of their own educational destinies to the extent that their goals and actions are not contradictory to peaceful group accommodation on the basis of liberty, responsibility, and equality of opportunity. With this rough standard, we can proscribe both publicly supported "private" schools for whites in the south, because their obvious intention and probable result is to preserve a traditional inequality based on color, and also the "lily white," neighborhood schools of the north, because their existence rests on illegal and unethical segregationist housing patterns which strike at the very heart of equality of opportunity. We would also reject those ethnic proposals which are grounded on reverse racism and the ways of violence, because they take us not towards peaceful accommodation but towards war. In addition, we can exclude from public support those ethnic efforts which are truly exclusive in the sense that they exclude members of other ethnic groups from instructional programs. Again, we can reject exclusivity because it forces us to exclude people from the benefits of publicly supported educational programs because of their color and national backgrounds and thus denies equal protection of the laws. We would have to take the same position if a non-Catholic were denied access to the Catholic institutions on the basis of religion, particularly now that public funds are allocated to Catholic institutions with increasing frequency.

In the latter sense, one might argue that, by the same token, ethnic control of ethnic programs would have to be proscribed because it does deny equal access to the boards and smacks of denying equal protection of the laws because of race, creed or color. It is a fine point. We have been grappling with it in the courts and legislatures, on questions of fair housing and parochial education, among others, for many years. Perhaps the best that can be said is that ethnic control is a way of attempting to remedy years of unequal treatment. It is designed to give some minorities the opportunity which whites have had in controlling their own educational destinies because of their majority position. Perhaps the only way minorities, particularly those at the lower end of the economic scale, can ever experience the same kind of educational advantage is to have control of some institutions of their own, and to have them publicly supported because the minority groups cannot afford to do that by themselves.

It can even be argued that we have already been doing this, at least in some measure, for the educational institutions of religious minorities. Public funding has certainly been coming their way in increasing amounts, although often rationalized in terms of national defense. Yet, there has not been an enormous cry to take Catholic or Lutheran education out of the hands of Catholics or Lutherans on grounds that Presbyterians do not have equal access to their boards of control. We may be discovering that a pluralist approach to education is not necessarily destructive of democracy or other aspects of our society and can even lead to the diminution of conflict rather than its heightening. In this regard, the experiments with ethnic control may be profoundly useful in leading toward the resolution of some basic conflicts in our society. Certainly, our current recipes for a resolution have not provided us with much evidence of overwhelming success. Ethnic control of ethnic programs seems to have promise.

There are other aspects to the control issue that are not so promising. They relate to the nature of the control envisaged. While men who prize the goals of independence from political influence for the university might agree that ethnic control of ethnic programs is desirable, they would still want to know what this means in operational terms. If it means that properly representative members of the ethnic communities are to have the deciding voice on broad policy questions— such as the kind of formal educational training most suitable for their young in terms of solving some of the problems of the minority ethnic people and better equipping them to assume useful and satisfying roles in American society—then there would be little argument. But if it means that the members of the communities, through their boards or through the ethnic minority students themselves, are to intervene in the determination of the content of courses, in questions of expertise and the make-up of the staff, then serious questions arise in the minds of many academicians.

In the first place, those who would subject a professional staff of the university to a closer control by members of the community, students or otherwise, need to overcome traditional arguments supporting academic freedom. Although under attack from this student generation for complicity with the military-industrial complex, the university still appears to have retained much of its critical function as a free and independent marketplace of ideas. While the insidious and sophisticated pressures for conformity and orthodoxy have made their way into the university, mostly through the pipelines of monetary support, it is still possible for a professor to make intellectual challenge to the most basic aspects of our conventional wisdom. Vital as this academic freedom is to the existence of the free university, it may at times be quite vulnerable to the onslaught of tyrannical majorities or minorities bent on seizing the university for their own political or doctrinal ends. In the name of adherence to a narrowly defined world view, professors can be hired and fired, courses can be shaped, and students can be indoctrinated. But an ironic outcome is the result of this effort. By capturing the university they no longer have a university. A political action group, perhaps, or a diploma mill, but not the free marketplace of ideas which is the main distinguishing characteristic of a university. It is not at all clear that the substitution of ethnic-minority control for majority control would enhance the chances for the survival of academic freedom and the university if that control means intervention. The San Francisco State experience seems to suggest that, if power over the courses and personnel ever really does fall into the hands of "the people," the traditions of academic freedom will be greatly endangered if not destroyed. For example, when a political science professor took exception to some of the ideas put forth in a black studies proposal, he was apparently singled out by the "people" for a range of intimidative acts culminating in efforts to shout him down in the classroom. That this behavior threatens to become a way of life can be surmised from a report of the first semester's operations of black studies at State. In an open letter from the undergraduate dean's office, the following incidents were reported: "harassing telephone calls—followed in one instance by slashed tires and smashed windows in the instructor's car. . . . threat to 'haul you before the central committee' made to instructor who gave examinations and refused to allow the committee's teaching assistant to take over the class for political discussion. . . . friendly warning that 'somebody would probably shoot you tomorrow' . . . . published report [*Black Fire*] that certain faculty members should be treated as 'enemies of the people' . . . . faculty members have been told to leave their class and if they don't, the class is simply disrupted by continuous 'discussion' making instruction impossible. If the faculty member does not leave the hour is given to a function determined by the Central Committee."

It is instructive that these outrageous actions were mirrored by an insidious attempt at intervention from an opposite direction when President Smith was given to understand that he could solidify his position with certain trustees if he denied tenure to an economics professor who was out of favor with some of the board of trustees. In either case, one might suggest that there is need for less community control of the interventionist type, rather than more, and that matters of expertise in personnel and curriculum should be left mainly in the hands of professionals where the commitment to academic freedom is perhaps most firmly entrenched. It has yet to be shown that any other group will operate as well in the tradition of tolerance for dissenting opinion as the academic profession. That tolerance is what makes the true university possible.

There is a second reason other than the preservation of academic freedom for questioning the intervention of community controllers into the day-to-day academic workings of the college. That reason is wrapped up in the question of why we have colleges or universities in the first place. The colleges live many lives. But there would be no college if there was not a body of knowledge to be discovered, imparted, and even changed. While we cannot deny that the college of hard knocks teaches a lot, it does not exist for the reflective examination of man and nature nor does it have many built-in mechanisms for self-criticism. Living in a reflecting, criticizing, knowledge-exploring institution, the academician claims to have something to impart— some style of discovery, some ways of thinking, some methods of operating, some statements about the relationships among the facts of life, and some commitment to a peaceful style of persuasion. In the marketplace of the mind he has these things to sell. Collectively they are known as his expertise, his *profession*. Those who enter this marketplace do not come entirely as equals. Although students in the broader community should have an equal personal right to accept or reject the theories, explanations, and ways of thinking of the professionals, their limited experiences and lack of knowledge and other training would not seem to qualify them to be equal judges of professional competence nor curriculum.

One may grant that there must be regular and formal opportunities for the students, and at times the broader community, to make their judgments an effective part of the evidence in weighing the worth or competence of the professionals, particularly as they perform in the classroom. They may even share the examination of curricular relevance. However, it seems ludicrous to suggest that partially trained or untrained learners or laymen should be equal arbiters of professional competence and decisive developers of the curriculum.

One would readily agree that students are competent to judge whether they are learning anything, but it is doubtful that they are equipped to chart the course of academic ships. In a sense the drive for student power may be as irrelevant as the worst of our curricular efforts. If students want faculty to tell them what they want to hear, then they are perhaps no better than the reactionaries who also want the faculties of the college to tell them that "God is in His heaven and all's right with the world." One would hope that students would recognize that the preservation of academic freedom is the surest way to insure an opportunity for hearing and making the full range of analysis and thus of challenging the dogmas of the day. But when control is defined in interventionist terms, it threatens not only the destruction of the independence of the professional—whether in ethnic programs or elsewhere—but also the continued existence of a particular way of gaining and validating knowledge and competence. It is an escape from freedom. It attacks that aspect of the university that is most precious. In its worst form, such control may result in know-nothing-ness masquerading as wisdom and mere expediency pretending to be relevance.

Clearly, the traditional place of the college as a part of society but somehow apart from it is at stake. Now, as in the past, this pressure group or that pressure group appears desirous of capturing the college to further its own political and social ends, which are defined in terms of goodness and desirability. Although it is unquestionably true that the larger society has made the college in part an instrument of the establishment, many if not most American colleges have had a reasonable degree of success in walking that fine line between necessity to respond to the wishes of society and the obligation to maintain their critical independence. How else could one explain the fact that criticism of societal involvement in Vietnam and of other unsung popular causes, from the abolition of capital punishment to the demand for racial justice, has in large part centered in the colleges? To deliberately structure a program so that it invites interventionist control from any group seems unwise, both from the standpoint of society at large and, in this case, of the ethnic groups concerned.

What seems most needed, as the scholars in the ethnic programs go about their academic business, is this awkward independence, so that they can freely put their intellects not only to the business of accurately describing the situation but also to the profound job of searching for answers to the racial dilemmas in American society. One is tempted to urge that those who already have answers should start a political movement and propagate their ideologies to the believers, existing and potential. Certainly, the colleges can and should be a spawning ground for various solutions, but they probably cannot survive as captured instruments for propagating some particular group's favorite solution. In doing that, they would lose their crucial independence.

In addition, most sober analysts of American society would agree that if the self-defined minorities attempt to capture institutions for propaganda, instead of educational purposes, they will very likely precipitate a reaction of major proportions with undesirable outcomes. It seems certain that publicly supported academic institutions or any of their institutional parts, from ethnic studies to philosophy, have very few chips of their own to play in such a confrontation. Perhaps they can only protect their interests by being intelligent, clever, and true to their mission. A job of those in the college is to use their arts and sciences to propose solutions to society's problems and to persuade the people to accept them within the framework of the scholarly style. This does not mean that in their roles as citizens scholars must remain aloof from working in the buzzing community confusion to solve the problems. It means that in the scholarly role they must retain their commitment to the tentativeness of knowledge, the tolerance of differing views, and the arts of peaceful persuasion. And, finally, one might hope that they would bring the same attributes to their broader societal roles. It is a good trick. Given the tensions of our present society, they may have to be magicians to bring it off.

Community Action: In a sense the question arising about the community action aspect of the strategies for the solution of the educational problems of minority ethnic groups is closely related to the question of community control. What kind of action is it going to be? Normally, there is little quarrel about those aspects that project tutoring, cultural programs, and adult education in the ethnic communities. There has already been experience with these types of activities, and the college is regularly reaching out into the various communities as part of its continuing education program and as part of its training of specialists in fields of education, social work, government, and so on. The college community is even experienced with programs that seek to engineer conditions of better motivation and higher educational performance among the ethnic minorities. What is new (in addition to the extent of the direct action envisaged) seems to be that members of the ethnic communities themselves are to be in control of the action and that the action is to be based on an emerging set of assumptions which we have already examined.

Perhaps it might be of some value to recall the basic argument at this point. A major reason for the plight of the ethnic minorities in the United States is that they have been denied a positive self-image both by segregationist and integrationist attitudes and by practices of the dominant majorities. To remedy this situation we need programs in ethnic studies designed to right the historical record, to emphasize the virtues, accomplishments, and contributions of people of minority backgrounds, and to provide a better self-image, thereby breaking the chain of historical untruth, self-hate, apathy, and despair. These programs, in turn, must be under the direction and control of the ethnic communities themselves so that they will not get whitewashed in the process. They must include a community action component in every course or activity. And, all members of the ethnic communities who wish to attend college must be permitted to do so.

Nathan Hare contends that it is the community action aspect that makes the program new, different, and truly revolutionary. While the kind of community action envisaged is not entirely clear and a good deal of debate among various members of the ethnic communities themselves continues, there seems to be growing agreement that community action programs at the very least must have a political-ideological base in the sense of promoting ideas of group cohesiveness, group dignity, and group action. In addition, at San Francisco State there seems to be a convergence on the strategy of "revolutionary nationalism," which is a somewhat vaguely worded call for the formation of a coalition led by the ethnic minorities to organize politically (perhaps militarily) to end racism, to gain self-determination, and to seize political power in order to destroy capitalism and install socialism.

This uniqueness, highlighted by the community action tactic based upon the above political ideas or variations of them, raises questions about the propriety of the actions proposed. Let us make it clear that the right of members of various ethnic groups to make such proposals and to work to get them accepted is not under discussion here. They have the same right to make political proposals as any one else and a good deal more cause to make revolutionary proposals than many groups in American society. What we will briefly examine here is the propriety and wisdom of a *higher educational institution* as a participant in a particular political strategy for solving the problem. Most of the argument against the college institution assuming this role has been presented in the discussion of community control and is well known. It is bound up with the idea of the university as a relatively independent place for free expression of contending ideas, not a place for manning the political barricades in an effort to seize political power. The university as one of society's institutions is not prevented from seeking to end society's inhumanities through peaceful persuasion, but unlike its individual professors, the power of the university is probably strengthened by abstinence from partisan political activity. While we would be foolish to deny that academic institutions are rarely strictly academic, and that a measure of political involvement is almost unavoidably part of the university experience, it seems clear that at least the most militant envisage a radically different role for the academic institution in its ethnic studies program.

A quote from *Black Fire* (October 15, 1969) provides evidence of the contention that certain proponents of ethnic studies have something in mind other than an academic program: "Black studies across the nation cannot become *a part of* the existing institutions of higher learning, but act as a vehicle for perpetuating revolution," (italics added) writes a member of the Black Students Union central committee at San Francisco State College. Some academicians believe this is an admission that our existing academic institutions cannot contain ethnic studies.

However, we need to reserve final judgment on statements of this type until we have better answers to what sort of community action programs eventuate and to whether sentiments like these are the prevailing ones. In particular, we know that we need to seek continuing answers to the following questions about community action programs. In their community action efforts, will faculty demand that students follow a particular line or vice versa? Must they, as workers in the community, swear allegiance to the principles of "revolutionary nationalism"? Will they be evaluated in terms of their qualifications as revolutionaries or as good tutors or professors? Or are the terms interchangeable? Will contending views be presented in the various community programs or only one view? Will doctrinal purity be demanded at the point of a gun or the show of a fist? Will a reign of terror by students or others serve as a substitute for a reign of reason and peaceful persuasion? More generally, will a scholarly or academic style of respect for the truth and dignity of an opponent win out over tactics of expediency and intimidation in the college-supported community actions of the ethnic minorities?

Unfortunately, at this point in time a satisfactory and satisfying answer to these questions is not to be found. If we are to judge from the perspective of the most inflamed rhetoric of some of those in the ethnic studies program, there seems little prospect of preservation of what we have called the scholarly style, in the community action programs or anywhere else. "Have you killed a white man?" was scrawled on one of the walls in a Chinatown basement which housed one of the community action programs for some of the students at San Francisco State College. Whether this was simply a sign of the underlying rage and discontent of a member of an ethnic minority, or a conscious prescription for tactical behavior, or a conditioning statement showing how far they must be prepared to go in order to get the whites to redress their grievances, or merely a tactic of intimidation designed to influence whites who saw it is not easy to ascertain. But what would seem to be certain is that action programs encompassing this "premise" have no place at the college. Whether there is a place for the *college,* as we have known it, in these tense moments of social change is by no means clear. Perhaps there is no time for scholarship but only for political struggle.

The ominous fact may be that increasing numbers of people in the minority ethnic communities seem to be entertaining drastic alternatives based on the view that the situation is desperate and desperate remedies are needed. "Our lives are at stake" was a frequently uttered phrase at San Francisco State, as the ethnic minority students pleaded their case to the academic community. This phrase suggests how desperately students are searching for some institutional mechanism to help mobilize their communities in a struggle for a better life. It seems that they feel so little success in getting traditional political institutions to respond to their felt needs that they are now attempting to base their strategy on educational institutions as preliminary devices for building the group cohesiveness necessary for gaining the maximum political strength that minority numbers will allow. The dilemma for them and for the larger American society is obvious. If the students push for politicizing their own educational experiences, they may well precipitate action of a more severely debilitating kind, including the withholding of monetary support and the destruction of academic freedom. If they do not push, the psyche-shattering situation seems likely to continue. The kind of revolution that is needed is clearly a revolution in the attitudes and behavior of the white majority. That that can be brought about by violent revolution on the part of a challenging group would seem to be doubtful in the extreme. But can it be brought about by *peaceful* means?

Access to the Colleges: At first glance, the demand that students from minority backgrounds be given unlimited access to the colleges and universities of the nation strikes again at some of the most basic views about the college. The traditional view has been that college education is to be open to students on the basis of merit, at least in the tax-supported colleges and universities. Various devices have been used to determine merit, ranging from the possession of high school diplomas to performance on entrance tests like college boards. These devices are based upon the twin assumptions that only the best qualified can truly benefit from a college education, or are indeed capable of handling the difficulties of knowledge at the highest intellectual levels, and that the society does not need nor could it afford universal college training. Given these assumptions, it is not surprising that the demand that *anyone* of a minority ethnic background be permitted to enter college conjures up unwelcome images of a flood of the unlettered and unqualified into institutions already overcrowded with students that meet at least minimal standards. Leaving aside the question of whether such an inundation would really occur, it seems fair to ask what is objectionable about this demand.

American society has been increasingly demanding that its young people pass through the rite of college if they are to be given full privileges of membership in the tribe. Yet, American society cannot, by any stretch of the imagination, contend that it has invested as much money and skill per child in the education of the children of the poor—including the ethnic poor—as it has in the children of the middle and upper classes. Visits to a school in a poverty area and to a suburban school quickly reveal the truth of this assertion. It is true that some equalizing efforts have been made, but they have been puny in comparison with the magnitude of the problem. The problem, of course, is that unless and until a massive amount of additional funds and talent is poured into the schooling of the poor, the contention of equal opportunity will remain a sham and a myth. The whole question of equality of opportunity in education is intimately connected to the broader problem of poverty in America in the sense that an attack on one necessitates an attack on the other. As long as the society moves closer and closer to the point where it insists upon highly sophisticated skills—both human and technological—grounded on intellectual access as the price of the good life, then a clear conscience requires that it provide equality of educational opportunity for our poverty stricken. And that is what the ethnic minority demands for unlimited access are.

While one can reasonably contend that money should not be

invested in the colleges before it is rushed into the elementary and secondary schools, the argument may not be entirely on point. The active ethnic minorities believe it is necessary to begin at all levels at once. The immediate need is for trained educational manpower that can successfully communicate with the children of the minority groups. It seems possible and desirable in terms of righting an ancient and present wrong to take many of those who have fallen by the educational wayside because of lack of incentive and other emotional blocks and train them quickly to assume some of the needed positions in all walks of life, but particularly in the educational institutions. This would provide badly needed role models for children in these communities, and it might also bring the myth of equality closer to reality. There is a massive job to be done and many hands would seem to be needed to do it. Rather than look with consternation at the prospect of flood into the colleges and universities of the society, we should welcome it as one of the great challenges in human history. But the academic profession cannot possibly do it justice without a massive input of resources according to some well-conceived plan of action. To open the doors of the university to all who would come without providing special academic and financial help would merely be visiting another educational failure upon people who have experienced failure far too frequently already. No reasonable educational purpose could be served by such strategy. What form such massive input of resources would take is a book of its own, but we will make some tentative suggestions below.

There remains one final aspect of the tactic of unlimited access that has raised serious question. If it is true that the supporters of unlimited access see it as a device for increasing the power of the ethnic minorities in order to make the university more malleable and more responsive to their needs than it has been and is, then we must discern what is meant by malleability and responsiveness. Certain supporters of unlimited access define educational responsiveness as meaning that the university, or at least the ethnic studies aspect of it, is to be a direct launching platform for seizure of political power by revolution, armed if necessary, and that those who become involved are to be considered troops in the field. Quite obviously, it is this aspect of unlimited access that arouses doubt and consternation in many people, both within the university and in the broader community as well. If ethnic

studies programs are to be recruiting grounds for violent revolutionaries and unlimited access is going to swell those ranks, then many
would raise even greater doubts about its advisability.

Most of the pragmatic and purposive arguments about the independence of the university are brought into play by the proposal to
use the university as an active instrument of the violent revolution,
but in a sense they are not on point in terms of the question of access.
That a political group may seek to enlist the support of incoming students is not a reason for keeping the student away from the university
even if the proposals of the political group are revolutionary. Political
groups have long had their campus branches, and the underlying principle of the university as the place for the examination of ideas and
programs would seem to demand that this extracurricular effort continue. The constitutional principle of freedom of association would
also seem to apply. What is relevant to the discussion is whether the
ethnic studies program and curriculum in which many of the students
are likely to be involved are appropriate for the university.

What Is To Be Done

Our discussion suggests that the present situation in ethnic
studies is complex and grave. The way the winds of strategy and for-
tune will blow is difficult to forecast. On the one hand, the prospect
is for a war of the races, variously defined as a war of liberation and
insurrection, a guerilla action, a revolution, a fight for law and order,
and so on. On the other hand, the pleasant prospect is for programs
that they will contribute to a peaceful solution to America's racial
dilemmas. A sober analysis of what has transpired at San Francisco
State suggests that it would be foolish to portray the current scene in
optimistic terms. It is true that by the fall of 1969 a faculty for a
black studies program was partly in place, courses were being offered,
and a large number of the students had enrolled. Unfortunately, it is
also true that rumors and instances of intimidation, indoctrination,
politicization, and violence against persons and property have become
a part of the campus scene. If these continue, there is every likelihood
that part, if not all, of the ethnic studies effort will be destroyed, at
least for the near future and perhaps for much longer. Thus, a movement that promised hope will reap despair, and Americans of all backgrounds will once again have failed in an attempt to resolve their
greatest dilemma. Perhaps it is not too late to make a few tentative

proposals about what might be done but in doing so we cannot be unduly optimistic that these proposed solutions will do the job.

These proposals rest mainly on the assumptions that a major part of the current difficulty stems from a paternalistic attitude and performance by the members of the majority ethnic group when dealing with the educational problems of the minorities. In the current atmosphere, whenever a member of the majority (no doubt including these authors) makes a decision or comment or attempts to give some advice, a growing number of people of ethnic background are psychologically unable to listen. Perhaps the time has come to lessen the voice of the majority and agree to develop institutions that come under the direct supervision and control of the ethnic minorities themselves and are technically apart from our current institutions. Several new federally supported centers or colleges of ethnic studies could be created across the country. Primary focus of these colleges would be on the arts, humanities, and social sciences; they would be basically concerned with problems of educational motivation and relevance from kindergarten through college and would be centers for the celebration of ethnicity through historical cultural programs, art, art shows, cinematography, and so on; they would be a source of learning about the people and problems of the minority communities and a source of proposing solutions to these problems. Like other publicly supported educational institutions, they would probably need to be denied institutional participation in partisan politics or in institutionally supported programs (modeled perhaps after the Peace Corps rule which is imperfect but serviceable). Partisan political activity by the institution might be denied in order to preserve the independence of the colleges and on the purely pragmatic grounds of getting the support needed to establish and maintain the colleges. Nonetheless, they would be encouraged to serve the various ethnic communities in many capacities, from tutorials to advice on numerous social problems. Rural communities have long had governmental support, with special institutions designed to aid them in their struggle against the inequities of nature and of society. Similarly, these new institutions might be viewed as institutions designed to aid the ethnic minorities in their struggle against the inequities of a prejudiced society.

The colleges would be controlled at first instance by a board of governors elected by members of the ethnic communities according to some principle of proportional representation. Places on the board might be reserved for representatives of faculty and students, inaugurating a welcome practice in the constitution of boards. The board would play the same general role as boards of trustees and school boards in the best sense of representing the needs of the colleges, arbitrating disputes, and serving as a cushion between the legislature and the workers in the academic vineyards, but, hopefully, not in subverting the principles of academic freedom. At the outset, the boards would select the main administrative officers. Those appointments would be subject periodically to the advice and consent of the entire faculty and elected representatives of the students. The faculty would originally be appointed by the administrators so selected, with consultation with student groups where appropriate. The basic principle for staffing the departments would be that the professors would be qualified professionals or experts in their fields with suitable evidence of professional preparation and specialized interests in the areas of minority ethnic studies or problems of minority ethnic communities. Faculty would have tenure rights based on the judgment of their peers and evidence of their effectiveness in the classroom.

Access to these ethnic colleges would be given to any student, regardless of ethnic background, who had completed an accredited high school program or its equivalent. The only exception would be that students of minority ethnic background would be given matriculation preference if spaces turned out to be severely limited. A massive effort should be made to accommodate all those who wish to attend. In this connection, now is the time to inaugurate a sweeping educational bill of rights for the sons and daughters of low and middle income families. The children of the poor and even of the middle class often do not have the ability to stay in school or to apply themselves thoroughly to their studies even though attendance is free. Perhaps the only way we can make equality of educational opportunity become a quick reality for ethnic minorities and for many others is to provide full four year scholarships which would cover books, fees, and living allowances comparable to the resources provided to our veterans. There is a widely held belief that one of the wisest educational investments that this country ever made was the G.I. bill after World War II. Might we not look upon the universalization of access to higher education as an equally significant step in bringing the dream of equality of opportunity closer to reality?

A few additional words need to be said about the curriculum

of the ethnic departments in the new colleges or centers. We have suggested that they might emphasize the arts, humanities, and the social
sciences. This would give them an orientation towards exploring the
life styles, needs, histories, and so on, of the peoples in the ethnic communities, with an eye towards remedying the motivational and informational inadequacies of the past. While there might be some temptation to cover the whole range of collegiate instruction, that temptation
probably should be resisted on two grounds. First, to water down the
social and motivational focus by taking on the responsibilities of vocational and professional training might lose some of the opportunities
of concentrated focus and study whose absence has been a plague of
the traditional curriculum. Second, the chances for continuing monetary support for such a broad effort would seem to be minimal. Moreover, an attractive aspect of the new colleges might well be that they
would become an excellent supplier of ethnically-oriented people for
the whole range of professional and vocational programs in other colleges and universities.

In this connection an experiment with the principle of educational reciprocity would seem to be worthwhile. In practice, this would
mean that any student attending a new school would be permitted to
take classes at any of the other service area institutions (hopefully,
both public and private, but certainly public) without additional fee,
and that he would be accorded the same academic rights and privileges as students in the other institutions. In exchange, students in the
other institutions would be permitted to enroll in courses offered by
various departments in the new school. While new school majors would
have preregistration privileges much as majors in departments in other
colleges, students from other institutions could undoubtedly be accommodated. The exciting possibilities for this reciprocal intercultural
learning might prove one of the most significant outcomes of the new
school experience. To those who support the idea in principle but dismiss it as too cumbersome in practice, it should be pointed out that
reciprocity arrangements now exist in a number of places in the
country.

Even if the formidable and perhaps insurmountable fiscal, political, and psychological obstacles to establishing these new colleges
are overcome, they cannot come into full operation overnight. Consequently, some provision for the transition period would seem to be
desirable. This may already be at hand in the growth of ethnic stud-

ies programs in several colleges and universities across the country. The experience and knowledge gained from these efforts may provide the most effective way of planning these new colleges, and also some of the planners. Whether these on-going programs should remain in their present positions in the colleges and universities should be for those in these colleges and universities themselves to determine. One would expect that those most interested in the ethnic studies effort would find the new colleges a powerful magnet if there is major discontent with the practice and prospect of the present situation.

What is proposed here, in rather sketchy outline, is a truly dramatic, massive, and unique effort to begin to provide equal educational opportunity and, importantly, a significant measure of control by the ethnic minorities over their own educational destinies. The proposal rests on the faith that from these ethnic minorities themselves will come a major part of the basic solutions to the societal problem of achieving a more satisfying and meaningful life in American society, and that the entire society will be immeasurably enriched by a full understanding of the communities and by a greater recognition of their actual and potential contribution to the human story.

In its uniqueness and scope, the proposal is revolutionary. Given all the ways it could go wrong, it might be unwise to attempt it. Yet, in another respect it is counterrevolutionary. It is counterrevolutionary in the sense that it proposes to accomplish by peaceful, rational means most of what some revolutionaries hope to accomplish by violent means. It proposes to give the minorities something that at least some of them desperately want, and it proposes to do so within the broad framework of the American democratic system. The proposal is put forth with the shaky hope that the American system will be able to meet this most serious challenge of rooting out racism and providing equality of opportunity to all the people. It is also put forth with the recognition that the violent revolutionaries may be right when they contend that our present system does not permit them to escape fast enough from material and psychological bondage to a land of liberty, equality, and fraternity. However, the stark tragedy is that even if these revolutionaries are right, their prospects for accomplishing change by violence seem hopeless. Indeed, they are likely to worsen their situation and the situation of all of those who passionately believe in the right of a dignified existence for all men.

The trouble with the current slogan "Power to the People" is that the majority of the people do have the power. At least as far as our racial situation is concerned, "the people" *are* the problem. The fatal flaw in the analysis made by the violent revolutionary seems to be the belief that it is simply the power structure, the power elites, which confound their aspirations when the fact more likely is that the power elites are really men of the people, rising out of the people, sharing their superstitions, bigotries, and inhumanities, sometimes to a greater, sometimes to a lesser, extent. It is easy to see why revolutionaries have wanted to believe that it is a small class, a clique, or a few hundred manipulators of power that need to be destroyed. The task of overthrow seems so much easier, so much clearer, and so possible in that kind of situation. Yet, in the United States in this era there is sufficient evidence—as exemplified by votes on fair housing, by racial discrimination of labor unions, by the popular flight to lily white suburbs, and by the cries for crackdowns on the students—to confirm the thesis that "the people" are indeed the problem. Thus, the task is to change them rather than to give them an excuse for playing out their own violent fantasies. It is a tough, perhaps an impossible job. Who is to say which is the most effective way to do it? There are no social engineers with tested tools and fine blueprints to help us bridge the problem. This essay suggests that the arts of peaceful persuasion and careful analysis both exemplified by the scholarly style may be the best means available. While Mao Tse-tung may be partly right in saying that "political power grows out of the barrel of a gun," it seems foolishly adventurous to flaunt that "truth" when the preponderance of the gun power is in the hands of the majority. One might hope for a return to the truth of the saying that "the pen is mightier than the sword."

FIVE

Administration of
Student Justice

It has become axiomatic in the recent literature on student unrest that once police are brought onto the sanctuary of the college campus to attempt to restore order and arrest those responsible for disorder the battle is virtually lost and escalation and polarization will soon severely damage the campus. It is now becoming equally apparent—given the goals of some militant students—that unless the faculty, students, and administrators of a college face up to the difficult and unwanted task of formulating acceptable rules of conduct and enforcing these codes as a community, police intervention is inevitable. The events at San Francisco State College provide a classic case study of the failure of an academic community to come to grips with the realistic need for internal self-discipline and of the concomitants of police intervention and institutional chaos. It is possible that a dedicated band of revolutionaries could, under any conditions, force a college to bring the blue-coated, crash-helmeted forces onto the campus, no matter how seriously the academic community addresses itself to internal control. But at State the hostility of faculty, student liberals, and student personnel administrators to the concept of law enforcement precluded the opportunity of testing this thesis.

Not only does this institutional failure to discipline its own ranks usually insure police on campus, it also encourages additional confrontations and the loss of public confidence. After hearing more than forty hours of diverse testimony, the California Legislature's Select Committee on Campus Disturbances made this point quite explicit in its final findings:

> The low level of public confidence appears to relate to disorder and disruption of campuses characterized by overt acts of violence, walk-outs, sit-ins, strikes and physical intimidation of students, faculty and administrators. The failure of those in charge to cope with violent offenders, and to respond to the legitimate need for change has diminished public confidence.

Not only did the academic community at San Francisco State not cope with violent offenders, but—as other sections of this book attest—it was slow to respond to the legitimate need for change. Beyond question a wiser, more dedicated commitment to adapting the institution to the needs of modern students in our troubled technological society, especially the needs of the black and Third World students, would have obviated much of the anti-institutional behavior and the resultant demand for student discipline. It is equally true that if the state of California had recognized the financial and governance needs of modern higher education or if the Board of Trustees of the California state colleges had provided the colleges with enlightened rather than inept leadership, San Francisco State would have made more progress in responding to those changing demands. The purpose of this chapter is to underscore the problems in the administration of student justice on a campus responding to the new student ethic and embroiled in confrontational student politics.

San Francisco State has not been alone in its inability to come to grips with the complicated issues of acceptable conduct for the current activist, challenging student generation and legitimate procedures for insuring such conduct. With the emergence of a new generational ethic at deep variance with the conventional morality of most of those accorded power over institutional life—the public, legislators, trustees, administrators, and faculty—and with the disappearance of the ancient dictum governing student-institutional relationships, in loco parentis, conflict and deep-seated problems have been the fate of most colleges. This divergence in value orientation is accentuated by the introduction into the academic community of a group with a still different conception of approved personal behavior—the Third World students, militant or just quietly angry. The drive within the younger generation to gain control of their own lives—or as it is sloganized by the Third World students, "All power to the people"—assures that the resolution of this generational value conflict will not be a peaceful arbitration. Students are demanding that they have power in the development of a new code of conduct and in any court system established to evaluate alleged misbehavior.

The problems of San Francisco State in this area of internal discipline are only understood in the context of the broader concern in American higher education for a new student ethic, the drive for white and Third World student control of their own lives, Third World standards of conduct, and the problems of confrontational politics in the fragile campus setting.

New Student Ethic

The generational gap in values and ethics is not a problem for the college campus alone. Any parent, any legislator, any officer of the law is fully aware that the tastes and life styles of those "under thirty" contrast with those of the "up-tight" generation. Rarely can one pick up a magazine without being informed of some lurid details of this gap. At a superficial level the differences in hair styles, clothing, musical tastes, and leisure activities are most obvious. Many conclude from this that these differences are merely contemporary forms of the traditional resistance of the young to placid acceptance of the mores passed on to them from their elders.

Yet, penetrating studies and analyses have indicated that the claims of the young that they are a different breed have considerable substance. A lack of inhibition, a willingness to risk, a freer attitude toward sex and other taboos, a deep drive for fulfilling and intimate human relationships, a revulsion against societal hypocrisy and establishment power, a yearning for peace and racial harmony, and a capacity for personal involvement and commitment: all of these tendencies appear to be documented as reflecting a variant culture.

Of particular importance for this analysis are the attitudes that find expression in the college environment, that threaten the value system of those in power, and that produce conduct which—in the minds of some—should be disciplined. Two of the most important of these student perspectives concern the basic concepts of codes of conduct and of punitive institutional actions. In line with a general societal permissiveness, students increasingly resist do's and don'ts in favor of the attitude "do your own thing." If this means smoking pot on campus, engaging in a range of open amorous activities, walking around semi-nude, or studying—even practicing—guerrilla warfare, so be it. After all, isn't it *their* institution and *their* lives? And if they prefer to drink or engage in sexual activities or induce mind and emotion expansion in their dormitory rooms, what's wrong with that? Nobody would inhibit them in a pad in the Haight-Ashbury district. But to some faculty, many administrators, and most of the public, many of these activities are incompatible with the traditional image of a character-building institution, especially one supported and therefore controlled by taxpaying citizens. They contend that codes of conduct should be developed and regulations should be enforced, even if it means punishing, possibly expelling, errant students.

But punish is another disappearing concept among the norms of the new breed of students. Many subscribe to the psychological research that disparages punishment as a means of inducing changed behavior. Instead, they see police enforcement as simply a means for those in power to insure their own values and continued hegemony. Even those among the student body who are squeamish about some of the new norms are reluctant to identify with the "illegitimate establishment" through support of punitive action. From this antipunishment perspective, many students would simply do away with regulations, police powers, and courts.

The issue of legitimacy adds still a further complication. Discipline rests upon authority. In swelling numbers modern students question the legitimacy of the current authority structure, in society in general and in the colleges. They question this legitimacy on two fundamental grounds. First, they contend that an authority structure that derives its power from a corrupt, hypocritical society becomes the agent for that corrupt society and therefore has no right to sanction those attempting to reform or revolutionize the culture. In their pronouncements on this point, student activists invariably enumerate the ties between the college trustees and the military-industrial complex and believe no more need be said. In *The Closed Corporation: American Universities in Crisis*, James Ridgeway documents this point in great detail.[1]

For the majority of students who question the legitimacy of the

[1] J. Ridgeway, *The Closed Corporation* (New York: Random House, 1968).

authority of college trustees and administrators to devise rules of conduct for students and to enforce these rules, the simple declaration that students should govern their own lives is very persuasive. In broader institutional relationships this means students should totally govern their educational environment, or at least that they should have full power in some areas, shared power in others. The black students made this point pellucidly clear in almost all of their utterances: We must have absolute power to control our own destiny in a racist society. Third World student control of their own curriculum and teaching personnel was one of the ten demands that neither side would negotiate for the four months of the strike. In the minds of most students this posture is also totally valid on the issue of who devises student rules of conduct and who adjudicates cases of alleged violation. Many students do not trust faculty or administrators—who are of a different generation and are hooked into the power structure—to create rules students can live by or to make equitable judicial decisions.

This major irritant between white students and the authority structure becomes a matter of "our lives" to most black students. They are more aware, even than the sympathetic whites, that the black culture is more in conflict with the accepted ways of academe than are the evolving norms of the new student generation. Their living, breathing reality has been one of resistance to enculturation efforts of the "superior" white culture and its array of sanctions, inducements, coercion, and power. Consequently, "illegal" behavior becomes almost a matter of cultural survival and personal identity. Societal rules by their very nature have no legitimacy. Police enforcement automatically produces a visceral resistance and is interpreted as the mechanism of their repression. After resisting at considerable risk the laws and the official enforcement agencies of society, many of the young black students simply cannot take collegiate regulations and campus courts seriously. Correspondingly, guilt-ridden liberals among the students, faculty, and administration shy away from the application of such codes and courts to black students, and many in the academic community of all political persuasions retreat—frequently from fear—from the efforts of black students to defend themselves.

Many black students also bring to the campus a life style alien to the traditions of the academy. Their spontaneity runs counter to the deliberate rationality that colleges accept as a bed rock goal. Their interpersonal conduct resembles the behavior through which the new student generation expresses its emerging values and therefore is also in conflict with the comportment expected by those in power. And most important, what the college calls violence the blacks recognize as survival traits in the ghetto. The tempo of their rhetoric frightens some in committee meetings, their mass invasions of campus legislative or administrative meetings is considered coercion, and their attempts to "stomp" the enemy—a reflex action for some of the ghetto-bred— brings cries of "bring in the police and throw them in jail" from many of the faculty and most of the public. Thus, the culture of a large segment of the black community, as it inevitably invades the lily-white, middle-class college environment, creates serious additional problems in the administration of justice on the campus.

The new student ethic, the infusion of minority cultural values, and the student urge to govern their own lives would produce more than enough difficulties for administrators oriented more towards conventional academic morality and unquestioned authority. When the task of controlling the conduct of those among both white and black militants tending toward confrontational tactics is added to the administrators' burdens, many fail. Such failure was central to the San Francisco State scene. Paradoxically, confrontational politics not only magnifies the difficulties for college officials in controlling student conduct but also produces public anger and resultant pressures that make the task almost impossible. Disciplinary action amidst a vast media and political hue and cry for heads to roll is interpreted by much of the student body and many faculty as yet another example of the complicity of the institution with a corrupt power structure. Distorted media reporting of incidents certainly inflames this tender situation. And the general impression among students and faculty in California— of the Reagan administration as a prime symbol of an anti-intellectual, repressive power structure committed to strait-jacketing colleges, youth, minorities, and liberal impulses—makes bowing to this kind of shrill political demand for punitive action appear as craven obeisance.

Thus, a cyclic reaction develops—increased polarization, lack of public confidence, repressive control, further student and faculty alienation, escalated aggressive actions on the campus, more punitive pressures, and on and on and on. The educational climate disappears, administrators resign or are fired, faculty seek other employment or institute feverish adversarial relationships with each other and the outside world, funds necessary for the institutional changes that might

decelerate this escalation are lopped off by an angry legislature or ve-
toed by the governor, and what was once a proud, productive college
becomes little more than a battlefield for contending forces on the left
and right in a society in crisis.

Currently the description fits San Francisco State College; in
the near future it may apply to many colleges. The obvious way to
resist the cyclic events and the resultant institutional destruction is for
the college to decide to modify its traditional, inefficient and self-indulgent academic stance and make the changes demanded by learning
research, the critical student body, and the troubled state of the nation.
To assure the funds and public faith requisite for such changes, colleges must create some sense of internal order out of all of the difficulties enumerated previously. This the academic community at State
neglected to do despite the 1964 warning of the Free Speech Movement
at Berkeley.

Preconfrontation Student Discipline

For the most part San Francisco State could afford to indulge
itself in the liberal posture toward student discipline in its preconfrontation, pre-Summerskill period. Breaches in even conventional academic morality were infrequent on the streetcar campus. A bureaucratic unit called the Dean's Committee handled transgressions as well
as student petitions, and its monthly meetings usually adjudicated such
sticky issues as student requests to secure admission although deficient
five grade points, or to obtain an extension of time to make up an
incomplete grade. Maybe once in two years a case of cheating in-
truded, but most faculty either overlooked such incidents or handled
them individually. Virtually no students were warned or suspended,
no lawyers demanded due process, and no detailed transcripts were
required of the committee's proceedings. In 1962 the college joined
the trend to give students a fundamental role in their own discipline
by creating a Student Judicial Court, but student discipline was so
infrequent and of such a low priority that the court was seldom ac-
tivated.

This absence of concern or procedures for insuring student order and justice fitted nicely with the evolving liberal ethos of the college and the "student personnel point of view" that dominated the
administrative unit responsible in this area. Increasingly State created
and enjoyed its own self-image of a swinging campus where, as long

as faculty and students were allowed to operate with a minimum of rules, peace prevailed. The prevalent view was that people who are allowed to be creative and to fulfill themselves have slight need for aberrant behavior. The operation of the Dean of Students office was almost totally oriented philosophically toward the student personnel goal of facilitation, not repression.

Experience seemed to confirm the wisdom of this philosophy. Behind the leadership of a series of bright, dedicated social and educational reformists—Tom Ramsey, Joe Persico, Terry McGann and Jim Nixon—the Associated Students developed a new conception of student government, one that attracted national attention as it went into the ghetto and as it created its Experimental College at home. As the neighboring and resented Berkeley campus shuddered in the throes of its Free Speech Movement, San Francisco State complacently said "it can't happen here" because State had the formula: facilitation, not constraint; an absence of tight rules, not a detailed code of conduct; a speakers platform for open discussion, not stringent time, place, and manner regulations and restraints on advocacy.

San Francisco State went into the academic year 1966–1967 with great confidence, and a virtual void in the area of the administration of student justice. Its hallmark was a philosophy on student conduct that is epitomized by the statement, "The college faculty, administration, and student government assume that each student has, or is hoping to develop, an earnest and useful purpose." The college deeply believed in its obligation to promote maturity and responsibility by giving students freedom to act and to accept the consequences of their actions. The explicit disciplinary attitude and limits of student conduct are clarified in the college catalogue statement on student conduct: "In the few instances where disciplinary action is necessary, because students have failed to respond to the positive approach which is emphasized in dealing with questions of conduct and responsibility, the college is guided by the California Administrative Code. The code provides that a student may be placed on probation, suspended, or expelled for any one of the following reasons: (a) Disorderly, unethical, vicious, or immoral conduct; (b) misuse, abuse, theft, or destruction of state property." But the college had failed to define "disorderly, unethical, vicious, or immoral conduct" in terms of the new student ethic, Third World values, or confrontational tactics. It acted as though such definitions would indict student motives, and rather than do this the college relied upon the authority of the ancient Administrative Code devised by the state board of education in a different age for different purposes.

By contrast, the University of California at Berkeley learned from its travail that explicit limits of conduct were needed so that students could know what was permissible and what was not and the judicial process would have precise guidelines. On February 19, 1968, it promulgated a code that defined twelve specific limits. Some referred to conventional prohibition of dishonesty, forgery, theft, or narcotics. Others spoke specifically to the problems of campus disruption and prohibited: obstruction or disruption of teaching, research, administration disciplinary procedures, or other university activities, including its public service functions, or of other authorized activities on university premises; physical abuse of any person on university-owned or controlled property or at university sponsored or supervised functions or conduct which threatens or endangers the health or safety of any such person; violation of university policies or campus regulations including campus regulations concerning the registration of student organizations, the use of university facilities, or the time, place, and manner of public expression; disorderly conduct, or lewd, indecent, or obscene conduct or expression on university owned or controlled property, or at university sponsored or supervised functions; failure to comply with directions of university officials acting in the performance of their duties; conduct which adversely affects the student's suitability as a member of the academic community.

The California Legislature became so convinced that reluctance of the colleges to define these limits contributed to the many campus disturbances that it required by law that California public colleges "shall adopt or provide for the adoption of specific rules and regulations governing student behavior along with applicable penalties for violation of such rules and regulations." It further decreed that every student upon registration should be provided with a copy of such rules and penalties. Eventually the trustees of the state colleges acted even more explicitly than did the University of California at Berkeley. While the University of California wrestled with a code of conduct that would apply to the tactics of a minority of students who were convinced that their virtuous ends justified all kinds of disruptive means, both the student personnel administrators and the Academic Senate at State sat back, smugly content with their open-ended reliance upon freedom and responsibility and certain that this reliance inhibited rather than facilitated difficulties. When the battle was finally joined with the militant students, all parties were so busy avoiding the flak of blame that it was too late to cooperate on rules that might be acceptable and enforceable.

In addition to failing to define the limits of student conduct, San Francisco State failed to provide the means or locate the responsibility for prosecuting alleged misconduct and failed also to provide a workable judicial process. In an age of accelerated disruptive behavior, and at a college that witnessed more than its fair share of such disorder, this can only be construed as institutional malfeasance. Responsibility again rests with the deans of students and the Academic Senate, with partial implication of the transient presidents of the college and the Associated Students. Created in the post-World War II academic climate that stressed individualization of the depersonalized college environment and student responsibility for his own development and conduct, the student personnel services at State had moved even more clearly in this service direction in response to the new student constituency and the mood of the movement. Student activities counselors were hired who were simpatico with the hip student activists. Sweet music was made and the college flourished.

The only warning came from these same counselors and some faculty, who spoke not of laxness but rather of institutional tendencies that were frustrating the new breed of students. This warning was listened to but not acted upon. Oriented as they were to service and believing that few outsiders really understood the student movement, the student personnel administrators were reluctant to jeopardize their simpatico role with the additional responsibility of securing evidence against transgressors and prosecuting them. Such activities smacked of police enforcement, not educational endeavors. This contradiction in roles has always been a problem for those in student personnel. One answer is to separate the administration of student justice from the personnel area, as State attempted briefly under President Hayakawa. But this approach also poses a dilemma for personnel administrators, because this disassociated role does not give them the opportunity to temper justice with humane considerations. Yet somebody needed to act at San Francisco State, for transgressions of even the vaguely worded "disorderly conduct" code became routine as student protests accelerated,

Judicial procedures were as deficient as the prosecution mechanism. At a time when student personnel leaders throughout the nation had been working for six years with representatives of the National Student Association, the American Association of University Professors, and the American Association of Colleges to develop a bill of rights for students which included model disciplinary procedures, State had available a cumbersome Board of Appeals and Review (that replaced the Dean's Committee) and an inactive Student Judicial Court but no precise procedures to insure both due process and justice. When the college finally had to face the necessity of adversarial action against the *Daily Gater* attackers, it was in the embarrassing position of having the individual nominally responsible for prosecution, the Dean of Students, sitting as chairman of this judicial body!

The Academic Senate shared responsibility with the student personnel administrators for the lack of minimal rules of conduct, machinery for the administration of justice, and a viable judicial process. According to the Constitution of the Academic Senate, the faculty through the Senate had final policy authority for student control. Operationally this power was vested in a Committee on Student Affairs (COSA) which recommended policy to the Senate. Except as an advisory body to the Dean of Students and the Associated Students, this committee had been virtually defunct. In an era of great attention to student affairs, it had recommended little policy to the Senate. The Senate, wrapped up in its battles with the administration or the chancellor's office and hardly admitting student affairs to be an academic concern, had been more than happy not to intrude into this state of apathy. The Associated Students, who believed that neither the faculty nor the administration had much legitimacy in student business, did not challenge this vacuum, for no policy was good policy. Certainly the Associated Students did not complain about the failure of the faculty and administrators to intrude into student discipline. The student personnel administrators never did accept the transformation of COSA from an administrative advisory committee into a faculty policy committee, and they were quite satisfied that they could work best with student leaders in this loose, unstructured, untrammeled situation. Implicit, even explicit at times, was the point of view that you couldn't really trust faculty to understand student personnel philosophy. Very few senior faculty served on COSA, because schools selected faculty sympathetic to students or of slight tenure—and those in the Associated Students and student personnel encouraged this tendency. While this policy may have made for a more receptive committee, it also meant a policy body that did not carry much weight in the senate.

In early December of 1966, during the first year of the presidency of John Summerskill (who had been a vice president of student affairs at Cornell University) the assumption that students free to do their own thing would eventuate in an active but trouble-free campus began to tarnish.[2] During the cafeteria boycott, first by the ragtaggle SDS cadre, then joined by the BSU, the Associated Students leaders, and even many from the silent majority, the administration played it cool, in fact so cool that the students found that they had no opponents. Although this attitude certainly defused the situation, the event itself also convinced the activists that they hadn't come close to pressing the limits of behavior. Their tactics were rather mild in this initial skirmish, but they did bring in their own substitute caterer without permission and they did actively intimidate students with a shoulder to shoulder picket line well sprinkled with black students.

With the advent of the underground newspaper, *Open Process,* the contradictions in taste were joined, and with the inaugural ceremonies picketing, the limits of disruptive behavior were pressed. *Open Process* was closed temporarily by President Summerskill, but the semester was over and so this meant little. Shortly after the beginning of the fall semester *Open Process* was in full swing again. No student penalties were invoked and the college mechanism for some control of student publications fell into disuse. The inaugural fiasco proved that the dean of students took no responsibility for anticipating student disruptions, had no capacity to inhibit them, and saw no need for disciplinary action, although the ceremony was thoroughly discredited in front of a large public gathering, and trustees and other notables were actually physically harassed. The senate also disregarded the incident, because summer vacations were ahead of the faculty. For the militants it was a complete victory.

The year 1967–1968 saw an unending string of victories for those bent on coercing and disrupting the college. First the BSU students attacked the *Gater* editor. Before this situation was settled students had become convinced that the mass attack was justified by

[2] See *By Any Means Necessary,* pp. 10–65.

institutional racism, the college was on the defensive, the Board of Appeals and Review proved inadequate for the sustained BSU lawyer-dominated defense, an appeal for amnesty was carried to the Academic Senate, and ultimately President Summerskill quietly minimized two of the four suspensions that were meted out. The attempt to prosecute students for the first time in many years revealed to all who looked and cared that the college machinery was anachronistic and falling apart. The black students quite legitimately raised the issue that testimony on their part in the prior college trial would threaten their defense in the more important criminal courts. State simply had not anticipated this problem, although it is basic to student discipline in the modern confrontational scene. Assemblyman Willie Brown, one of the lawyers for the accused black students, commented in his minority report to the legislature's Select Committee on Campus Disturbances that "campus disciplinary procedures—frequently, and in the specific case of San Francisco State—are less protective of the rights of the accused than anything we would subject ourselves to." On the other hand *Gater* personnel testifying against the invaders were appalled at the contrast between their slight legal assistance and the battery of high-priced legal help available to those accused. The incident also vividly underscored the problems and dangers of a predominantly white college attempting to discipline black students according to vague white codes of conduct. Hanging heavy over the students testifying against the black students and the judges on the court was the implicit threat of retaliation—a relatively new phenomenon in the groves of academe.

The student personnel administrators, the Senate, the college president, and the Associated Students leadership all failed to move to remedy the egregious flaws in the college's approach to disciplinary action revealed by the prosecution of the *Gater* attackers. A month later the irate black students threatened the total campus with the all-out attack on December 6, 1967 that saw the invasion of the locked Administration Building through broken glass doors, mob action in the quadrangle that encompassed fights, weapons, fires, and building damages, and the disruption of many classes in a concerted attack by roving bands of Third World students. In defense of the decision not to bring police on campus, college officials stated publicly that it would prosecute the culprits within the campus community. This was never done. Although the militants had publicized both their timing and tactics, no effective arrangements were made by the college to gather evidence against those responsible that could have been a basis for disciplinary action. The dean of students' office had neither the heart nor the organization for such an effort. The dozen-plus campus police were totally inadequate to the task. No faculty volunteered to fill the void. Even by the vague terms of the Administrative Code limits of conduct, "disorderly, unethical, and vicious conduct" had occurred and "abuse, theft, or destruction of state property" had resulted. The incident was quietly swept under the rug. Instead faculty reacted aggressively to the Reagan-dominated board of trustees' attempt to question Summerskill's stewardship and to invoke emergency regulations for the administration of justice—regulations that would have handcuffed a president in the exercise of his authority.

Time and again in the past this same amalgam of chancellor-trustee overreaction had insured no constructive faculty-administration approach to the college's basic problems. Time and again in the future, the counter thrusts of these same two self-righteous legions— chancellor-trustee vs. faculty-administration—were to dominate affairs to the detriment of wise problem solution. Such faculty energies as were focused on the exceedingly important issue of student disciplinary procedures during this post-December 6th period concentrated on an attempt to secure a Christmas amnesty for the *Gater* attackers rather than on repairing the gaping flaws in the college's procedures and code. Although classroom disruptions were bemoaned repeatedly, no codes, machinery for prosecution, or sound judicial procedures were developed. During the spring semester students harassed military recruiters, YMCA representatives, and the Dean of Admissions, but according to the new college norms these conflicts were considered minor and were absorbed with no college action.

Events had proved to Dean of Students Ferd Reddell, however, that the cumbersome faculty-administration oriented Board of Appeals and Review was inadequate for the task of administering confrontational justice, that it implicated his office too heavily in the process, and that it was not in accord with the national trend for giving students both better due process and more responsibility for their own discipline. So, he finally reactivated the student judicial court which all had simply forgotten about. As this court composed of five students and two faculty members wrestled with procedural problems, it agreed that if all its decisions could be reversed by President Summerskill, it would be a waste of time for the court to operate. Accordingly, the

court requested of the president that he delegate final responsibility
for student discipline to the court. Dean Reddell supported this request. Summerskill, generally sympathetic to the student demands for
more power, acceded to these urgings and quietly signed his powers
away. Thus, major policy was made in this area of vital interest to
the college, the trustees and the public, and no academic senator or
administrator was any the wiser. The ratio of faculty to students on
the court was derived in 1962 for a different range of problems. Few
colleges even in the modern period have given students such power.
Of the four students already appointed by the Associated Students to
the court, one was president of the SDS, one was on the BSU Central
Committee, and one was deeply involved in the Associated Students
programs aimed at radical reform.

The final major disruption during 1967–1968 was the May
sit-in that sought to achieve the elimination of AFROTC and submission of the college to the first of the Third World demands. For eight
days approximately the same cast of characters that had been involved
in all previous disruptions, but now augmented by numerous radicalized recruits and some scattered Third World students, laid siege to
the Administration Building and almost had the college on its knees.
In the course of the battle administrators were held hostage in an office
for four hours, the Administration Building was taken over as a bar-
racks and planning center, secretaries and other personnel were harassed in a mill-in, and at one point the doors of the Administration
Building were chained shut. Police were called on three occasions
and made more than fifty arrests. For all of the disruptive activities,
threats, and coercion, at the end of the eight day siege there were no
college accusations, no trials, no suspensions or warnings. Student militants had been controlled only by the dangerous expedient of police
enforcement. At no time were the ranks of the disruptors depleted by
the law enforcement; those arrested were soon out on bail and leading
the next charge.

Student Discipline and Confrontational Politics

Although there was little excuse for the college's procrastina-
tion and ineptitude in developing an adequate student disciplinary
process, the advent of confrontational student politics created problems and a hostile climate that made the solution of these problems
extremely difficult. The confrontations introduced ranges of student

behavior that administrators simply hadn't considered when creating codes of conduct in the past. But more important, they made detection hazardous and conviction—especially by a student-faculty court—a slim possibility. This is a point rarely grasped by an impatient public. Many of the infractions occurred in mob scenes where arrests or even citations were dangerous. Certainly San Francisco State's campus police, administrators, or faculty could not have handled the situation even if they had had the desire to do so. Later, in November 1968, even plainclothes policemen found it difficult and on occasion had to fire guns to escape crowds when attempting arrests. Identification also posed problems, although here the college could have been much more successful if it had done a minimum of intelligence work and had used cameras. But this educators avoided.

When guerrilla rather than mass tactics were employed by the ever resourceful students, the difficulties of apprehending the hit-and-run attackers or gathering evidence that could stand up in college courts were increased. Few witnesses would come forward from either the student or faculty ranks. Many were fearful. Others simply did not care to identify with the repressive forces of society, or with Governor Reagan or Chancellor Dumke. Still others sympathized with the goals of the dissidents and so felt justified in turning their backs on the disruptions. Not surprisingly, convictions were extremely difficult in the civil libertarian, anti-punishment, due process environment of the campus. Probably nothing infuriated the public and the legislators more than the academic community's unwillingness to protect itself.

The mass nature of many student confrontations posed another problem. Which out of, say, four hundred violators do you attempt to discipline? For the courts this presents an even larger dilemma. Nevertheless, some colleges such as the University of California at Berkeley have stubbornly tackled the cumbersome issue, feeling that if the colleges do not discipline even obvious violators, the police and courts will inevitably usurp the colleges' disciplinary process. Selective citation makes the college vulnerable to charges of injustice or discrimination against the leaders, but it is one of the realities of college action in mass situations. The University of California and other colleges have proved that solid staff work, grubby attempts at identification, and sound due process procedures can often make headway in solving this problem. San Francisco State chose to avoid mass campus discipline.

Apprehensions and convictions under confrontation conditions are also handicapped when black students are involved. The guilt-ridden collegiate environment is deeply afraid of racist accusations. Many people are also simply physically fearful of becoming involved. Many Third World students are aware of this tendency and encourage it in various ways. The tactics of the new student dissent would challenge any campus judicial process, but courts where faculty and students share the judicial role are particularly vulnerable. This is accentuated when a campus becomes polarized, as happened at San Francisco State. Many faculty and students simply would not punish a student for "laying his body on the line to correct injustices others are too complacent to move on." Such judicial actions would be susceptible to the current dichotomous trap of "you're either for us or against us." Few faculty or students want to be "against" black students or student activists and, by the same token, few want to be "for" the police, the establishment, the administration, or, in a more personalized fashion, for Hayakawa, Dumke, Rafferty, Swim or Reagan. Joining the "enemy" on any issue is sacrilegious. This attitude is an intriguing reverse twist to the reactionary attitude that liberals castigated so bitterly during the McCarthy era—that if one supported a cause that the communists also supported, one was a fellow-traveler or communist. Such parallels are not infrequent between some of the new left and the old far right.

Again the element of personal fear enters the process. Few on the campus aware of the facts believe it was mere coincidence that Edwin Duerr, the first faculty member to volunteer to administer justice, found his house firebombed shortly thereafter. The law of averages would also not have predicted that the faculty member most involved in faculty grievance and disciplinary procedures involving black faculty would have his house go up in flames. The harassment of John Bunzel, a faculty critic of some basic assumptions in the black studies curriculum, penetrated faculty ranks and enhanced natural timidity and the urge to become noninvolved.

The potential severity of the penalties involved when the student-faculty courts are considering cases of alleged disruption or violence is another complicating factor. It is one thing to recommend a warning or even probation for a panty-raider; it takes quite a different attitude to expel twenty-five black students for whom college is the last means of escaping the ghetto. The fact that college discipline might well mean loss of loans or scholarships for the guilty students serves as a brake on student-faculty court discipline. This judicial tenderness on the college campus became quite apparent to the California Legislature's investigating committee. That group attempted to put "some steel in the spine" by specific statutory enactment mandating college discipline when criminal courts have convicted the same students for disruptive behavior.

With both the campus and the criminal courts wrapped up in adjudicating certain alleged transgressions, yet another complication arises. Rightly or wrongly, this double jurisdiction is alluded to as the problem of double jeopardy. Simply stated, the college is reluctant to prosecute while the student is awaiting judgment in the criminal courts for the same offense, for fear the student's testimony on the campus will jeopardize his case in the courts. Many colleges currently refuse to act in these cases until the courts have made their rulings. Given the pace of urban justice, this could mean that the student involved could be active in dissent on the campus for a year after his arrest—to the dismay of the authorities and the public. Such delayed campus justice is not undertaken after the intervening year with any enthusiasm or efficiency. During 1969–1970 there were no campus trials for any of the students convicted by the courts. A few mild penalties were invoked by the college coordinator of internal affairs.

The cry for amnesty that has become the concomitant of most student confrontations interjects still one more complication, and one more public exacerbation. Unlike most transgressors of the past, the modern rebel believes he should not be punished because his goals are just, and so he invariably includes amnesty as a tacked-on final demand. For faculty and administrators intellectually aware of the dangers of escalation and emotionally desirous of getting out of the disruptive mess and back to "normalcy," amnesty has a siren call. To those on the outside, it represents the final, permissive capitulation, one certain to encourage further attacks.

When in the midst of massive student confrontations, those living in the college environment appear to be overly sensitive to these difficulties of administering justice. Those paying the taxes for the colleges and those exercising final control seem to have slight awareness of the tangled thicket of apprehension, evidence, due process, double jeopardy, a court involving one's peers, and the time factors during these moments of stress. So, while the campus mills grind slowly and imperfectly and miss many grains, the irritated public asks for instant, certain justice. "Get rid of the troublemakers to make room for those you turn away" becomes the common advice.

The Smith Interregnum

The summer of 1968 would have been a good time to attempt to correct the concatenation of tragedies that had overcome the San Francisco State student disciplinary process, but students and faculty are not particularly available during the summer. One sluggish attempt was made. A black administrator, Edward Reavis, was employed by Reddell to work with the student judicial court. But by the time the fall semester had rolled around, events overtook the leisurely pace of academic reform. Eruptions that began November 6, 1968, found the college once again without specific rules of conduct understood by all and acceptable to students, faculty, and administration, without an administrative unit that would accept the responsibility for gathering evidence and prosecuting alleged transgressors, and without an effective court system. When the storm broke, President Smith interceded with a warning on acceptable conduct and a pronouncement on an interim faculty-student court. Neither had much impact during the hectic final three weeks of his stewardship. On November 24 he attempted to move more systematically to correct the glaring deficiencies when he addressed a memorandum to Reddell:

> During the past several weeks we have discussed in our numerous meetings with the vice-presidents, deans, executive members of the Senate, our failure in turbulent situations to identify students, collect needed evidence, and make charges within the college against those students engaged in direct disruptive action to upset the programs and processes of the college. It is apparent even from the disruptive events of Thursday, November 21, that a number of the same students who have contributed to earlier disorder leading to the closing of the campus were active in both the direct build-up and in leading Thursday's invasion of buildings and classes, harassment of personnel, and other acts which may merit suspension or dismissal. I want to urge you formally to work with your staff, the deans, department heads, faculty, and staff and others you believe can be of help in reviewing the data on individual student's participation in promoting and engaging in recent campus disorder. In repeated statements to the college community I have, after extensive consultation with your and our administrative colleagues, insisted both on fair and due processes for those charged with acts of violence, coercion, and disruption—and I am aware that you are moving on a number of

cases. I want you to place a high priority on this with my full backing. Would it be possible to have by Monday, December 2, a statement *for campus distribution* on our intent in relation to specific acts of violence and disruption on campus. . . . By Monday, December 9, could you have a specific proposal for streamlining and updating campus disciplinary proposals? To date we have largely depended on police reports arising from arrests. I have steadily urged that we develop much more rigorously our own means of reviewing reports, documentary data, and eyewitness accounts to expedite the intent to hold individuals accountable for their behavior in the college community. . . .

The memorandum was too little, too late. Most administrative energies during Smith's brief tenure had been spent on attempts to solve the root problems that contributed to disruptions, not in shoring up the disciplinary process. In some circles it was even felt that disciplinary efforts would only antagonize the students and interfere with this process. No organized college attempt was made to apprehend the many students who were interrupting classes, engaging in sabotage, or disrupting the college operation. The arrests that were made were undertaken by plainclothesmen, and the students who were arrested were prosecuted in the courts, not on the campus. In effect, November 1968 was a rerun of the previous year's scenario, except that the disruptions were more extensive and attracted more public attention.

This public concern was reflected in the demands of the trustees when Smith met with them in Los Angeles on what proved to be his final day in office, Tuesday, November 26. Whereas Smith came prepared to suggest a range of college actions to meet the total problem, including student discipline, the chancellor and the trustees focused purely on the absence of any satisfactory college disciplinary effort against the student militants. To correct this condition, which had long puzzled and irritated the trustees, they presented Smith with a virtual ultimatum that prescribed in great detail exactly how the college must go about punishing the students and faculty and thus restoring order. Their proposal pivoted on the idea of declaring an emergency condition so that "normal" procedures could be suspended and temporary rules substituted that would insure instant justice or, in the language of the proposal, "prompt disposition" of the charges. Detailed plans for mass arrests were outlined. Those arrested would be both temporarily suspended and prohibited from coming on the campus. Justice would be dispensed within seventy-two hours by a hearing officer who might well have the powers to determine both guilt and the magnitude of the penalty, including suspension or expulsion. The chancellor-trustee document suggested that a one semester suspension might be appropriate.

This turned out to be a historic proposal. Smith found it impossible to accept, and this fact, along with others, became the basis for his resignation. On the other hand, S. I. Hayakawa and his Faculty Renaissance group had made a similar proposal to Smith the preceding day. They suggested that such measures were the only means of terminating the appeasement approach to the militants and placing them on the defensive. Thus, Hayakawa was the ideal man for the task Smith refused to perform. When Hayakawa accepted the presidency, it was with the understanding that he would bring peace to the campus by invoking his system of mass, instant justice. This he attempted to do within his first week in office. The following account of student discipline under Hayakawa is a tragic reminder that the administration of student justice is a delicate and sensitive process that cannot be created and sustained by administrative fiat during the polarized, adversarial climate of all-out warfare any more than it can be prosecuted by the avoidance mechanisms employed by faculty and administrators in the pre-Hayakawa period.

Barrelhead Justice under Hayakawa

After a long Thanksgiving Day weekend, President Hayakawa announced on December 2 a "Declaration of Emergency" that outlined illegal acts and a policy of temporary suspension for students charged with violating the emergency rules. "Due process" would be obtained for these students within seventy-two hours of suspension by a hearing officer appointed by the president. Administering the policy proved to be much more diffiult than pronouncing it.

In the battle that developed the Academic Senate became the champion of the students and of the traditional canons of due process. The Senate challenged Hayakawa head on as it had challenged his predecessors on other important issues. Because the new president still had vestiges of respect for the official faculty policy formulating body and had yet to receive his overwhelming mandate of power from the public, he buckled. Although the faculty senators had been apathetic about filling the student disciplinary void themselves for the past four years, they knew for certain what they did not want. Emergency conditions smacked of dictators. Temporary suspension invoked a serious academic penalty prior to the establishment of guilt. A hearing officer, especially one chosen by Hayakawa, offered none of the protections of even a faculty court, let alone of peer group judgments. And due process, which provides the essentials of opportunity for legal advice, time to prepare a defense, gather evidence, and challenge witnesses, was impossible within seventy-two hours. By comparison, the criminal court hearings for some of these same students did not take place for as much as eight months and once begun lasted up to seven weeks. When these protests were made, Hayakawa recanted. Thus, his first attempt to cut the legs out from beneath the strikers by invoking the arbitrary conceptions of student justice developed by Dumke, the trustees and the college Faculty Renaissance group, died a-borning. The few hearings before those faculty who volunteered for the hearing officer detail were very sad affairs and had to be repeated.

In attempting finally to create fair student disciplinary procedures, the Senate drew heavily upon the widely accepted AAUP-NSA-AAC student bill of rights documents. To the surprise of the Senate, President Hayakawa was willing to go along with their suggested procedure—which diverged widely from that proposed by the chancellor and the trustees—with three exceptions. First, and most important, Hayakawa would not agree to the basic proposal that he should delegate his final powers of review to the student-faculty court. Second, he initially opposed the idea that the college delay any college discipline against a student who had been arrested for the same offense, the double jeopardy issue. And third, he aggressively resisted the idea that the president of the Associated Students, Russell Bass, should select the student members of the panel from which the individual student-faculty hearing groups would be chosen. In the latter instance Hayakawa believed that both the student legislature and Bass had forfeited any claims to impartiality when they decided to support the student strike totally. Beyond these points of dispute the president was willing to accept a rather liberal process, and one that substituted four man hearing panels composed of two students and two faculty for his one man, presidentially-appointed hearing officer.

These points of dispute underscore the extreme difficulties associated with creating procedures aimed at achieving justice in the midst of a polarized confrontation. Although in the abstract many administrators might agree to the emerging concept contained in the student bill of rights—that the president should delegate his powers of student discipline to student-faculty courts—this becomes a hazardous act of faith when lines have been drawn in a campus battle involving the formal student officers. Increasingly the outraged public, trustees, and legislators judge the president in the current climate of student unrest by his capacity to maintain order and punish violent disruptors. The California Legislature felt so deeply about this that they directed the chief administrative officers of all the state colleges to take disciplinary action against any student, faculty, or staff member convicted in the courts of a crime arising out of a campus disturbance. This action was demanded in one of the two major pieces of legislation that the legislators were able to agree on out of almost one hundred proposals. These elements of the power structure hold the president responsible for disciplining students. They believe discipline, not permissive appeasement, will solve the problem of student unrest. And they do not trust faculty or students to administer justice to students.

The act of presidential delegation of authority is further complicated when large segments of the faculty and students have already taken positions on the issues—in this case, the ten demands. With many supporting these demands—even totally committed to them— and with amnesty one of the demands, it becomes difficult for the involved parties to take a cool, detached judicial view. To allow student body officers—who were wedded to the conceptions that the president was all evil and that the means justified the ends—to appoint the student members to the courts to which the president was to delegate his powers seemed insanity to President Hayakawa. In the one instance where the college did have elaborate due process procedures that could please even the most devoted civil libertarian—the faculty disciplinary and grievance procedures—faculty hearing committees laced with faculty on strike absolved almost every faculty member and registered one noteworthy conviction, Hayakawa.

By the same token, those hostile to the ten demands would have had an equivalent problem in maintaining objective detachment while on a jury. This became the crux of the problem when President Hayakawa eventually established his own faculty juries, and liberals and moderates among the faculty boycotted them. Any decisions the juries reached were immediately suspect. Once a campus becomes as embroiled as San Francisco State was, with faculty and students lining up on one side or the other, the issue of impartiality and objectivity becomes almost an insurmountable one in judicial decisions. In the larger society this issue is sometimes settled by bringing in outside judges or remanding the adjudication to another community. The new spirit of polarization might force the adoption of some similar process, even though it violates the cherished concept of local autonomy. The trustees eventually acknowledged this problem late in 1970 when they developed systemwide disciplinary procedures giving great power to a one-man hearing officer.

The case for the presidential delegation of powers is equally strong. It hinges on two points. First, how can the individual with final responsibility for prosecution of student violators reserve for himself the ultimate judicial role? And second, how can he do this when under excessive political pressure, from the governor on down, to punish any suspected troublemaker or lose his job? In essence both student-faculty courts and presidents as final arbitrators of justice are heavily tainted in a politicized environment. President Hayakawa was particularly suspect, because when he took the job he was committed to "throwing the radicals off the campus," and because he derived his power not from the customary sources of faculty and students but rather from the aroused public. He needed a record to run on. A student-faculty court of last resort might not give him that record. And such a court might not be able to administer justice in a manner that would promote public confidence.

This same public had little awareness or respect for the fine legal distinctions in the so-called double jeopardy issue. It is well known that the courts mete out justice at an exceedingly slow rate. How, then, could a college allow an obvious troublemaker the privilege of continued attendance and even revolutionary leadership while he was awaiting trial in the community for a year or so? Besides, there were lawyers in the chancellor's office who told one and all that testimony in campus courts could not be demanded by the criminal courts and that contradictions between campus court statements and criminal court statements could not be prosecuted. Actually there was also considerable evidence to support the position that prior campus disciplinary action might well become a basis for out-of-court reduction of criminal charges or even dismissal of the case.

For two months the Academic Senate and President Hayakawa were locked into this dispute. After the president had agreed to the Senate's position on double jeopardy and to a compromise system of choosing the student panel members by lot, a solution appeared to be in sight. However, a majority of the Senate refused to compromise and negate the powers of the duly elected student body president, Russell Bass, to make student appointments, and it would also not bend on the delegation issue. Rather than participate in what might smack of a political compromise and become suspect of selling student rights down the river, the Senate declared it had enunciated official college policy, and that if this policy wasn't implemented the onus would rest upon President Hayakawa. In the meantime the weary public and trustees witnessed a continuation of San Francisco State's apparent dedication to no student justice, even under the hard-liner Hayakawa.

With the impasse apparently unresolvable, President Hayakawa finally stepped in with his own modified system. It featured three-man faculty hearing committees chosen from larger panels, attenuated due process during the hearings, reliance upon police evidence, the burden of proof on the accused student, and final power resting with the president. The Senate promptly denounced the process and urged all faculty not to participate in this travesty of justice. To the surprise of many this Senate position was overwhelmingly supported at a well-attended faculty meeting.

Ferd Reddell, Dean of Students, continued to resist having the student personnel area perform the disciplinary functions. Hayakawa resolved that dilemma by creating a new administrative unit, the Office of Internal Affairs, and persuading his fellow Faculty Renaissance member, Edwin Duerr, to take on the unpleasant task of administering student justice. The semester's history of that new office offers positive proof that justice administered without a semblance of community support is no more apt to solve college problems than no justice. At every turn Duerr met resistance. Few faculty volunteered for the hearing panel. When it was discovered that those who did volunteer came almost uniformly from the conservative ranks of the faculty and were concentrated in the areas of business, industrial arts, and physical education, the decisions of the hearing committees became suspect. At one time the Senate had before it a motion to censor those faculty who defied the Senate injunction not to participate. The Senate itself, however, in eschewing any further collaborative effort to develop moderately acceptable procedures and in urging faculty not to participate, found itself hoisted on its own petard. Criticize though the faculty might, students were still being convicted in the tainted courts and the faculty could not provide these students with any protection.

Due to the flaws in the procedures, the inexperience of the college in administering student discipline, and the reluctance of faculty and students alike to participate as witnesses, few convictions were obtained by this unwieldy system. When some students secured skilled lawyers for their defense, these lawyers revealed so many discrepancies in the system that even the hearing panels hesitated to carry on. At times students picketed the proceedings. Many charged with violations simply didn't appear. When faced with the massive numbers problem Hayakawa tacitly agreed to the recommendation of the Select Committee to End the Strike merely to warn those suspected of nonviolent, but disturbing behavior, and to remove even the warning record from the files after a semester of peaceful behavior. By the end of the school year the record of the new Hayakawa system of internal discipline was: twenty students suspended for nonappearance in the campus court, thirteen placed on varied periods of probation, and one suspended by court action. Many of these suspended for nonappearance were readmitted on probation during the 1969–1970 school year.

Not only did the system flounder because of the judicial process, but the new president never solved the equally complex problem of how to secure reliable evidence in a confrontation scene, evidence that could not be shredded by experienced lawyers. The poor record of the college in the spring semester is placed in perspective when one compares the emergency rules of conduct promulgated by Hayakawa with the overt student actions in defiance of these regulations. Efficient prosecution of all of those who assembled illegally or who disrupted the instructional process would have produced several thousand convictions. Try as Hayakawa and Duerr might, the disciplinary void was never effectively filled. To the outside public the illusion of commitment to the principle of college self-discipline was partially sustained, primarily through skillful use of the mass media in creating the image of President Hayakawa as a no-appeasement administrator. Near the end of the semester the Senate swallowed its pride and reestablished a negotiating committee to work with the president on discipline. The issues still remain, and if confrontations develop again, as they almost inevitably must, the climate of mistrust would make effective college action extremely difficult. Systemwide mandated rules of conduct and disciplinary procedures eliminated the pervasive ambiguity, but the only major attempt by the college to operate within these rules, in November 1970, revealed the same ineptitude that had plagued San Francisco State College for four years.

In the absence of any effective internal control over student behavior, Hayakawa finally had to rely on a mass police arrest and criminal prosecution in order to test his hypothesis that a hard line was the only effective means of breaking the strike. On January 23, 1969, the police quickly surrounded a strike rally of over four hundred that was testing the president's no-assembly edict and arrested the entire group. After a confused period of booking and bail the action shifted to the municipal courts, where the 453 were to be tried for unlawful assembly, refusal to disperse, and disturbing the peace. In one of the least troublesome and provocative of the many student disruptive activities, the full punitive might of society was used to break the back of the strike.

There seems little doubt that the mass bust was vital in terminating the student strike in the spring semester. Although many other factors contributed to the eventual "negotiated settlement," the prospect of more mass arrests, jail sentences, excessive bail costs, large funds needed for legal aid, and revolutionary energies spent in legal defenses rather than in producing "one, two, three more San Francisco States" certainly dimmed the revolutionary ardor of many. The threat of time in jail under the control of the hated "pigs" was particularly discouraging to the Third World students. For some this was not a new experience, and they felt deeply about what the black man could expect behind bars.

At first the bust became a situation for the strikers to capitalize upon as the desired example of the reliance of the corrupt power system on punitive repression for the maintenance of its illegitimate power. The strikers were both elated and furious. A legal defense committee was established, rallies were held to raise funds, students were urged to attend trials for their own education, and witnesses were sought. A large organization developed that was devoted to protection of the persecuted brethren and furtherance of the revolution through the use of court prosecutions to radicalize liberals.

For a while the effort was sustained and some students were radicalized. Although the district attorney's office was willing to compromise in order to reduce the load on the court system by offering the "deal" of a ninety day suspended sentence, two years' probation, and a fine for those who pleaded *nolo contendere,* the most dedicated radicals refused the deal. One hundred and three had accepted it by mid-August of 1969. Originally the YSA and SDS believed that they could beat the rap by shrewd, committed legal defenses, thus avoiding the risk of probation, which could effectively cut them out of the movement. The dangers of militant activity while on probation were made quite vivid. Several students who were on probation when found guilty in this arrest were sentenced to jail from six months to a year; others in the same group and found guilty, but who had not been on probation, were given suspended sentences or no more than thirty days in jail. Zealous radicals came to the political conviction that some students could also defend themselves by speaking to the larger corruption of society and thus educating people. When convicted these students also received long sentences, making this a hazardous defense.

As the group trials of ten or more students went on and on, and as the conviction rate increased, the militant students began to have second thoughts about their original strategy of not accepting the *nolo contendre* deal. This is realistically expressed in an article in the *Gater* on August 8, 1969 by Dianne Feeley, of the YSA:

> The high proportion of acquittals has caused the DA's office to cut the original "deal" in half. As it now stands, it involves a 45-day suspended sentence, a year's probation, and a fine. As time drags by, as the movement's resources in money and lawyers dwindle, and as the center of activity shifts from the mop-up of last year's strike to the coming strikes and anti-war actions of this fall, it makes sense to realize (as many defendants are now doing) that a four to seven week trial is a waste of time, that the chances of conviction are going up, and that the "deal" may be the best tactical response for political activists. We urge every political activist to consider a tactical shift, to gear up for the fall political offensive, and to get free of the courtroom swamps as quickly as possible. We have all done the best we can in terms of political defense, given the limitations; the odds against further acquittals rise daily. We are fighting a serious battle, a battle in which we must keep the initiative. To have the best San Francisco State activists stuck in the courts or languishing in the jails, at the precise time when a new offensive can be launched, is unnecessary and unwise. A serious political activist should consider these factors carefully, and set them against the rather dubious value of going to trial, with the results more and more certainly against him.

The trials indeed were tedious, dreary, expensive affairs. Between impaneling the jury, conducting the trial, and the jury's consideration, from four weeks to seven weeks could elapse. The time lost cut seriously into the student's academic program or his outside work commitments. Most were truly re-runs of earlier trials, and with only twenty accomplished by late August there was the prospect that they could continue into the Christmas holidays.

The college role was minimal in the courtroom. A presidential assistant testified regarding the official police warning to the students and the reasons therefor. Usually one of several Hayakawa friends in the Faculty Renaissance attested to the fact that the assemblage was disturbing the educational process. Arthur Mejia of the history department was a star witness. Faculty friends of the defendants (frequently from the AFT ranks) would refute his testimony and make other points for the strikers. Police representatives delineated their role, assuring the jury that the assemblage was disruptive and that it had been warned to disperse. Technical questioning on a particular point could take a full day. The district attorney's office used a bevy of young assistants to carry the prosecution. Sometimes students defended themselves, sometimes they used public defenders, sometimes paid legal aid was employed. Originally there was heavy press coverage; as time wore on the results of a particular trial rated only a small box fill-in back in the entertainment section of the paper. Standing room only audiences dwindled and finally only the cast of participants was present. While the defendants made much of the absence of representatives of the "people" in the early juries, the rank and file jurist more often came from the lower middle class or the lower class. Their sympathies with those accused of trying to destroy the system seemed less than the sympathies of jurors from the upper middle class.

The cost to the city of San Francisco was vast. Four courts were tied up for most of a year. The delay in adjudication of cases that normally would have been heard in these courts created great hardships. But the power structure of San Francisco, supported by that of the state, was determined to secure justice and break the strike, whatever the cost. Even the prosecution of the more than seven hundred that sat in Sproul Hall at Berkeley in 1964 did not come close to this investment of time, talent, and money.

At the conclusion of the twenty-four group trials (eleven months after the arrests), the box score was: 109 convictions on one or more charges; 55 total acquittals; 12 dismissals of charges; and 242 pleadings of guilt or no contest. Whether convicted or acquitted, most students were accused of the same crime. This inconsistency of verdict seemed, to the involved students, to underscore the injustices of our judicial system. The fact that leaders, especially those who had prior records, received much stiffer jail sentences was interpreted by the activists as proof positive of political suppression. On the campus these results could have been used to radicalize the average liberal student yearning for justice in our society, but because these decisions were handed down in the courts in the city, they had little influence on the movement.

In part the radicals were unable to capitalize on this bust because many students caught up in it eventually felt they had been used by the radicals, especially by certain leaders who were not around when the bust came. Many of the students were fringe members of the movement or only intellectually curious. They had little awareness of the potential threat to themselves and their academic careers. To them it seemed far-fetched that attendance at a rally at the speakers platform could ever lead to their arrest. Such rallies had been going on for years and were part of the local scene. Some students were not even particularly interested but were not going to bow to Hayakawa's illegitimate emergency edicts. A few had been innocently caught in the middle of the campus and had had no intention of being part of the rally. For those students, being pawns in the radical game was very disillusioning. The court trial, while it did not endear the city's system of justice to them, also frequently did not cause them to cherish their radical comrades. Instead of radicalizing, the trials made many yearn for the studies that had been interrupted by the entire strike episode.

In perspective it is quite clear that mass arrests and mass prosecutions through the criminal court system do not provide an acceptable answer to the problem of campus disturbances. The hard-line approach has its attractions for those who relish the prospect of dirty, long-haired radical students being forced to spend time behind bars with hardened criminals. To those who are committed to suppressing campus rebellions at any cost, mass arrests appear on the surface to be effective. But a judicious analysis of the total cost of this one mass arrest at San Francisco State College—the cost to the city, to those other citizens desiring the use of the court system, to the college, to the atmosphere desperately needed for productive learning, to the generation gap, to the students—can only conclude that it must at best be an absolute last resort and that there must be more effective, healthier means of maintaining a learning rather than a revolutionary climate on the campus. The fact that this ultimate weapon had to be employed merely attests to the inability of the academic community at San Francisco State over the years to solve the vexing but critical problem of disciplining its own ranks.

In the fall of 1970, new student disciplinary procedures were invoked by the chancellor and the trustees for the entire system. Faculty and students have had minimal influence on the critical features of these new policies. The new procedures emphasize judicial expedition, the elimination of student-faculty judicial panels in favor of a legally trained hearing officer, concurrent college and civil court trials for the same offense, if necessary, and ultimate presidential authority. When faculty failed, trustees stepped in. It remains to be seen whether these streamlined procedures can solve the difficult problems enumerated in this analysis and elicit sufficient campus acceptance, or tolerance, to become viable.

Under normal campus conditions this disciplinary function has had slight attraction for students or educators. When those who administer this function must wrestle with the complications of a new conception of acceptable student conduct, of a new student commitment to shared power, of the Third World attitudes toward appropriate behavior and equitable law enforcement, and of the strategies and tactics of activist dissent, it is understandable that students, faculty, and administrators retreat from the responsibility. Understandable, but not defensible. This retreat does not solve the problem, but rather invites public, police, and trustee intervention on terms unacceptable to most in the academic community. More critical, this retreat from responsibility for whatever reasons predictably insures the absence of freedom, of financial support, of understanding and mutual trust that are totally requisite if the college is to address itself to the paramount problem, to the disease not the symptoms. In late twentieth-century American society, this disease is sufficiently acute that a symptomatic approach borders on societal suicide.

SIX

Challenges to
Faculty Governance

All governmental structures in higher education have been seriously threatened by the challenge of managing student confrontations in a hostile political climate, but none as much as the institutions of faculty governance. Nourished in a more benign atmosphere, many academic senates discovered that they had neither the wisdom nor the commitment to create policies that might obviate or control student dissent. Managerial and establishment powers, restive during the reign of the faculty, moved swiftly to grasp the levers of control at the very moment of faculty vulnerability. At this juncture in the history of higher education, the future of faculty power remains dubious. The rise and fall of the faculty at San Francisco State College reflects many significant facets of faculty governance; their problems are the problems of the profession in the 1970s.

For the first three centuries of the existence of American colleges and universities, management patterns bore a close resemblance to the governance structure of United States industrial and military organizations. Faculty controlled their classrooms but had a minor voice in the determination of college policy. For the past four decades faculty have chipped away at the prerogatives of administrators and trustees, first in an advisory role in the determination of academic policy and more recently in a quasi-legislative fashion for a wide range of college decisions. With business being governed more democratically

177

and unions paving the way for enlarged employee power, it just followed that the institution that had pledged to develop citizen skills and commitments for the future generations would take on democratic forms. All enlightened administrators were expected to employ the wisdom of the faculty and to gain the consent of the governed.

San Francisco State College kept in step with the national trend. After having their affairs directed during the post-bellum decade by a highly competent, paternalistic president, J. Paul Leonard, the faculty began to press for more involvement in college decision making. At the transition from Leonard's administration to the tenure of Glenn S. Dumke they achieved unity in urging creation of a representative Faculty Council with ultimate advisory power vested in the collective faculty. Dumke, realizing that he could profit from countering the managerial image of his predecessor, and apparently believing that the collective faculty might well become a powerful force in moving the college in the direction of his desired "Harvard of the West," quickly enfranchised the faculty. The decade from 1957 to 1967 saw the emergence of the hegemony of the faculty during the tenure of a succession of transient, anxious, vulnerable presidents.

President Dumke acted as though his educational ambitions for the college were so consonant with historical destiny that inevitably he would be able to persuade a democratic forum of the essential rationality and goodness of his views. Thus, faculty power seemed to pose no threat but rather appeared to be an opportunity and a challenge for a new form of leadership. Events did not corroborate this expectation. When the new president attempted to impose the essentially traditional and elitist values that he had developed at cloistered Occidental College on the egalitarian, vocationally oriented, upwardly mobile faculty and student constituency at State, he discovered faculty government served as an impediment rather than a facilitator. Four years of resisting Dumke's insistence on national fraternities, a classical general education pattern, a slowing down of the growth of professional programs, and an emphasis on traditional academic standards transformed the Faculty Council from an embryo advisory structure to a major source of antiadministration power.

The faculty at State enhanced its authority by insisting on a virtual advise and consent consultative role in the choice of Dumke's successor when Dumke left the college to become Vice Chancellor for Academic Affairs in the system created by the master plan for the governance of all of California's state colleges. Paul Dodd, a product of the democratic faculty ethos at the University of California, Los Angeles, where he served as Dean of the College of Arts and Sciences, immediately endorsed the concept of faculty governance. The faculty consolidated its power during his wavering tenure. All administrative appointments required faculty approval. More important, in a constitutional revision Dodd ceded his ultimate authority for all major policy formation to the faculty and its new instrumentality, an enlarged Academic Senate. In a brief span of six years the faculty had moved from minor advisory status to legislative power, and all was accomplished with little risk, commitment, cost, or proven accomplishments. A vacuum existed, the time was propitious, and the faculty moved. At other state colleges strong administrators blunted some of these encroachments on their power. No other state college president agreed to faculty legislative authority.

Two developments at the statewide level contributed to the amazing San Francisco State faculty feeling of manifest destiny. When Buell Gallagher resigned abruptly after a mere six months as the first chancellor of the California state colleges, the San Francisco State faculty led the overwhelming state college faculty resistance to the trustee move to slip Dumke in quickly and quietly as Gallagher's replacement. (In the final showdown, Democratic Speaker of the Assembly Jesse Unruh cast a critical vote for Republican Dumke, believing a weak chancellor enhanced the politician's power. Governor Ronald Reagan reaffirmed the political wisdom of this strategy when he used the harassed chancellor to facilitate his image as tough-minded controller of student dissent. Ironically, Unruh was never able to counter this successful image in his campaign to unseat Governor Reagan.)

Failing in this venture but feeling self-righteous, the San Francisco faculty bided its time, then blasted Dumke and the trustees for inept, overcentralized administration in a widely publicized faculty petition to the governor and the legislature. Heavily pressured, the trustees agreed to a blue-ribbon investigation of the administration of the system. As college after college reported criticisms of the central administration, the San Francisco State faculty judgment gained validity and respect. But these aggressive actions were to color the relations of the college with Dumke and the trustees all through the college's subsequent travail. These blatant challenges to established authority and their widespread support also produced delusions of

power, virtue, and unity that were to plague the college in the days
ahead.

Nothing during the fading days of the Dodd tenure, the brief
interval of Stanley Paulson's acting presidency (Paulson had been an
earlier chairman of the Faculty Council), or John Summerskill's first
year disabused the faculty leadership group of its impression that it
fundamentally ran the college. Its victories were achieved rather easily
and largely consisted of challenges to administrative power and drives
for rectification of purported administrative error. Only here and there
could the Academic Senate point to productive educational achieve-
ments. Much energy had been expended on saving the faculty and
the college from the acknowledged enemy without—Chancellor Dumke
and the trustees. In this atmosphere, self-criticism seemed ultraconservative. Nothing during this period prepared the ever victorious faculty for the powerful challenge by white student activists, the Black
Students Union, the California political establishment, or President
Hayakawa in the three years from 1967 to 1970.

The two years of Summerskill's reign and the brief six month
tenure of Robert Smith were dominated by student insurgency and
by trustee, legislative, and public reaction. Faculty government proved
inadequate in providing leadership for this entirely new range of college problems. Explanations for this inadequacy are multiple. Some of
the explanations are indigenous to the specific history of faculty governance at San Francisco State College; others speak more generically
to the basic concept and operation of faculty governance. The nature
of student confrontations has been fully described in our earlier volume, *By Any Means Necessary,* and by now these styles are familiar
to most who have been following newspaper accounts of the rise of
student unrest on United States campuses. In stressing the flaws that
appeared in the academic governance machinery as it attempted to
cope with unprecedented college conditions, we do not mean to imply
that the faculty alone stumbled. Those possessing direct power in
American society, many of whom are represented on and through the
board of trustees which controls the state colleges, have contributed
deeply to the social malaise that is being discharged in American colleges. This ruling sector directs the state colleges, and its prior and
current decisions have both sown the seeds for revolt and distrust and
added fuel to the rebellion. But their culpability is analyzed elsewhere;
this chapter concentrates on the problems of faculty governance.

Fundamentally, the challenge of student confrontation is a challenge to college administration, not to policy formation. Wise faculty policy formulation might obviate confrontations or, once underway, might provide means for containing them, but the delicate task of coping with student demands and student tactics is essentially an administrative task. If the faculty through its consultative procedures has not produced capable administrators whom it can support, little can be accomplished through faculty governmental structures once students have violently challenged the administration.

The faculty at San Francisco State, long accustomed to intervening in administrative matters because they did not trust administrative wisdom, continued in this tradition during the three years of student confrontations at State. History proved that the collective faculty all too often contributed to the problem rather than to the solution. This transpired not because of an absence of concern or effort but primarily because the containment of this new phenomenon demanded administrative action. The mechanism of faculty governance, developed for rational legislative debate on educational policy, could not act with the wisdom, unity, expedition, and force necessary at these critical moments. Instead of uniting the college and reinforcing the administration at its moment of trial, faculty action proved divisive and undercutting. Administrative difficulty in coping with these nonacademic problems assured faculty intervention. The administration, accustomed to seeking Senate advice, was unprepared to act unilaterally and face the inevitable faculty criticism.

In addition to this basic shortcoming, faculty governance at San Francisco State evinced other weaknesses when confronted with a student revolt, especially a black student revolt. By serving so often as the cutting edge of faculty resistance to the bumbling actions of the chancellor and the trustees, the Academic Senate deluded itself by believing it had full faculty support. The issue of student dissent was to prove that on critical issues the Senate frequently did not reflect faculty wishes. The Senate, by a sizable majority, desired to close the college so as to mediate with the students; the total faculty, by more than a two to one majority, supported its president in his decision to keep the college open. Not only was the Senate out of step with the total faculty, but it had for so long dictated faculty policy that it was unwilling to turn to its constituency for direction. Blithely it believed it had power in and of itself.

When the Senate finally did seek faculty opinion, it discovered that it had burdened itself with a governmental mechanism that was totally inadequate for policy development during a crisis situation. Although the more conservative members within faculty ranks had pressed for some time for more use of faculty referenda and for the elimination of policy determination through open faculty meetings, the liberal leadership cadre had opted for the prevailing structures of Senate authority and, where necessary, participatory democracy through open faculty meeting for developing wise courses of action in confrontational settings. Despite frequent clues to this deficiency, the Senate never moved to correct this structure. Thus, faculty meetings all too often exacerbated the problem, undercut the administration, and contributed to wide public and trustee disenchantment with the faculty.

In treating "the disease rather than the symptoms," faculty governance at San Francisco State also proved deficient—along with most senates and administrators across the nation. The problems on the academic horizon demanded a degree of skill, wisdom and commitment that faculty did not recognize was necessary or, when so recognizing, were not able to produce. Their mores and customs and leadership were vested in another era, an era of peace not violence, an era of outside enemies rather than urgent internal tasks. Chapter Five on the administration of student justice depicts the faculty unwillingness to face the delicate but critical problems of limits for student conduct, an operative judicial process, and means for enforcing codes of conduct. Chapters Two and Four spell out the inability of the faculty, despite its liberal educational and social allegiances, to anticipate the needs of those seeking educational reform and ethnic equality. Once confrontations with black students had revealed the slowness of the college in responding to ethnic frustrations, the Senate moved with force and speed to accommodate the ethnic demands. But by then too little was provided too late. The pace of faculty governance and institutional operations was simply not attuned to the imperatives of the black, brown, and yellow students.

Once the battle had been joined by the dissident students and the college, faculty governance proved chronically unable to contribute to the containment of student confrontations. The policeman role was totally alien to the faculty ethos, particularly because such discredited symbols as Reagan, Max Rafferty, and the police had coopted this law and order role. Time and again the faculty through its Senate cast its vote for compromise, mediation, and amnesty, devoutly believing that rational people could achieve a rational solution. Few faculty had any insight into the goals and tactics of the radical black and white students. This faculty mediation posture strengthened and legitimized the student activists and weakened the role of the administration in coping with the rebels. In retrospect, it would seem that, for better or for worse, faculty must support their administration in moments of crisis—or else commit themselves to the risks and hazards associated with eliminating incompetent leaders. The good guy role of compromiser has a seductive appeal but would appear to be a luxury that faculty can only infrequently afford.

This pervasive stance of conciliation rather than tough-mindedness proved fundamental in the mushrooming public and legislative disillusionment with faculty and colleges. The image of faculty prostrate before rampaging students was made indelible. The fact that faculty were attempting by their own lights to avoid bloodshed and bring peace back to the campus made slight impact. Those public figures who had access to the media and were deeply critical of higher education as currently constituted and controlled, such as Reagan, seldom failed to capitalize both on this faculty tendency toward compromise and on the occasional involvement of a few faculty in some portion of the student attack on the college. The goals of these critics ranged far beyond the momentary crisis, for they saw the moment as an unexcelled opportunity to diminish the status and power of that segment of higher education—the faculty—considered most responsible for the liberal social and political stance of the colleges.

The basic commitment of most liberals to elaborate due process procedures for students accused of academic disruption equally incensed those in power. Faculty seemed ever in the posture of demanding due process for those who appeared to be attempting to destroy the colleges, while never participating in the responsibility to control and penalize these students. Undoubtedly pervasive guilt feelings about complicity with institutional racism and membership in the establishment contributed to this reluctance to discipline militants, especially black militants.

The years of Academic Senate involvement with the confrontational campus scene revealed other flaws. During the earlier period of faculty potency, the Academic Senate occasionally attempted to use the machinery of faculty government to impinge on the larger and ominous problems facing the nation. The Senate took its actions in response to moral pressures from students and out of a sense of bewilderment as all forces in society seemed moving toward a tragic climax. Unfortunately, the Senate actions seldom satisfied the student critics, made virtually no impact on the political situations, created grave schisms within faculty ranks, and diminished faculty credibility with the body politic.

Once the public became deeply concerned with what was transpiring in its colleges, faculty sadly learned that previous attitudes of disregard for public views and unwillingness to spend time communicating with this public—including listening—had isolated them and their values from this basic source of power. Regaining a sympathetic ear became almost impossible, because by now many in the academic community had set themselves apart from what polls indicated was majority opinion. When those faculty disenchanted with Senate impotency united under the AFT leadership and took strike action, organized faculty governance lost its impact on affairs and became just another group attempting to give advice.

Once student militancy, black and white, had propelled colleges into the center of American politics, powerful forces new to the academic scene but pervasive in other sectors of society began to dominate most college decisions. In this battle of tanks and bombers, Academic Senates discovered they were using peashooters and slingshots. Advisory powers contributed little except to nourish an illusion. Collective action offered the only hope of real strength, but faculty governance was not geared for such action and the AFT was not able to generate sufficient faculty support in this context to counterbalance determined political opposition.

The nature of the new politics used in repressing dissent played into the hands of those in political positions. Exaggerated, oversimplified, hostile, emotional appeals through the media became powerful tools for the ambitious and experienced politician. Faculty, with their addiction to rationality and the delineation of the complexities of problems, proved to be no match in the appeal to public opinion. Faculty governance had little to contribute to this competition for public sympathies. Reporters recognized this by giving only scant coverage to Academic Senate activities and pronouncements; Reagan, on the other hand, seldom operated at trustee or regent meetings with less than a dozen television cameramen in constant attendance. It remained for a new breed college administrator, S. I. Hayakawa, to employ similar techniques successfully.

The future of faculty governance, now that student dissent and politics have engulfed colleges and universities, remains precarious. In states and communities less troubled by student confrontations and less dominated by conservative politics, faculty will undoubtedly continue to have a major though diminished influence on customary educational policy personnel decisions, and classroom operations. In California, the establishment has utilized this rare opportunity to move powerfully and quickly to neutralize most centers of faculty influence. Executive orders flow from the chancellor at a torrential rate. Presidents are increasingly chosen from the conservative sector with only minor faculty consultation. These presidents are expected above all else to insure law and order, follow trustee and chancellor directives, and maintain a tight ship. Institutional democratic forms have been replaced within a year by a hierarchical system that makes the lowest level administrator, the department chairman, a line officer to be chosen by and beholden to the president rather than an agent of his faculty. A system posing the possibility of economic sanctions has been substituted for fairly automatic salary increases to insure merit and faculty cooperation. Dumke proposed to the trustees that the probationary period be extended from four to seven years. Regular review of even tenured faculty—with power ultimately vested in the administration—has been offered as a system counterproposal to the threat of legislative removal of tenure. These threats of economic and job security sanctions are expected to produce "professional" behavior— and to reduce faculty to their proper roles of employees of the public. Should these threats fail to induce faculty to accept administrative orders gladly, to eschew political activity, and to teach more conservatively in the classroom, new rules for faculty conduct and new procedures for enforcing this conduct have been decreed by the trustees. The most recent act in this accelerated trustee takeover occurred when the trustees substituted their own faculty disciplinary and grievance procedures for those that had been cooperatively developed by the statewide academic senate, the college presidents, and the chancellor's office over a six year period, and that had been in operation only a year. But these laboriously established procedures, with ultimate power given to a faculty appeals committee, had refused to support the chancellor's attempt to dismiss the president of the AFT at San Jose State

College. The new regulations vest ultimate power in the chancellor and diminish the protections of the faculty member at every point in preference for expedition of justice and protection of the institution. With dismissal from his employment at stake, the faculty member has much less guarantee of due process than he would in the civil courts for a driving violation.

Central to all of these recent managerial actions is the philosophy that threats and sanctions will serve to persuade faculty to perform their duties in the manner desired by their employers. In our judgment this approach is doomed to failure. Stated simply, we believe you can not coerce professional behavior. You can nudge, lead, urge, facilitate. But when a faculty member stands before his class or works alone in his laboratory or study, the public simply has to depend on his professional conscience and his allegiance to his peers. This dependence upon the personal commitment of the individual faculty member has proved difficult for those in power to accept, accustomed as many are to inducing desired behavior by rewards and punishment. The only certain outcome of the current drive to coerce faculty is the diminution of professional commitment. Some in the state apparently might prefer this.

All of these moves by the Reagan-dominated trustees and legislature to strip faculty of powers have had strong public support. Faculty do not seem disposed to struggle to preserve their influence. Some faculty prefer the new managerial regime to control by their liberal faculty colleagues. Many have opted for withdrawal from power struggles so that hopefully they can teach in peace, quietude, and personal independence. Even those who were formerly aggressive appear to judge the new risks as too great, particularly with faculty ranks so divided. One wonders whether the risks stemming from the withdrawal of faculty moral influence in the current climate are not equally heavy, and whether peace and independence will ever again be the lot of the college professor.

If traditional faculty governance is to reassert itself as an important instrument of collegiate decision making, several obvious conditions will need to be met. Most are the reciprocal of the weaknesses revealed previously. Governmental procedures must be developed that can transform the sacred status quo into viable policies for a new age and a new constituency. This task will prove extremely difficult in view of the deep faculty cleavages on these issues and the gulf that exists between the liberal educational tradition and the emerging conservatism of American society. Violent revolutionary acts by the alienated young and violent repressive acts by those in power will complicate such an endeavor and possibly make it incapable of achievement. Even wisely developed faculty governance procedures will succeed only if faculty commit themselves to them to a degree seldom observed in the past. Distasteful issues, particularly those that involve modification of faculty prerogatives, must be faced and dealt with or the faculty will have little credibility. Curriculum and teaching procedures cannot continue the traditions of the early 1900s, power must be shared with students and the lay public, faculty must police their own ranks and accept responsibility for the preservation of the institution, and freedom of speech must be preserved for all if faculty expect it for themselves.

In developing new policies, faculty governing organizations will need to involve the full faculty so that ultimate decisions reflect majority wishes and are therefore likely to produce a degree of united support. This consensual academic politics will prove difficult for those on both extremes of the academic political continuum. But without the degree of unity that stems from broad involvement in policy development, faculty will never obtain the strength needed to achieve college policies that conflict with those supported by large segments of the body politic. And some such conflict is inevitable, for a number of values basic to the academic community are diametrically opposed to those emerging from the silent majority in the nation. As much as they may dislike many characteristics of their colleagues, in the future faculty will need to choose either collective potency or divided impotency. For many it will be a hard choice.

At San Francisco State College and in the California public colleges, the prospects are slim that the established authorities will voluntarily relinquish their new-found powers to a more mature, self-critical, effective structure of faculty governance. No matter what policies faculty develop, no matter how much faculty commitment, wisdom, and unity, events seem to have bypassed traditional faculty modes of influence. What remains as the basic faculty option to trustee sufferance is collective bargaining through some private organization, not cooption by means of state-supported (and controlled) academic senates. Only when faculty are willing to unite and take the risks that will certainly be pressed on them when they withdraw their services at a point in the bargaining process can they achieve power in the new climate. Many former prerogatives and values will certainly disappear with the advent of such employer-employee adversarial relations. But the choice is slowly being pressed upon faculty by those now in authority who are using their new-found force so indelicately. Just as blatant faculty misuse of its authority precipitated the counterreaction, so crude political pressure on colleges and faculty and students by the public is escalating the battle to the bargaining tables and picket lines.

In prior years such collective faculty action and its ultimate success seemed inevitable. But in the current epoch in California higher education, events seem to have splintered and frightened faculty and consolidated and strengthened their opponents. Collective bargaining has surged forward with elementary and secondary teachers, nurses, social workers, police, and other public employees. In California colleges, the price for disunity has not yet become painful enough to produce faculty who are willing to unite and take risks for what they believe in. Many have been scarred by the past. The move to consolidate the two most aggressive faculty organizations—the Association of California State College Professors (ACSCP) and the California Federation of Teachers College Council (AFT)—into a single organization committed to collective bargaining has gotten off to a shaky beginning because of jurisdictional bickering and an unwillingness to make major ideological compromises in order to obtain a broad faculty base of support. In the constitutional convention for the United Professors of California, ACSCP was liquidated and the AFT controlled the new organization. The AFT image and tactics might well repulse the reluctant majority of the faculty unless the hard-riding, reactionary trustee leadership and a reelected Reagan, fortified by a Republican legislature, decide to hire, fire, punish, and control in accord with their basic impulses and delegated powers. If so, the faculty choice might become either an academic wasteland or faculty power through collective bargaining. Such a choice could well produce strange academic bedfellows.

Professional and
Unprofessional Ethics

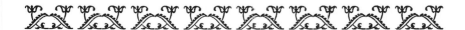

Passion, bitterness, irrationality, and a host of other emotion laden reactions are inevitable at a college confronted with crisis—certainly they
were at San Francisco State College. The air is filled with charges,
countercharges, allegations, inflamed rhetoric, and suspicion. Mis-
understandings, misconceptions, doubts, feelings of betrayal, and a
creeping dismay seem to shatter whatever sense of a unified community there is. Significant light can be shed on the problems of the
institution and profession by noting crisis behaviors. Because crisis
provides a dramatic display of an institution and profession seeking to
solve immediate problems, it highlights structural problems which
unfortunately have been countenanced in more placid times and which
raise questions about accomplishing goals with justice and dispatch.

Systemic Problems Revealed by Crisis Behavior

At San Francisco State crisis behaviors of faculty and others
highlighted problems about: the nature of academic due process; the
meaning of professional conduct, academic freedom, and license; and
the character of sanctions on behavior. To provide some perspective
for further discussion a brief description of some crisis incidents or
situations seems appropriate. These incidents occurred during the
the years in which San Francisco State was in a crisis situation, from
1967 to 1969. There is no intention to single anyone out for special

189

criticism; names and departmental affiliations will be omitted. None-theless, some of the incidents are sufficiently well known so that any effort to preserve anonymity will not succeed, particularly within the community itself. The incidents are included to give us some oppor-tunity to reflect on common problems, not to provide further grist for the conflict mills that continue to grind on at the college.

A faculty member plunged through a window of the Adminis-tration Building which had been locked to avoid a threatened student mill-in. The faculty member then appeared at the door of the building, which had been broken in, and invited students to enter, assuring them that they would not be punished.

Subsequent to the settlement of the strike, two faculty members engaged in a verbal interchange which resulted in one of them de-livering a knee to the groin of the other.

A number of faculty members putatively on strike continued to meet their classes and draw their pay. Others on strike refused to report their absences from the classroom even though by the faculty's own rules they were obliged to do so.

At least two faculty members joined students on the stage of the auditorium for the purpose of interrupting or perhaps preventing a presidential address to the faculty.

A faculty member, active in the crisis, was denied tenure by the president despite the fact that all appropriate evaluating levels had recommended it before the acute crisis of 1968–1969 began. A state-ment of charges for alleged unprofessional conduct was never made nor was a hearing held. No official explanation was provided by the president for his action.

A faculty organization executed a strike vote despite the fact that it was not the elected bargaining agent of the faculty.

An ode to masturbation appeared in *Open Process,* one of the student newspapers supported by compulsory student fees.

A picture of a nude young lady exposing pubic hair and geni-tals appeared in the "Summer Love" edition of the same newspaper.

A group of students enrolled in the class of a professor and pro-ceeded to shout him down whenever he tried to speak.

A faculty member pulled wires out of a sound truck parked on the street off-campus, silencing it.

At least two faculty members interrupted the classes of other faculty members and attempted to dismiss the classes.

At least one student requested to be permitted to drop a class because the instructor was using his control over the grading process to demand adherence to a particular ideology.

Another student requested similar permission, alleging that a distinguished faculty member had threatened grade retaliation if not granted sexual favors.

At least one student received more than fifty-six hours of almost straight A grades in one semester. Some students received high grades without attending classes, writing papers, taking exams, or talking with the instructor.

At the end of the fall 1968 semester it was learned that at least one instructor had abandoned his class in early November without notifying anyone in his department.

Some faculty members supported student demands that a fellow faculty person be dismissed without a hearing or statement of charges and that another be promoted without going though the regular faculty-centered procedures of the college.

An alleged invitation by a faculty member to students to bring guns on campus apparently did not violate any explicit rule or code of professional conduct of the college.

A student who challenged the fairness of an instructor's grade had no real recourse even though a review committee examined the charge and decided in the student's favor. The professor was free to accept or reject the findings of the committee according to his own personal conviction.

Almost any professor at San Francisco State could present a similar list documenting this supposedly unusual (some say absurd) character of our college times. While incidents of the kinds described above may not be so unusual as we now tend to think, it is certain that they are gaining more attention than ever before. How can we make sense of such incidents? What courses of necessary action (remedial or revolutionary) do they suggest? Although many issues are raised and many different ways of discussing them are valid, the plan here is to focus on four major topics: professional conduct, academic freedom, academic due process, and academic sanctions on behavior.

Unprofessional Conduct

The term *unprofessional conduct* probably arouses more than its share of difficulty and misunderstanding. In a relatively benign climate this situation does not cause much of a stir because there are not enough cases to shake our complacency. But in times of increased social stress, particularly now, the problem of its meaning generates anxious attention. Incidents such as those recounted above suggest not only that academicians are under attack from various quarters, but also that they operate in a very uncertain climate when faced with frequent demands to give meaning to charges of unprofessional conduct. No doubt a considerable degree of confusion and uncertainty has always existed about unprofessional conduct in most professions, but the somewhat different current circumstances challenge academicians to become more precise about its meaning and its implications.

That the concept of unprofessional conduct is vague and imprecise is beyond question. One searches almost in vain for codified efforts to give it operational meaning. Although some attempts have been made to develop a code of ethics for the teaching profession, none appear to have gained widespread acceptance at the college level. Most colleges and universities are undoubtedly in the position of San Francisco State, where judgments about unprofessional behavior are made almost exclusively on an ad hoc basis without the benefit of a guiding standard. No professor can be reasonably certain how behaviors such as those listed in the opening illustrations in this chapter will be treated. The professional remains in the dark about what precise behaviors are forbidden by his membership in the profession. Unfortunately, the absence of precision in our code of behavior can have dangerous effects both in transforming freedom into license and in using the vagueness as a weapon in the hunting of unpopular academic heads.

At San Francisco State, significant evidence demonstrates that there was doubt and confusion about the meaning of unprofessional conduct, and that these vague professional norms—with their consequent inability to precipitate deep internalization—offered little restraint on the behaviors of faculty in times of acute crisis or in more normal times. Equipped with only the general belief that they should behave professionally, faculty often permitted the expediency of the moment to prevail. This contributed to a tendency toward license that was surprising in its scope and intensity. Three situations in particular were indicative of the extent of our disarray and the nature of our confusion. They were the matters of grade intimidation, the departure from honesty and responsibility in the reporting of absence from the job, and the ignoring of regular processes for change of the vital grading system. (Unlike many jobs in the business and governmental worlds, the academic profession does not usually have an attendance system that places responsibility on supervisorial or administrative personnel for reporting absence. Instead, each professor assumes the obligation to notify the students and the administration when he is not going to meet his classroom responsibilities. The statement that there was a departure from honesty and responsibility in this instance refers to the obligation of the individual to tell the truth about his job performance.)

The question of grade intimidation, whether for sexual or ideological reasons, appears more often than not to have been skirted by the professional academician, at least at San Francisco State. In part, this is because students are reluctant to push charges of this kind and bring the matter forcefully to our attention—they vaguely understand that most, if not all, the cards are in the hands of the professor. In this connection, it is also probable that our vague views of academic freedom and professional conduct seem based on the questionable assumption that the professor can do no wrong in the classroom, particularly after he has tenure. While few among us would condone the intimidative behavior exhibited in these instances, we seem to have done very little either in a substantive or procedural way to encourage redress of grievances concerning such behavior. Thus, unscrupulous or unfair behavior is rarely if ever penalized. The lack of provision for handling such situations is an invitation to license and to authoritarian behavior. Behavior of the sort reported in the two incidents of attempted intimidation for sexual and ideological purposes may not seem crisis connected, but they are another symptom of the deep crisis in which the academic profession now finds itself. They cry out for a reevaluation of the relationship between teacher, student, and the whole educational process. Yet this is unlikely to be done as long as we have a vague code which enshrines professional infallibility by refusing to be explicit about what is forbidden.

There is yet another aspect of the crisis-related behavior that raises questions about whether we know what we mean by professional conduct and academic freedom. Surprisingly, it focuses upon the question of honesty and integrity. In our idealized view of ourselves and our profession, we usually claim honesty, integrity, and the search for truth as among our distinguishing virtues. If the society wants men who are fair, turn to the university; if the society needs men who will

tell the truth of the matter, turn to the university; if the society is looking for an honest man, turn to the university. This has been our preferred image and often the perspective shared by others.

Whether our devotion to these virtues has ever been as solid as
we imagine is doubtful. Like most groups, the men and women of the
academic profession have their share of human frailty. Yet, little in
our previous experience at San Francisco State suggests that significant
numbers of our best people would deliberately disregard the obligation
for truth and responsibility in reporting their absence from the job during the strike. Perhaps some background is necessary to understand the
willingness of men who value truth and integrity highly to subordinate
these values during the crisis.

Although the list of faculty grievances was a varied one, there
can be little question that off-campus intervention in the affairs of the
campus by the chancellor and some trustees was one of the root causes
preparing the way for a significant number of our faculty to go on
strike. And in so doing, many chose the tactic of refusing to report
their absence from the classroom. There was a widespread feeling that
off-campus meddling from afar, stimulated by sensationalized newspaper reporting, was violating due process. This was accompanied by
a tacit agreement that a high degree of local autonomy was the right
of the institution. Although it is doubtful that anyone stated it just this
way, the striking faculty seemed to be saying—by their actions on
absence reporting—that the cord of institutionalized obligation had
been cut by outsiders (the chancellor and the trustees) and, therefore,
that they, the striking faculty, were in a no-holds barred political
struggle where tactical questions rather than obligations to report absences were decisive.

After the Smith resignation, the appointment of Hayakawa
to the interim presidency seemed the catalytic act that destroyed
legitimacy of the local administration for the striking faculty and others
as well. Not only had Hayakawa been a member of the elected Presidential Selection Committee at the college, and thus by the agreed
upon rules of the selection process not available for presidential can-
didacy, but his selection had been made with no official consultation
whatsoever on the local campus. Thus, the striking faculty could violate
what might be called canons of the profession concerning institutional
honesty and responsibility in the interest of the greater good and the
higher obligation wrapped up in their opposition to unethical and

questionable behavior of others. It is doubtful that many striking faculty felt any sense of guilt or remorse when acting in this fashion. Rather, it is more likely that they felt a sense of righteousness and high morality for risking their pay and perhaps their jobs by standing against the evils of the system. In this particular situation they felt legitimacy had been destroyed, and it is perhaps unlikely that they would have behaved radically differently if there had been a clear code of conduct which forbade departures from honesty and responsibility. However, there is a chance that prior agreement to such a code would have pushed them strongly to reject this tactic, both as a matter of conscience and of possible consequence.

The violation of regular procedures in the allocation of grades with a fair distribution through the range from A to F was apparently another matter that struck not only at integrity but also at the respect for due process. This is surprising because perhaps nowhere outside the legal profession is the cry of support for the principles of due process more resonant or more frequent than in the academic profession. We often portray ourselves as stalwart pillars helping to prop up the principles of due process. Yet it probably did not occur to most involved faculty that their skirting of normal decision making in grading was an important, direct, and unequivocal avoidance of duly constituted procedures and thus a violation of due process. The story of how this came about is too complicated for extensive treatment here, but we can trace the main outlines with brevity. Analysis of trends in grading during the five years from 1964 to 1969 demonstrates clearly that a revolution in grading practice has been going on with or without the existence of acute crisis. Although the faculty has not changed the formal requirements on distribution of grades, with the exception of partial introductions of the Pass/No Report system, grade point averages for the entire college have steadily increased from 2.57 (on the four point scale) in the fall of 1964, to 3.06 in the spring of 1969.

By the fall of 1968 more people were receiving A's than any other grade. Some of the trend can undoubtedly be attributed to the acute crisis. The figures of 1968–1969 show the most dramatic increases—in some departments, grades reportedly averaged out at straight A. Nonetheless, a different more basic hypothesis seems consistent with the evidence at hand at the time of writing: Individual faculty members, largely on their own and for a number of reasons ranging from sympathy with the draft-haunted male undergraduate to deep philosophical convictions about the utility and justice of grades, find the traditional pattern of grade allocation contradictory to the educational mission of the college. Recognizing that grade point averages have become a substitute for more personal and detailed kinds of evaluations, many faculty seem to be carrying on their silent rebellions in the grade book. Apparently few have given much thought to the probability that this was an example of license in our professional behavior and that this kind of action might conceivably be considered unprofessional. The appointment in September 1969 of a faculty committee to consider the whole matter of grading at San Francisco State gave belated recognition to the need for institutional rather than haphazard personal treatment of an important issue.

If one were to grant (and many would not) that there were extenuating circumstances in the three matters, is there anything left to be said about the situation in connection with the problems of academic freedom and a code of professional conduct? Perhaps not. But again, maybe there is. Some questions come to mind. Are we not falling into the trap that often has meant a threat to freedom and justice when we justify excursions away from principles like honesty and responsibility in quest of a good cause? Do our protestations for due process in other matters lose some of their moral and persuasive force when we have by our acts suggested that it is the ends and not the process or means that are most important? If the strike action was essentially a moral act of conscience (as we believe it was for most), was the cause served by refusal to report one's absence as the faculty manual explicitly directs, thereby bringing the purity of the protest into question? If the grading system is unfair, anti-intellectual, and contrary to learning, do we put the argument in the best light by private anarchistic flaunting of due processes of our community? Does not the uncoordinated, individualistic attack on the grading system result in significant inequities for students, making the system a mockery? When students are faced with required courses and limited choices of professors, are not some bound to receive differential treatment of an unusually unfair sort? What happens to our defense of proper process when we cavalierly abandon the open procedures for orderly change? Can we as powerfully rail against violations of due process by trustees or a chancellor or a president when our own hands are unclean? Can we really lay claim to moral leadership when our pursuit of the good is shaded by methods that are questionable at best and outright dishonest at worst?

The issues raised by these situations and others like them are not new, of course. They reach back into the past and are simply receiving renewed attention today. A position on them may be heavily influenced by the perspective one has of the university and, particularly, by whether one believes the current social order of which the university is a part can be changed by adequate reforms or must undergo a radical revolution. To the revolutionary, invocations to obey those supposed universal canons of the profession are drowned out by the cannons firing on the pragmatic political line. For the reactionary, there probably are no real questions, only obligations to return to some idyllic past. Nonetheless, in the battle that is now being fought—whether for reform, revolution, or reaction—one wonders if the academic profession can any longer countenance vagueness and imprecision about the consequences of widespread departure from honesty, integrity, and due process, no matter what the cause.

In addition to the dangers of license, there is another aspect of the vagueness of unprofessional conduct that seems equally dangerous. Where professors can be dismissed on the grounds of unprofessional conduct—as they can in California—without significant statutory precision, the way is open for academic headhunting of the most devastating sort. It does not stretch the imagination to contemplate politicized raids on professors who take unpopular or controversial positions. If the standard of unprofessional conduct can be used almost indiscriminately and with terrible finality, we may be in more serious difficulty than we imagine.

The discussion up to this point has attempted to suggest two things. First, the concept of unprofessional conduct is somewhat vague and thus open to the twin evils of violating of academic freedom from outside the university and inviting academic license within the university. Second, the crisis behaviors at San Francisco State underscore widespread disagreement, lack of reflection, uncertainty, and even confusion about the limits on behavior, if any, implied by membership in the academic profession.

Crisis should force us back to first principles about professional conduct. But if the actions at San Francisco State, including the actions of its disciplinary and grievance panels, are indicative, crisis merely forces us to retreat into the vagueness of the concept itself, with the chance for erratic, capricious, and almost irrational results being increased.

For example, one panel found a faculty member unprofessional for interrupting a speaker, while another panel dismissed the charges on a roughly similar incident on grounds that "San Francisco State College faculty does not have an adopted set of principles which determine professional behavior for its members." In both cases, reference to a clear statement reflecting a basic standard for decision making was apparently not possible for the competent faculty involved. Nor should this be surprising, given the crisis context in which the hearings were held and the general conditions of our norms. The truth seems to be that we do not have an adequate standard. Consequently, the absence of a previously agreed upon set of standards that are reasonably precise and available in print tends toward no action on the one hand and capricious or inequitable treatment on the other. Vagueness encourages politicized headhunting of controversial or unpopular academics and a tendency towards license. It also, paradoxically, provides an opportunity for the good-guy, work-a-day faculty, suddenly thrust into the judge and jury role, to avoid making judgments. Even more seriously, such vagueness may increase the possibility that intimidative tactics now being explored by some students and faculty will become more effective, because the determination of unprofessional conduct is now so much a matter of ad hoc definition by the jury of the moment, unguided and unsupported by a solid statement of norms or principles.

We have neither a consensus based on time-clarified tradition nor a clear agreement based on a written statement of rights and responsibilities. We have rested secure in the feelings that our liberties and our duties as professionals were understood and shared by us all, if not always by the outer community. Although we recognized that violations would occur, we either did not expect widespread challenges to the presumed commonsense tenets of the profession, or we believed that—like a family—a university which must rely on a formal code to maintain its sense of justice and common purpose is lost. Given either of these perspectives, it is not surprising that most of our statements about principles of the profession are largely concerned with procedural matters and say little about what might be causes for dismissal and thus violations of the standards of the profession. For example, a widely-supported statement on the code of the profession, *The 1940 Statement of Principles on Academic Freedom and Tenure* by the American Association of University Professors, provides little that is substantive beyond an affirmation that academic freedom is essential to the profession and that tenured professors should be terminated only for "adequate cause." Perhaps only in the 1958 statement of the national AAUP Committee on Professional Ethics do we have a hint of what adequate cause might be. But even here we find a rather ambiguous listing of responsibilities of faculty members which focus largely on their commitment to their students, their institution, their profession, and their community. One can infer what sorts of conduct are proscribed by these rather general statements of responsibilities, but the charge of vagueness and imprecision seems justified. There is apparent opting for a system of ad hoc or common law justice in the matter, possibly based on the underlying feeling that this permits necessary flexibility and invites a contextual or situational treatment of each case.

Perhaps this vague, largely unspoken system can still serve the purpose of justice. Undoubtedly, many capable people continue to believe so. We do not share that belief. The profession needs to put its ethical house in order. It needs a clear and reasonably specific statement of the ethics of the profession. While no formal enunciation and adoption of a code will reduce ambiguity and the need for an ad hoc judgment to a vanishing point nor restrain some faculty who are powerfully influenced by other values, it would have a socializing effect. Such a code would reduce the possibility of capricious results; it would help limit headhunting of academics; and it would provide a deterrent to behavior that has been proscribed by the code.

To the argument that the university, like a family, is lost if it has to rely on formal codes, one can respond that even the family needs codified principles for ending the relationship, and more important, the absence of a strong sense of community on most college campuses makes the university less like a family and more like a political society of divergent interests in need of some consensus and a quasi-legal framework to moderate its conflicts. To the argument that the alleged lack of precision and consequent confusion is more apparent than real, that professors really do know what behaviors are forbidden and deserving of sanction, one can respond that this position fails to take sufficient account of the contribution towards justice of a clear set of legal standards. It is not by accident that men have sought to establish codes of behavior from the very earliest times. To limit capricious judgment by the sovereign and to provide clear warning of potential illegality to the subject, men have developed the written law. That no man should be penalized by the society without a clear statement of charges against him based upon the citation of the specific rule violated is one of the great principles of our legal tradition which protects against arbitrary action. The academic profession might do well to follow this tradition.

In addition, members of the profession both old and new need to tackle the question of unprofessional conduct at their own institutions because, given the atomized nature of our profession, statements only have effective teeth if they are accepted at the local level where the professors are. Although this is not the place, nor is there space, to consider what such a code might be in any detail, it may be provocative to put forth some ideas about a professional standard.

Before we attempt that, it may be useful to examine what are emerging as radically different views about the nature of the university and the academic profession. Only by examining these emerging views in some detail can we understand why the issue of unprofessional conduct has suddenly become so important. Radically different views of the nature and mission of the college and university tend to make questions of the limits of conduct more frequent and more important.

What are these positions? One is the view of the university as a handmaiden or servant of the established order, a sort of mirror-image of the guiding institutions in our society, and an important but subordinate cog in the societal machine. Adherents to this position point out that the university is run on societal money, either private or public, that nonprofessional boards of directors, regents, trustees, and so on, supposedly representative of the public interest, are the main controllers of the system, and that the university, as presently organized, is constrained to respond to the wishes and desires of the establishment or the community. Ironically, the people who hold these views tend to be radicals and reactionaries located at opposite ends of the political spectrum. Although they may have very different prescriptions for what needs to be done, both wish to make the university reflective of their own particular belief systems and are bent on destroying or at least greatly changing it if they cannot have their positions affirmed. Many if not all of the radical groups believe that the university must be destroyed and rebuilt anew along with the rest of the decadent institutions of society, or that somehow it must be preserved to be used as an active instrument of radical social change or violent revolution. The reactionaries believe that the university must be preserved, but that the dissenters, the critics, and the political activists should be kept out or kicked out of it. Freedom for them is all right as long as it does not threaten the established order and professors stay in their ivory towers.

In the San Francisco State experience some of the radicals and reactionaries were apparently willing to see the college close down—perhaps for good—if it would not respond as they thought it ought to. For people of these persuasions, academic freedom and professional conduct are viewed mainly in expediential terms. The radical who plunged through the window of a locked administration building in an effort to close the college seemed not particularly concerned that the academic freedom of others to teach and learn was interrupted by this coercive act. Yet almost in the next breath he could invoke the principle of academic freedom in defending a fellow faculty member from suspension, apparently because this person was important for the revolution. The trustees who criticized the radical students and faculty as "dangerous to academic freedom" apparently saw no inconsistency in pushing strongly for denying tenure to a faculty member without benefit of hearing and without proof of alleged inflammatory statements. Apparently for the radical and for reactionary, the outcome is what is important, not the process nor the protection of abstract principles like academic freedom. Those who tend towards the reactionary extreme and those who tend toward the radical extreme thus meet in a bitter contest for the body, soul, and buildings of the university, both believing all the while that the university now belongs to the other when it should belong to them. Freedom as the keystone of professional conduct is not likely to survive in the hands of the reactionary; what its fate would be in the new order of the radical remains uncertain in the extreme.

There is a second view of the college or the university. In times of increasing polarization in the society, it could become a declining view. Those who hold this view see the university as an institution that is at once of society and outside it. In the intellectual spirit of John Stuart Mill and John Milton, they contend that the proper function of the university is to provide a free, unfettered, wide open opportunity for the testing of ideas and beliefs. For them, the university is the citadel of freedom from coercion where no man is suppressed because he holds and advocates unpopular views, where truth is tested in the fires of hot argument and not in the gunfires of the true believers. While they recognize the inherent difficulties in attempting to have an institution that serves society yet is not its slave, they argue that the delicate balancing act must be attempted. They realize that the college or university is forever vulnerable to the passionate onslaughts of the believers. The institutional conservatives who view the university this way seem to regard it as essentially a neutral arena where anyone can get his licks in. The institutional liberals argue that it need be neutral only in the sense that it does not coerce or suppress anyone. The latter group views the university primarily as a place for the development and expression of the conscience of mankind and its members as having a commitment not only to the search for truth but also to the spread of humanity and brotherhood in the world. The former group believes that the university has primary responsibility for the search for knowledge and truth and for preparing people to assume society's roles.

The liberal faction regards the university, in part, as a Society for the Prevention of Cruelty to Human Beings, a society that not only facilitates the search for knowledge but also concerns itself with the inhumanities of today and tomorrow. Although both conservatives and liberals might agree that the university has an obligation to hold up a mirror to society and deplore its inhumane treatment of human beings and nature, they tend to disagree that the university has an obligation to actively participate in the often bitter, confused political struggles of a society in change. Here one finds a real dilemma that splits the advocates of this second view into two camps. The liberals ask: If the university is to be a place for the conscience of mankind, how can it avoid entering the social and political lists to battle evil wherever it is found? Does it not risk the supreme irrelevance if it only deplores evil and does not practice what it preaches? In the rhetoric of the time, must it not "put its body on the line" if it is to be something other than a human safety valve letting off potentially revolutionary steam so that the boilers of the establishment do not blow up?

The conservatives respond: What happens to the function of the college as a free marketplace of ideas, where men are to be free from ideological coercion, when it sallies forth in the political arena armed with an institutional orthodoxy? Is it not likely that a zealous pressure for unity of action will tend towards suppression of the lonely dissenter when there is consideration of competence to perform in the university arena? Moreover, in putting its "body on the line" in a direct political action even to the point of violence and counterforce, does not the university expose itself at its most vulnerable point? Where are the arms, the armies, the men and numbers, the war treasury, the massive outside support in the sense of indispensability that are to be used to win the battles and force society to do the university's bidding? Thus the conservatives raise not only questions of appropriateness but questions of strategy.

Both factions of this second view would probably agree that the only force that the university has and should have is the force of argument, the power of articulate persuasion, the power of intellect and perhaps the force of noncooperation. In a world power struggle where arms rather than ideas and votes rather that logic are actively decisive, the university may be weak indeed. Yet the liberal faction would have the university act as a body to provoke change in the interest of justice and humanity despite such obstacles, while the conservatives tend to believe that the university must be free from institutional position-taking both in the interest of its own survival and in the cause of freedom from enforced orthodoxy. Although both might deplore the radicals' seeming willingness to risk the survival of the university in half-baked efforts at violent revolution, they tend to diverge on the question of responsibility for an institutional role and for peaceful social reform. The conservatives, at least some of them, do not deny that the individual professor can, perhaps should, involve himself in the political issues of the day, but this remains largely a matter of individual choice. The liberals, on the other hand, want the collective conscience of the university to be brought to bear upon the political and social issues of the day. It is almost as if the liberals want the university to be at peaceful war with the inhumanities of the community, while the conservatives opt merely for an uneasy truce between town and gown so that the search for truth can go on. The question for them both is how to set a path for the university that will preserve its basic freedom from coercion and freedom for dissent and yet facilitate a relevant and open persuasion of the true, the good, and the beautiful.

It would be foolish to contend that faculty members can easily and once and for all be assigned to one of the two basic views that have just been discussed. The truth probably is that except in times of acute crisis, there are only tendencies in one direction or the other with a possibility that most faculty share the second view or variations thereof. However, when an acute crisis is in full flower there is movement along the spectrum, and a need for agreement upon a standard of professional conduct becomes apparent. It is difficult to operationalize because of these conflicting views of the role and mission of the university. Despite this difficulty we are now ready to plunge where even devils fear to swim and to propose the outlines of a basic code for the profession.

Any brief discussion of a standard is likely to suffer from some of the vagueness which has been criticized above, particularly in the space available here. Perhaps the presentation of a few basic principles will take us steps away from the vagueness. If we start not in the usual manner of stating freedoms and responsibilities, and instead deal with the behavioral question of how a professional shall operate in his profession, we may find a better perspective for viewing the matter. The first general statement might be that the professional shall operate in a scholarly style to honor the marketplace of ideas, to oppose those who threaten it, and to oppose the marketplace itself when it is only a shell and not a substance. In turn, what does each of these terms mean?

By operating in a scholarly style we mean that the scholar is obliged to seek and tell the truth of the matter. Honesty and integrity are his hallmarks, and he is unprofessional when he leaves them aside. He must bring not only a toleration and respect for dissent and disagreement to the argument but also a commitment to follow the arts of peaceful persuasion. Force and violence are proscribed as he operates in the free scholarly arena. But a scholarly man, like all men, cannot be denied the right of revolution when the prospects for freedom are no longer salient. In the desperation of revolution, the scholar exchanges his scholarly style for the style of the partisan; persuasion by logical argument then gives way to persuasion by gun and knife.

The scholarly style demands an effort to engage in rational discourse according to the canons of simple logic, particularly when the lives and reputations of others are at stake. Those who operate in a scholarly style recognize that academic freedom is not absolute nor anarchical; that it implies a respect for due process in decision making and an agreement to adhere to decisions made in this fashion (yet not antithetical to its existence); that tactics of intimidation both subtle and flagrant by professors, students, or society must not only be opposed but a system for redress of grievances must be established and maintained; and finally that a proper consideration of the viewpoints of the community must be extended, if not accepted.

In this latter connection, the scholarly style would not require adherence to outside community norms, except that the scholar, like other men, cannot under usual circumstances put himself above the law without expecting to suffer the civil or criminal consequences. Whether a scholar should be penalized by the profession for violation of the law is largely dependent upon the nature and context of the violation. If, in an act of conscience, the scholar is arrested for civil disobedience, one might conceivably find no cause for professional penalty at all. Yet another similar act, one that may be directed at the destruction of academic freedom, for example, on the shaky grounds that the university was somehow complicit because it was part of society, might call for penalty from the profession because the profession must have the right to discipline those who would destroy it.

Perhaps all that should be set forward is that the academic professional should not be freer than other men from civil penalty for performing illegal acts. But neither should the society demand that he be penalized professionally for acts that challenge the conventional wisdom and norms but are not illegal, or if illegal, not destructive to his role as a professor or to the rights of others in the academy. The professional academic may take on additional responsibilities by joining the profession, but he need not forfeit his social and political rights nor the obligations of conscience. To force him to do so would not only make him a second class citizen, but more importantly, would also deny society the high privilege of possessing an institution which places freedom of conscience at the pinnacle of human values.

Another aspect for consideration is the question of the limits of action in matters of taste and propriety. Here the basic position would seem to be that the college or university is the place for a very wide range of freedom. A university or college is a testing ground, a criticizing ground, an exploring ground. It is not a place for indoctrination nor for institutional approbation on matters of taste and propriety. The full range of human emotions and behaviors are fit subjects for the investigation and commentaries of the men and women of the university. In literature, humanities, the arts, and the natural and social sciences, the problem of the human condition grasps the attention of faculty and students alike. No subject is profane for study and examination. No faculty member should be subject to the charge of unprofessional conduct if his investigation or commentaries chart unfamiliar or unpopular routes, so long as he maintains the proper respect for the dignity and rights of others.

We always arrive at controversial matters when we get to the question of whether the professor should be free to visit his sense of taste and propriety on a captive audience. One might argue that he should, at least, be sensitive to the opinions of others when his actions take him beyond generally accepted limits of taste and propriety. One might entertain the idea that the student, the academic community, and the broader society have the right *not* to have challenges to their senses of taste and propriety forced on them with public displays which they have difficulty in avoiding. Thus, the controversial Spater sculptures at Long Beach State, although essentially anti-erotic, were nonetheless of such unusual theme that even though acceptable as a master's thesis and fit for a gallery show, they were scarcely acceptable for front lawn display to an unsuspecting public. No one has a right to coerce or trick the public into coming to terms with his personal world view. But by the same token, the public should have no right to silence any action that has redeeming social significance, limited though it may be. A man might run around nude at home and advocate nudity in his lectures and yet possibly be disciplined by the profession only for removing his clothes in the classroom or on the football field.

In matters of taste the public's right *not* to know or see or hear must be respected as much as their right to know if they wish. In no other way can we maintain the sometimes uneasy balance between freedom of inquiry and freedom from coercion. What was unacceptable about the unadorned nude and an ode to masturbation in the student newspaper was not that they challenged certain conventions of taste or propriety, but that they appeared in a medium directed toward the general student public and forcefully supported by them through compulsory student fees. One would have little cause to prohibit them if they were privately published and available to those who wished to buy. They were unacceptable because they were coercive in the double sense that they forced other students to support essentially personal bouts with convention, and they did not respect the rights of the unsuspecting not to see nor to read. While one might argue that the men and women of the university have a right and duty to level challenges to the conventional wisdom in all fields, there is a style for doing it that recognizes the feelings and values of others and makes no attempt to jam those challenges down the throats of others.

The Latins realized long ago that in matters of taste there is no arguing in the sense that no one can prove the other person wrong. The Danes recently realized that taste even in the highly emotional matter of pornography had better be left to the individual judgments of adults (anyone over sixteen) rather than legislated into a deceptively rigid standard whose base remains static as society changes. The men and women of the academic profession might recognize the wisdom in both of these approaches and insist only upon freedom from coercion and respect for the rights of others as a limit on the scholarly style in matters of taste. To that extent concern for prevailing viewpoints of the community must be accorded.

Implicit in what has been said about the scholarly style is what we mean by the professional's obligation to honor the marketplace of ideas. It is what we usually mean when we argue that the basic foundation upon which the academic edifice rests is composed of the three freedoms *of* inquiry, *for* dissent, and *from* coercion. It is certain that without these three freedoms, no college or university could exist—a trade school, perhaps, or a finishing school, certainly—but not a university. It has often been pointed out that freedom to inquire and freedom for dissent are necessary aspects of the search for truth. Without freedom for dissent, truth cannot be tested nor error exposed. Without freedom of inquiry discovery cannot be made, the frontiers of knowledge cannot be extended. The journey from ignorance to knowledge is often the distance traveled by the lonely dissenter accompanied only by his challenge to conventional wisdom. Many, if not most of the honored explorers of knowledge were controversial, widely condemned figures, sometimes suppressed, often ridiculed, and occasionally destroyed. Yet their spirit remains the spirit of the university. Those who argue that the college or the university has the privilege of these freedoms only at the sufferance of society miss the point. Society can indeed take away freedom of inquiry and dissent, but it cannot then have a university. The buildings may stand, the professors may remain, but the spirit would be gone, its void filled by the depressing aura of enforced orthodoxy.

Not as often have we discussed the freedom from coercion as a component part of academic freedom, yet it is surely a necessary companion to the other two (although sometimes there is a limitation on freedom to publicize). If the university must support freedom of inquiry and for dissent, it cannot do so without supporting freedom from coercion. Freedom from coercion permits inquiry and dissent to go on their unfettered way. The moment that coercion through force or more subtle forms of intimidation is countenanced at the university, the rare atmosphere of freedom will be fouled by the first traces of a pollution that can destroy it. It is difficult but necessary for the larger society to understand that the university can demand really no other allegiance than adherence to these freedoms, particularly the freedom from coercion. In the deepest sense, the men and women of the university can give ultimate allegiance not to the state or the nation, but to the free search for truth, beauty, and justice. In that search the force of argument accompanied by the commitment to listen rather than the force of power accompanied by bullets or ballots is the only force that is accorded legitimacy. In a peculiar way, the university, although infused with the democratic spirit, is not a democracy in the sense that the majority has the right to coerce support for any principle or dogma except for those principles of academic freedom which are necessary for its existence.

What is so shattering about the apparent willingness of some professors and students to look upon these freedoms as expendable is that there is so little recognition that these are among the very highest freedoms to which man has aspired. The academic revolutionary who defends them seems justified; the academic revolutionary who destroys them seems quixotic. What is it that the latter revolutionary buys that is half so precious as what he sells? One might argue that the protection or gaining of political and socioeconomic freedoms, like freedom from want and discrimination, would justify the sacrifice of these academic freedoms, and perhaps they might. However, it is likely that academic freedoms and political and socioeconomic freedoms are interdependent in the sense that a society that would destroy the former is unlikely to grant the latter.

It seems wise to remember that the story of the halting march towards academic freedom is largely the story of an effort to garner support for all of these freedoms and to weave them into the very fabric of society. They are intimately connected to feedom of conscience, without which all other freedoms wither. To derogate them as clever deceptions of the liberals or the power elite is to run the risk of placing them forever in society's expendable categories, subject to the passing whim of whoever is momentarily on top in the struggle for power and influence.

We may have believed that because so much has been written, said, and experienced about these freedoms they have become a self-evident part of the scholarly heritage. Yet our current circumstances suggest that they need rearguing every generation. It is up to the profession not only to reargue them but also, by example, to give them concrete meaning. What was unsettling about our behavior as a San Francisco State faculty during a number of the incidents of our crisis period was the failure of large groups to demonstrate, by our example, the high importance we assign to these freedoms. While significant numbers appeared to recognize the threat to freedom involved in the experience of a professor who was singled out for intimidation by shouting him down, there were few who seemed willing to do anything about it. One might argue that the entire faculty should have expressed its disapproval in an open and dramatic fashion. Or in another instance, many faculty gave little evidence even of recognizing that these freedoms were at stake when pressure from outside resulted in the removal of a faculty member from the classroom without benefit of trial. (Instead, significant numbers seemed so incensed by his inflammatory rhetoric that they apparently felt that the removal decision was justified indeed.)

We need to include as a part of our standard the obligation to oppose those who threaten these important freedoms. If we are to use the obligation to honor the marketplace of ideas in order to measure professional behavior and in particular to determine when behavior has been unprofessional, then we surely are obliged to agree that action to oppose must be demanded consistently from ourselves as well as from those who have leveled dramatic challenges to our work-a-day ethic. If we really do believe that the university must remain a free marketplace for ideas where the three freedoms are observed, must we not insist that there is not only the negative responsibility to discipline our own, but also a positive responsibility to oppose those from any walk of life who violate or threaten to violate these freedoms? By the obligation to oppose those who threaten the marketplace do we not mean simply, but no less profoundly, that members of the profession must be willing, in the still fresh words of the Declaration of Independence, to "pledge our lives, our fortunes, and our sacred honor" in defense of these academic freedoms?

The faculty strike at San Francisco State was, at root, an act of conscience in the great traditions of this obligation. The fact that it was tainted by human frailty and blurred by questionable means and some undesirable goals connected to certain aspects of the students' strike should not divert us from recognizing the risks that were selflessly undertaken in opposition to some of those who were threatening the free marketplace. It is risks involving fortunes and jobs that the professional must be prepared to take if this aspect of professional obligation is to be anything but hollow. This does not mean that the professional is obliged to go charging off on a striking steed at the first sign of threat, but it does demand that the profession pay some specific attention to the strategy and tactics of opposition.

The recent San Francisco State experience reveals that our means of defense, let alone our willingness to defend, are in disarray. For a profession with so much intellectual power, it is surprising that we have thought so little about how we can most effectively oppose those who would destroy the free marketplace. Must it be the cup of hemlock? Again, there is not space to treat this problem in detail here, but a few tentative comments seem to be in order.

The foolishness (yet somehow the nobility) of the San Francisco State faculty strike as a tactic was that there was so little really adequate financial staying power on the part of the strikers and there was no effective strategy for overcoming the five-day dismissal rule, whose effect was to make the strikers "sitting ducks" after the first five days of their absence from the job. Yet, what other carefully considered alternatives were available for faculty who wished to oppose? The answer is probably none. The truth of the matter is that the academician seems utterly without plans of action that promise a chance of success in the struggle to defend his professional integrity. To be sure, the strike is a weapon, but in its current state it is almost a doomsday machine for the professional at the university. The faculty strike at San Francisco State would very probably have been in that category had the administration been as truly vindictive as some believe. If unsupported by even minimal finances, uninspired by careful psychological and political preparation, and hindered by the lack of a common consensus on what professional obligations are, the strike is likely to produce a disunited faculty whose power is severely limited at best and utterly futile at worst. Given this situation, and it may be changing, have we any way to make such a risky tactic fall at the end of a graduated list of deterrents? Are there none among us who can articulate a strategy for opposition that will gain widespread support within the profession and perhaps on the outside? Do we need to clarify what kinds of attack would result in what methods of opposition and how the decision will be taken to oppose? Are we not obligated to use moral means for furthering moral goals? Where do we as professionals really stand on the question of obligation to oppose?

The professional conduct standard sketched here suggests that the professional is obliged to oppose the marketplace itself when it is only a shell and not a substance. By this we mean that the professional is obliged to oppose the college or university when it is no longer a free marketplace of ideas where the professional can enjoy academic freedom. At what point that opposition is demanded is, of course, extremely difficult to state precisely and we are in a sense back to the problem of the overgenerality of the concept *professional conduct*. Perhaps the following simple standard could be applied. Will the institution protect a professor whose unflinching search for truth makes him controversial? If it will not, then it should be opposed. What form the opposition takes will be determined by the nature of the situation. It may range from efforts at reform where the prospects of peaceful change are reasonably good to outright revolt when these prospects are absent.

Clearly, such a standard must be refined, extended, and debated. Now is the time to get on with the task and with the auxiliary task of developing better mechanisms for the fair determination of alleged violations of professional conduct. Yet incomplete as this sketch is, the mere brief discussion of the subject of unprofessional conduct may have served to make certain things clear, particularly that when we are talking about professional conduct we are focusing on questions of professional life and death, but we have little evidence of explicit agreement as to what it means operationally. Although in the past there may have been some value in maintaining a certain ambiguity about what is and what is not unprofessional conduct, we have contended here that the academic professionals now need to provide substantive definition in order to protect themselves. If the men and women of the profession do not, it will be done for them through the accretion of the common law, by the legislatures (California has already tried), or by harassed administrators attempting to serve two masters. The ambiguity or overgenerality of the term encourages license by the unscrupulous, gets us involved in the course of justice whose hallmark may be capriciousness, and increases our vulnerability to intimidative acts from outside and inside the community. A substantive code of the type enunciated here may not provide a magical solution to our dilemma, but it might help provide a more defensible system of academic justice.

Since a major part of the college effort on academic freedom and tenure has focused on the important matter of due process, one might expect that at least here our house would be in good order. A careful look at the San Francisco State College system and at the system sanctioned by AAUP suggests some possible weaknesses that raise doubt even on this matter. Because this is not intended to be a commentary based on extensive survey of the experience with various systems of academic due process, the effort is simply to raise questions about two underlying assumptions or principles upon which the San Francisco State and the AAUP systems seem to rest and then to comment on the crucial appeal aspect of due process. By raising these questions, we do not mean to suggest that justice has generally been lacking in the majority of the cases tried under the existing procedures. It is probably true that a reasonable justice has been administered in most cases, at least where professionals have made the final judgments. Nonetheless, there have been important flagrant abuses, particularly during crisis periods like the McCarthy era and the present time. While no questioning of assumptions nor remedies stemming out of this questioning will guarantee justice and protect academic freedom, the chances for justice may be increased by raising the issues. That is our intention here.

There are at least two basic assumptions upon which the structure of academic due process rests, both in the AAUP statement and in current San Francisco State college practice, which are open to question. For the sake of convenience, we will label them the *electoral assumption* and the *professorial assumption*. In addition there are pressing questions about the prospects for fair and just treatment in the new system of discipline recently promulgated by the trustees and chancellor of the California state colleges. It is to those three topics that we now turn.

In the administration of justice, a major question always is who shall determine the facts and apply the law. Both the AAUP and San Francisco State have answered: duly elected faculty members, at least in the first instance. (As this is written a new format for disciplinary action has been unilaterally announced by the trustees and chancellor. We shall comment on it below.) Not surprisingly, since faculty members seem to have a constitutional weakness for committees, the function of judge and jury at the original jurisdiction level is to be performed by an elected committee. San Francisco State has the additional fillip of an elected faculty panel from which committee members are to be drawn for each specific case. Apparently the electoral device has been chosen in part to prevent the administration from simply appointing its own committees and in part in the belief that the faculty will select the most judicial, nonpartisan types to serve on the committees. In addition, the San Francisco State device may have been designed to provide a reasonably broad reflection of faculty attitudes and biases.

All of these reasons for supporting the electoral principle are defensible, and during normal times the system probably works fairly well. Yet even during normal times, is there not room for lingering doubt? Does not the electoral principle tend towards the politicization of a process that is essentially judicial? While no system is going to eliminate politics in the sense of certain value orientations on the part of the judges and jury, it does seem that electing a group to carry out the combined function of judge and jury is a needless invitation to throw the process into the cauldrons of faculty politics. Moreover, the requirement that committees be elected often leads to selection of those who are most heavily partisan, particularly during times of extended crisis. This possibility seems antithetical to a fair and impartial system of justice. In fact, one might argue that the electoral process, open as it may be to politicization, may have the specific disadvantage of removing or downgrading the quality of impartiality as something to be sought in candidates for the committees. In turn, this may lessen the pressure on those elected to consider themselves selected by their colleagues on the basis of their impartiality and instead may pressure them to feel that they were selected as representatives of a faction or point of view. The tendency then may be to uphold the cause of faction rather than the cause of justice. Elections may be a democratic way to accomplish goals, but they are not the only democratic way.

Even if the problems of politicization were minor or could somehow be overcome, a case can still be made against the electoral principle. Perhaps one of the most serious problems of the academic enterprise today is its lack of a sense of community and common involvement. Far too frequently, alienated, isolated individuals inhabit the college campuses. Faculty as well as students often harbor this destructive disease. It is in this context that devices which permit or indeed encourage individual faculty members to opt out of responsibility for involvement in the decisions of the group seem most dangerous. Yet that is precisely what the electoral principle permits. So long as people must agree to be candidates and so long as it is so easy to refuse to run, the electoral principle offers the widest escape hatch imaginable. Faculty members on many campuses need not even feel the minimal type of involvement that the ordinary citizen feels in regard to his liability for jury service. Each is free to fly to the sanctuary of his home when tough issues of the judgments of his peers come into play. The spectator syndrome has become a powerful part of American life, and each device that permits escape from involvement reinforces this developing life style with its tendency to block a community of responsible men. In the splintered and shaky academic community, the two most important professional personnel actions that we take are hiring and firing of faculty. We remain heavily involved in the first, but we are disengaging from the second. The electoral assumption, ironically, may be abetting the disengagement. It does not seem wise.

Finally, the elective principle seems likely to be too heavily weighted towards the well-known older faculty, thereby losing the talents and rejuvenating qualities of the younger faculty. Although there is undoubtedly some value in relying on the judgment, wisdom, and experience of the grey eminences of the profession, a system which lists too much in this direction when it is not leaning in the political one leaves much to be desired. Should not the younger faculty member feel his chances or the chances of one of his peers for serving on grievance and disciplinary panels are random rather than drastically skewed? Judgments should not be made on the basis of youth or age, but it does not seem fair to exclude significant numbers of bona fide members of the profession from the process merely because they are late arrivals. Possibly an argument can be made for limiting their participation in tenure judgments where professional evaluation in the discipline is paramount, but it is difficult to see what good reasons can be advanced for limiting their opportunity for participation in disciplinary cases where questions of academic freedom are likely to be paramount.

If the electoral principle leads in the direction that we have indicated, then we must ask what other systems might be better? One answer might be that a variation of the jury selection procedures for the administration of justice in the larger society could prove useful. The device for selecting grievance and disciplinary panels from the entire voting faculty by lot could be utilized. The responsibility to serve, once drawn, could be avoided only on the basis of adequate cause. Thus, politicization would perhaps be incidental, the opportunity to escape participation would be diminished (or at least equal and random). And the possibility of exclusion on the basis of extraneous factors would be diminished. Such a procedure cannot be put forth as the solution to the problem of lack of community, but at least it would not seem to work in the opposite direction and it may contribute to a more impartial system of justice.

A serious charge that can fairly be leveled against our system of academic due process is that it is grounded on an assumption of professorial exclusivity. Professors have excluded the other side of the teaching-learning process—students—from the full protection of academic due process. In the AAUP statements on academic freedom and tenure of 1940 and 1968 one searches in vain for a statement of procedures for the protection of students from intimidation and mistreatment at the hands of a professor. The 1940 statement does include a passing reference to the protection of the rights of the student "to freedom in learning," the 1968 statement quotes favorably a Supreme Court contention that "teachers and students must always remain free to inquire, to study, and to evaluate," and the 1958 Professional Ethics statement contends that it is unprofessional for the professor to "use his relationship to his students to exploit them for his own private purposes." But none of these statements takes up the question of how the student is to secure his rights from possible violation by the professors or someone else. At San Francisco State there are procedures through which the student can register a grade grievance against a professor involving a professorial review committee, but there is no present way to force the professor to accept the adverse judgment of the committee even though it may be unanimous. We probably all know tales, either from our own student days or from more recent years, about professors who have used their positions of trust, authority, and responsibility to terrorize students in the most authoritarian fashion. We have already noted instances at San Francisco State, where grade intimidation of students occurred. We have dismissed these instances and many others as rather quaint idiosyncrasies on the part of some of our colleagues, or we have been reluctant to question the authority position of any of our colleagues, perhaps realizing that our own position was wrapped up in the same set of privileges.

The student enters the academic arena with few defenses against arbitrary and unreasonable action on the part of the teacher. Even his freedom to change instructors is severely limited by the overcrowded nature of most of our institutions and the abundance of required courses. Some might justify this situation on grounds that the professor is the trained professional most competent to judge the learning performance of students in his particular specialty, and that it is a rare occasion when a professor treats a student unfairly and unjustly. It can also be pointed out that charges of unprofessional conduct can be brought against a professor if his behavior against students is flagrant. But these justifications of the status quo are not persuasive. Violations continue to occur, rarely has a student had redress, and professors simply are not customarily found unprofessional because they have been judged unfair to a student. In the affairs of men, any system that assumes the infallibility of human beings in positions of authority is perhaps assuming too much, yet that is precisely what is assumed when the professor's judgment is pragmatically the court of first and last resort. Those of us who reject the anarchistic view that beauty is the defiance of authority and support the liberal view that beauty is the control of arbitrary authority, once again find a curious void in our past efforts to make this belief reality. Right here in our own back yard, we find almost a callous disregard of the need for a well-developed system of due process. It is difficult to see how we can justly sing its praises when it is to be applied to ourselves and yet forget the tune when we are considering the rights of students. Surely the right of academic due process, so much a part of academic freedom, needs to be extended to all in the academic community, if we are to have a community of freedom and responsibility. Too long the academic profession has neglected this problem. It does so now at its own peril.

If the electoral and professorial assumptions suggest that at least some members of the academic profession have not done their homework, the problem of the application of discipline points up the dangers that may arise if someone else does their homework for them. Perhaps nowhere has this been more dramatically demonstrated than in the aftermath of the time of troubles which San Francisco State College experienced in the three year period from 1967 to 1970. Apparently frightened by the disarray of college faculties as they attempted to deal with the problems of confrontation, the trustees and the chancellor of the California state college system promulgated a system of discipline for faculty that raises serious questions of propriety, equity, and justice. Indeed certain of its provisions seem contradictory to traditional principles of Anglo-American jurisprudence, one of the prized gifts of our past to our present. While these provisions undoubtedly came about because the faculties have not skillfully handled some of the issues raised so far in this chapter, this does not diminish the necessity for focusing a critical light on their implications for the health and welfare of the academic community across the nation. We are reasonably certain that in the months ahead many colleges and universities that have experienced confrontations will be pressured to follow suit.

In September 1970 the trustees and the chancellor of the California state college system announced disciplinary action procedures for academic personnel containing these main provisions: First, the president shall appoint a prosecuting officer who shall investigate all alleged misconduct, receive all requests for the pressing of disciplinary action and determine whether there is sufficient cause for proceeding with a formal charge. Second, a hearing officer shall be appointed by the chancellor from the state of California's Office of Administrative Procedure.

Third, hearings before the chancellor-appointed hearing officer shall be closed and confidential. The only persons permitted to attend are the person charged, the prosecuting officer, one advisor for each of the former two, representatives of not more than two statewide faculty organizations (one named by the president, the other by the accused) and witnesses, but only while presenting evidence. All evidence, proceedings, findings, and recommendations are not to be made public by the college or any participant except in formal court proceedings at a later date. The formal rules of evidence in court proceedings do not apply to these hearings. This specifically means that hearsay and other usually proscribed evidence can be taken into consideration. The hearing officer shall forward a written decision and his report on findings of fact to the president of the college.

Fourth, a disciplinary action panel consisting of the entire list of associate and full professors at the college shall be established. From this list, three members drawn by lot are to be impaneled if the president determines that the facts reported by the hearing officer warrant a consideration of the disciplinary penalty. The duties of the disciplinary action panel are to consider the findings of the hearing officer, but they may not receive new evidence nor go beyond the hearing officer's findings. The power of the panel is advisory to the president of the college. Its recommendations must be based upon the education code, whose main causes for action are immoral conduct, unprofessional conduct, dishonesty, incompetency, and failure to perform duties. The panel may recommend that action shall not be taken, or it may recommend the application of penalties from a list which includes dismissal, demotion, denial of access to campus, suspension, and written or oral reprimand.

Fifth, the president is encouraged to concur with the recommendations of the disciplinary action panel, but he clearly has the power to disregard their recommendations when in "rare" instances he has compelling reasons to disagree. Those reasons must be stated in writing and discussed with the panel. Once he has reached his decision he forwards his recommendations to the chancellor, who shall take such action as he, the chancellor, deems appropriate.

Sixth, apparently the accused has the right to carry his case to the state personnel board for a hearing de novo and then to the courts for a review of the case, but not de novo. Significantly, the new system explicitly states that it is not "intended that any of the procedures or error in application are relevant to or provide a basis for review by the state personnel board or by any court" reviewing the case.

Such are the new procedures for administering justice at the California State Colleges. There is much that could be said about them. For our purposes, we will only concentrate on those aspects which seem to threaten a fair and impartial system of justice and to retard the growth of a community of free and responsible men and women.

The first factor for our consideration is the apparent decline in importance of professional peer evaluation and judgment. While the provisions do make an advance in requiring widespread faculty availability for serving on the panel (thereby striking at the electoral assumption), they immediately lessen its effect not only by making the panel dependent upon the chancellor's hearing officer on matters of evidence and fact, but also by clearly making their power advisory. Thus, the final determination of what is unprofessional or immoral clearly rests with the president and the chancellor. Rather than take the model of the bar or medical associations as the guide for determining unprofessional conduct, the procedures clearly adopt the model of the old-fashioned, nonunionized business corporation where the employee's opportunities for justice depended mainly on the sufferance and good will of the boss. From this perspective colleges are not quasi-independent communities at all, but hierarchically organized corporations perhaps unduly subject to the whims, dislikes, and politics of the management and the board. Such a situation does not offer great promise for the college to live successful lives of exploration, social change, and criticism. While academic freedom may not die from exposure to this increasingly corporate model, it is doubtful that it will live a very healthy life in the years immediately to come.

Perhaps even more serious for the prospect of obtaining justice are the procedures which, in effect, combine the roles of judge, jury, and executive. Our traditions of justice argue most strongly for maintaining a separation of the functions of judging and executing. When the chancellor appoints the hearing officer, who is a part of the state administration in the first place, a distinct possibility arises that an interested party to the dispute (for example, the chancellor or his representative) will be selecting the parties to hear the case. While certain safeguards are apparently to be erected (the presiding officer of the state Office of Administrative Procedure will do the selecting of the specific officers), their connection to the chancellor and the administrative hierarchy of the state, even though minimal, makes the question of impartiality significant.

More significant is the fact that the determination of the hearing officer and the disciplinary action panels, as we have seen, are only advisory to the president and the chancellor. This makes it possible and indeed likely that the president or chancellor as parties to a dispute will become judges in their own case. As recommendations are channeled to them, they are clearly free to accept or reject those recommendations even though they initiated the action in the first place. Even some of the kings of ancient times did not have such a prerogative. It is clearly more power than the President of the United States has in dismissing or otherwise punishing a civil servant in the many branches of the federal government. The opportunities for intimidative and unjust behavior are inherent in such procedures. Unless the president and the chancellor possess no human frailties or are somehow infallible, one would expect them to err, at least occasionally, in the direction of unfair punishment or biased judgments.

Strikingly absent from these procedures is the right of appeal within the system. The right of appeal in a system of justice is an ancient and desirable right. It is based upon the recognition that error may occur in the heat of deliberations at the scene of original jurisdiction and that the community has an obligation to be doubly sure when it uses its collective power to penalize an alleged wrongdoer. By removing the case one step away from original combat, there apparently is a hope of obtaining a higher degree of impartiality and disinterest. This is not recognized by the new procedures. Although one would suppose that an employee could always beg for mercy, the absence of appeal procedures within the California state college system strikes another blow at our traditional canons of due process. We no longer have even the appeal prospects sanctioned by the American Association of University Professors which themselves are tainted by the fact that the governing board, a potential party to a dispute, is to have the final appeal authority. It is a chilling prospect for those who believe that one of our glories has been the development of the common law in which appeal or judicial review has played such a magnificent part.

The demand that hearings be confidential, almost secret, is another procedure that does not seem wise. The underlying reason for this confidentiality may well have been to protect accused, accuser, and witnesses from embarrassment, intimidation, and later vengeance. Given the fact that we have had attempts at all three at San Francisco State and elsewhere in the state college system, it is not surprising that some effort should be made to preserve the integrity and decorum of disciplinary hearings. Unfortunately, it may be that the effort to preserve confidentiality when linked with the waiving of traditional rules of evidence will compound the problem of obtaining a just decision by making it difficult for the members of the community to be watchful against possible miscarriages of justice. The ancient practice of open hearings functioned in part to keep people informed about the workings of the judicial system and thus attentive to possible injustice and need for change. As long as the hearing officer has ample authority to remove from the room those who would disrupt the hearings or intimidate the witnesses or other parties to the hearing, then the need for confidentiality or secretness would seem to be diminished. It is true that open hearings may increase the opportunities for unscrupulous people to intimidate and threaten, but probably not greatly so and this prospect must be balanced against the arguments that have made secret trials almost synonymous with oppression.

The new system of discipline carries with it a list of possible sanctions. They too present a problem. The problem of sanction on unacceptable conduct is closely related to the problem of shaky due process and the difficulties of determining unprofessional behavior with such a vague and imprecise definition of what conduct is unprofessional or immoral. Even though there may be less difficulty with identifying other proscribed behaviors such as dishonesty, incompetency, and failure to perform duties, the system of sanctions enunciated in the new procedures leaves much in doubt. For a system of justice to have a reasonable chance of success, it should not only be accompanied by a reasonably clear and precise definition of the limits of behavior and by the safeguards of the tradition of due process, but it also should include a system of sanctions which can be fairly fitted to the gravity of the offense. The view that the punishment should fit the crime suggests that all crimes are not of equal gravity, yet the academic system of justice here described seems to have failed to deal with this question at all.

As it now seems to stand the disciplinary action panel and/or the president or chancellor can use its own discretion as to which of the penalties should be invoked for a particular offense. It could mean in practice that a person could be dismissed or demoted because of an action which most reasonable men would consider petty or minor. When coupled with the present imprecision of concepts like unprofessional or immoral conduct, this kind of discretion seems excessive. Throwing a man out of an institution because in a moment of passion he behaves outrageously by interrupting a speech, or by breaking a window, or by silencing a speaker, or by directing a knee to the groin of a colleague, or by punching a fellow faculty member or student on the nose is all too possible under the system recently promulgated. Although we suspect a few would want to eliminate the discretionary power of the panel or president or chancellor entirely, many might want to circumscribe this discretion when the penalties of dismissal or demotion are proposed. Surely, it should be possible to define more carefully the circumstances and offenses which would lead to dismissal or demotion. It seems that an invitation to inequitable and unfair treatment has been presented to us. Who knows who will accept?

There is an added danger, not quite so noticeable, brought on by the combination of the unlimited discretionary nature of penalty application and the imprecision surrounding actions deserving penalty. Such a combination may mean that faculty will be unwilling to participate in a process so filled with ambiguity and dangers of inequity. What can happen, even if the faculty participate, is that they will recognize the overkill consequences of the vague and poorly articulated action and penalty situation and refuse to find any colleague guilty of violating the shaky code of conduct. One suspects that the path is so strewn with the possibilities of injustice that the faculty will tacitly agree to live with varying degrees of questionable behavior. The result may well be that we will continue to fail to provide protection for students, other faculty, and the community from actions that almost all of us would agree were improper and deserving of sanction. At that point academic freedom becomes license and we have lost our claim to virtue.

Underlying all of these specific criticisms of the disciplinary aspects of the California state colleges, and to a lesser extent of the American Association of University Professors, is a basic difference of outlook on the role and function of the American college or university. In our ideal world, we see ourselves as free individuals in a cooperative community of scholars and students whose major mission is to live lives of conservation, exploration, criticism, self-development, and social change. Many of us do not perceive ourselves as factory hands turning out semi-finished products to fit into the larger machines of the outside world. Instead, we view ourselves as members of a very special and ancient community whose job is to discern truth from falsehood, to discover or create beauty amidst ugliness, and to promote justice over tyranny as our life goals. Many of us hope that our small academic community will thrive for our own good, for the good of our nation, and most of all, for the good of humanity. Thus our differences with those who would view us as a corporation do not rest on pomposity or elitism but on the fundamental proposition that since our enterprise is different, so must be our life style.

In this context actions which tend to make us more like a corporation and less like a community are likely to be opposed. Many of us do not think that the humans occupying the hierarchies of our present structure are totally or even largely evil men and women. But we do strongly believe that to place us in a situation in disciplinary or other matters where authority and responsibility reside mainly in the president, the chancellor, and the Board of Trustees is to endanger our vitality and our promise. Most of us are convinced of the wisdom of our forefathers, who saw that to create a community of responsible productive citizens it was necessary to make the governors responsible or accountable to the governed. Thus, when faced with a structure modeled after a corporation, we are particularly aware of the dangers of tacitly assuming the rightness of executive authority and, indeed, the presence of executive infallibility.

While we realize that the managers of the educational establishment answer ultimately to the body politic, we suggest that there is another body politic, the academic community, that must also be served. The patron public may, in the end, call important shots but they cannot be the only shots if we are to preserve man's most precious possession, the free intellect. That can only be preserved in a climate of academic freedom where no man is presumed infallible and where the traditional protections of our time-tested system of justice operate. Viewed in this light, all power to the chancellor or the college president is a journey backward into a time when rulers ruled their subjects and lost their kingdoms.

In this chapter we have discussed some questions about professional conduct, academic due process and the problem of administration of justice in the academic corporation. In doing so, we have made little effort to be comprehensive. It is likely that other participants in the crisis at San Francisco State would have quite different perspectives and tackle different problems. Moreover, it should always be remembered that the authors of this book were not innocent bystanders to the unfolding drama, but active participants. As such, we were party to and share in many of the problems that have been raised in this chapter and thus have our own particular biases, failings, and blindnesses as well as our inside insights. Nonetheless, we hope that by making our positions rather clear we will stimulate colleagues and other interested public to do as we have. It is our expectation that by doing so, the state of the profession would be improved. After all, we do believe, with so many of our colleagues, in the free marketplace of ideas.

EIGHT

Intervention by
Police and Media

A number of college and university campuses are involved in struggles that continue from year to year with periodic outbreaks of direct action, violence and suppression. The experience at San Francisco State shows the fundamental wrenching of relationships such a cycle of disorder generates within the campus, and between the campus and the trustees and chancellor of the statewide system. The relationship of the campus to the society around is also altered drastically. The reciprocal impact on each other of a disorderly campus and various interest groups external to the campus is more difficult to describe and assess. It is clear to us in a gross way that a continuing pattern of campus disorder negates old ways of relating to the society and its other institutions and throws the college into intense patterns of interaction for which it is not prepared. Nor are concerned sectors of the community any better prepared to absorb and respond constructively to campus rebellions and the conditions that generate them. The college in turmoil is forced into novel relationships with executive officials of local and state government, the legislature, the police, the national guard, the courts, the alumni, civic organizations, and societies of clergymen. Relationships with insurance companies, employers of graduates, and the mass news media also undergo drastic change. All affect the immediate course of events on the campus and beyond and appear to have a cumulative impact of a more permanent kind in distorting the

225

future direction of the college and in fraying the fabric of support both on the campus and in the broader society. In brief, the college becomes a sitting duck.

We have chosen two patterns of college-community interaction for description and analysis: emergency police on campus and campus coverage by the media. In the following chapter we assess the unsolicited mail from a public agitated by campus events. These patterns were selected from a range of social forces because of their sharp impact on the college, its personnel, and its future and because we are convinced that each of the three patterns of response will operate powerfully in affecting the outcomes of any prolonged campus conflict. There is urgent need for more comprehensive analysis of the campus' societal relationships during a period of campus stress and conflict. Such analysis might point to effective reforms in the governance of higher education. Too much of the impetus for recent reforms in governance have come from raw feelings of anger, fear, and the urge to restrict, retaliate, and punish an entire institution. In California, the post-Sputnik scapegoating of colleges and universities is apparent in the face of community and campus unrest. When there is campus disorder, police on campus and the mass media interact to escalate conflict and distort solutions.

Police on Campus

The growing use of large numbers of off-campus police, sheriff's deputies or national guardsmen to control campus disruptions poses a number of acute dilemmas that threaten the future of higher education. The two academic years 1967–1968 and 1968–1969 placed most of those problems in bold relief at San Francisco State College as its cycle of disorders endured for months. Dialogue, encounter, and confrontation moved on to direct crowd action, destruction of property, and occasional physical assault during the year 1967–1968. In the fall of 1968 the strike led by black and Third World students introduced the war of the flea, an urban form of guerrilla warfare. The rhetoric of rebellion advocated violence against persons and property and the intent to seize power by force. Illustrative acts of arson, bombings, beatings, and other terrorist tactics occurred early in the student strike and continued into the spring semester of 1969.

It is probable that the trend during the past few years toward more potentially lethal provocations on many campuses has already bypassed the issue of whether off-campus law enforcement personnel *should* be called during sharp crises. They *will* be called. If the college president is slow to call police, then a mayor, a police chief, or a governor is likely to do so. In 1967–1968, the shift toward massed, uniformed police or national guard was yet to come, as was the resort to gunfire on the part of law enforcement personnel causing student deaths. Yet, beneath the growing violence and counterviolence the dilemmas persist.

The image of some Latin American universities, as sanctuaries for revolutionary movements marked with intimidation of campus officials and students, floated over the campus scene, hardening the rhetoric and the actions of proponents of law and order. Provocative acts on campus seemed to verify a drift toward Latin American patterns. The massive student struggles in Japan were forcing universities to close for months at a time. Faculty and students are deeply jealous of the college as a self-governing community, presumably cemented together by consensus. The open search for knowledge, teaching, and learning and the duty of responsible social criticism are supposed to go forward in a climate free from the taint of coercion, guided by empathy among scholars and the use of critical intelligence in a setting of academic freedom. On campus after campus, disorderly events have washed over this image without altering it in the minds of many who subscribe to it.

A campus administrator, seeking to absorb provocative acts and to hold provocateurs accountable without flooding the campus with police, takes major risks. In addition he suffers the wrath of the no-nonsense forces. Yet, if large numbers of off-campus police in riot gear invade the campus, its traditional image as a benign place of reason is shattered for the faculty. In 1968, outrage seemed to surge from all sides, almost independently of the provocations precipitating the call for police assistance and of the behavior of the police on campus.

Another dilemma arises from the decision to call the police to a campus. The president has usually considered the decision a last resort action necessary to protect safety on the campus and continuation of campus functions. Yet large sectors of the faculty and student body and some administrators immediately conclude that the decision is a mistake and they are prone to act accordingly, escalating the difficulties of both police and administrators. The administrator carries the burden of proof for the soundness of his decision in the face of many who are severely skeptical.

The quality of the information and advice on which the decision to call police on campus is made is often a crucial problem for the administrator as well as for the faculty and students. On a large and crowded campus, thousands of persons move about in remarkable anonymity. During a crisis, communication of accurate information to and from major sectors of the campus is very difficult. During continuing stress and growing anxiety, large numbers of people become highly suggestible and it is increasingly difficult to assess the accuracy of available information. The direction a disruption may take thus becomes hard to predict.

Introduce the guerrilla tactics of the war of the flea to which San Francisco State was subjected in November 1968, and caprice becomes an even more potent factor in decisions about emergency police action. Awareness by the administrator of the no-win choices confronting him is of little help. He must refrain from calling for assistance or else make the call, often without knowing whether reported incidents of disruption or violence are the prelude to intensified disorder or are isolated episodes. In fact, he may feel impelled to act even before the accuracy of the reports is established. As a result, large numbers of police may flood the campus before many of the people on campus know why the police were called.[1]

Still another paradox arises. The police on campus at the behest of a president may well protect persons and property, but they also have great potential for deepening and extending conflict. Hardnosed experienced activists and revolutionaries know all this well, and exploit the basic situation in their search for recruits and in their struggle for increased power over campus affairs. They know that disorder brings severe pressure to bear on the president from both inside and outside the college to call for police assistance. They believe that a major demonstration that does not bring police on campus can be at best only a partial success if not a failure. Many activists have learned that a small, determined group of a dozen or fewer can often contrive

[1] In April 1970, President Pitzer of Stanford University announced publicly that it was no longer necessary for other college personnel to clear with his office before calling police on campus. The refinement of guerilla tactics coupled with easy resort to assault and serious property destruction cuts into the feasibility of "clearance through channels."

a situation, or capitalize on a situation they have not provoked, to precipitate a call for off-campus police. Once on campus, police can often be provoked to counterviolence in ways that further radicalize students. Activists know that many students and faculty prefer having the campus closed to having extra police on campus. To have police there under the control of other jurisdictions, such as the city or the state, may be worse than having the campus closed, but better for provocateurs. The police control the campus but the president and his staff can still be held accountable for disorderly events arising from police presence, a fourth dilemma.

Ironically, many of the most active and socially concerned faculty and students urge that the college engage itself directly on as many fronts as possible with the society and the metropolitan area that sustains it. Faculty and students are urged by the changed circumstances to become change agents both on and off campus, precipitating "creative conflict" as they go. Further, they encourage more direct involvement of new sectors of the community in campus sponsored activities. Those inured to the dangers of violence of socially disorganized areas of large cities are welcomed on campus. Street patterns of conflict resolution come with them.

Engaging education with the problems of our time and thereby achieving increased relevance while making direct contributions to the easing of the urban revolution are laudable objectives. A significant part of the educational process should, it is argued, be based on real transactions between students and faculty and off-campus citizens. Yet, paradoxically, when sharp social conflict often rooted in the community and society turns to disorder, coercion, and violence on campus, resort to the services of law enforcement and peacekeeping agencies from the community throws many of the same persons into shock.

Faculty at San Francisco State widely assumed police should be excluded from campus-community interaction. For example, the Black Students Union arranged for as many young black men and women as they could recruit from the Bay Area to come on campus during a December 1967 campus demonstration. The day culminated in property destruction in three buildings, forcible entry into one, disorderly crowds, and some assaults. The visitors contributed to the disorder and violence. President Summerskill toughed the precarious day through without calling off-campus police and for that he was severely castigated by the trustees and chancellor. The faculty's public outcry was intense—directed only at the trustees. The BSU leaders who brought the young people from the surrounding communities on campus escaped faculty censure. That episode and its aftermath ended Summerskill's effectiveness as president. Whether police should have been called at the height of the danger on that December day was a matter of close judgment in the minds of both the police officials present and the president. As it happened, they concurred in not calling police. Those who set up the situation with potential for disorder and violence left the scene unnoticed while the issue of police on campus grabbed campus and public attention. Later, letters to President Smith told of sons or daughters, frightened or slightly injured on campus, and threatened suit (for administrative negligence) in the event of personal injury. It was a good day for the campus revolutionaries. The specific issues used to justify the confrontations became low priority.

President Summerskill sought in every possible way to avoid calling campus police, absorbing large risks in the process. Eventually, in later incidents and under severe pressure from Dumke, he called police. President Smith was reluctant to use off-campus police but did so to protect lives, property, and an open campus. President Hayakawa called police in whatever numbers appeared necessary to reduce or discourage disorder by whatever means he and police officials deemed necessary. In each administration, the president's posture toward use of off-campus police was a crucial factor in judgments of him formed by people both on and off campus.

A "double bust" of students and faculty during Summerskill's last week as president in May 1968 was judged too little and too late by trustees and the chancellor and was furiously resented by many faculty. After assuming the presidency a week later, Smith refused to intercede for amnesty for those arrested. That action helped stamp him as a hardliner with activist students and some faculty.

Smith's refusal to espouse a hard police line in public persuaded some trustees that he was weak. In a state that had fed law and order rhetoric into every major political campaign for half a decade, police on campus triggers conflict tied in different ways to the differing ideological positions described earlier. As positions crystallize, the issues of police as protectors of the status quo or as agents in provoking radical action gain in symbolic and emotional importance somewhat independent of the context into which they were called. The stance of a politician or an educational administrator about police marks him quickly as strong or weak, hard or soft, on the conservative or liberal side of the ledger. Those who dissent through direct action use the terms *repressive* or *progressive*. Both Hayakawa and the more trenchant militants accused each other of fascist tactics as they played on the emotional responses to the presence of police on campus.

Officials in California's public colleges and universities face a dilemma in relation to the use of off-campus police that goes beyond the administrator's judgment about whether and under what circumstances to use police. If a pattern of disorder and threat is building and dangerous crises are likely to arise, advance plans must be made to move quickly, whether the need is to close the campus or to bring sufficient police on campus quickly to contain disorder. (In the face of disorderly, emotionally aroused crowds, police are required, even to close and clear the campus.) In any event, police must be near at hand, well briefed, firmly led, and if possible specially selected for such precarious duty. However, since four public officials other than the president—the chancellor, the governor, the mayor of the city, and the chief of police—all assume that they too have a fundamental responsibility for order and safety on the campus, the judgment of the college president and his staff may well be brushed aside. If the campus is closed without a test of police strength, the president is charged with capitulation to anarchy. If publicized disorder endures with or without violence, discretion may pass from the president's hands. If police are called on campus amidst confused and contradictory feelings about police presence among students, faculty, and administrators, the stage is set for the kinds of provocations and brutalizing events cited earlier.

In this ambiguous context two things are explicitly clear: First, under present arrangements, once police are on campus the president's authority is replaced by the authority of those directing the police; second, students and faculty still hold the president—not the provocateurs lying in wait for the right situation—accountable for the outcome. In crowd situations provocateurs are present, sometimes among the students, faculty, police, media people, special agents, and onlookers. Nor does the faculty often associate their anger at the sudden appearance of police on campus with what we think of as the "Genovese syndrome" so dramatically described by Rosenthal.[2] There

---

[2] A. M. Rosenthal, *Thirty-Eight Witnesses* (New York: McGraw-Hill, 1964).

are paralells on campus to his account of the thirty-eight "nice middle class people" who refused to be implicated in action to stop the repeated open assaults and eventual murder of a young woman in a New York City neighborhood. When patterns of disruptive, provocative acts were developing on campus, few faculty moved firmly to contain or report such conduct. A fitful record of administrative support of scattered faculty efforts to uphold regulations in previous semesters encouraged default. Repeatedly the role of the college or university president as an administrator-educator has been destroyed by efforts to control disruption with off-campus police or militia. At San Francisco State this was no less true of Hayakawa than it was with Summerskill and Smith. (Presidents and chancellors have also been replaced after police-student confrontations at the University of California, Berkeley, Columbia, and Cornell. We assume Hayakawa's role as *educational* leader at San Francisco State *has* been destroyed.)

The precarious coming and going of top administrators at colleges and universities through the minefields of campus-police-political conflict will continue until a broader understanding is reached among faculty and students of the consequences of intimidation, coercion, and violence unleashed within the campus community, until an understood plan of managing and containing such forces is developed by colleges and universities that includes in the planning the policymaking trustees or regents and the state officers who impinge on them and also those who control supporting police forces. A cavalier resort to massive police action by the trustees and the governor at one extreme is offset to some extent by the romantic views of some faculty that the administrators (but not the faculty) must wrestle barehanded with guerrilla fighters in behalf of academic freedom.

Increasingly, as they face the spillover onto campuses of forces engaged in the sharpest social and political domestic conflicts of our time, colleges and universities are being described as the most vulnerable and fragile institutions in our society. If this is so, they must be made tougher and more resilient lest they be destroyed. This does not mean that colleges must become more rigid or repressive in their stance, seeking to balance incipient violence with a "preemptive striking force" threatening enough to discourage dissent and agitation. Such solutions will destroy colleges as surely as will a continuing inability to defend or redefine the institutions' central values and theses.

A flabby unwillingness to admit the need for limits on behavior of individuals both on campus and off poses another threat. The experience at San Francisco State during 1968–1969 set a disastrous precedent, especially during Hayakawa's administration. In effect—through massive police action—the students, the faculty, the college, the city, and the state collaborated to establish a conveyor belt that dumped several hundred students charged with a variety of misdemeanor and felony charges onto the unprepared court system. The cycle included disorderly or prohibited demonstrations, arrests, bookings, and trials. A San Francisco police official reported to the writer that, on January 23, 1969, the authorities who ordered the police to surround the crowd on campus that failed to disperse miscalculated the size of the crowd. That miscalculation resulted in twice as many arrests (453) as had been anticipated. And so the overloaded court system, even with augmented personnel, was engaged in group trials into the 1969 fall semester, delaying its agenda of civil cases for approximately a year. Arrested students were taught that the system of justice functioned badly, if at all.

The purposes of augmented police on campus during a period of disorder or crisis are not unique. They are there to contain disruption, enforce the law, protect life and property, gather information, and—if necessary—arrest lawbreakers. Large urban institutions that want to move into the explosive problem areas of our cities to "make education relevant" and to contribute directly to tension resolution and problem solving cannot have it both ways. Ivy draped tranquility does not mix easily with the tactics of the "university of the streets." Police presence will continue as part of the campus scene. Student, faculty, and administration leaders should work toward a common understanding of the relationships and hazards involved. The ability to develop this understanding is complicated by the image that police presence on campus precipitates, as well by their violent action in some stress situations.

Police cast up in the minds of activist students and faculty the image of ultimate enemy. Police accoutrements and behavior conjure up the prophecy of police brutality. Sophisticated radicals know all of this but see police differently. To them the police are despised but crucial tools who can assist in escalation of conflict and in gaining recruits with commitment born of strife. Police are trapped both by the threatening problem of crowd size and by demands from their superiors for unaccustomed restraint. They are trapped into the role of the heavies ("blue meanies") by their own professional subculture as well. Their job is not to protect academic freedom, which has already been set aside before they are called. Their job is not to protect the "long range objectives of higher education" during specific police actions. Their job is to be professionally proficient in keeping or restoring the peace, protecting lives and property, and enforcing the law. From experience they believe that when they are badly outnumbered and seriously threatened by large crowd attacks, aggressive counteraction is required both to protect themselves and to control the situation. They come to believe at a gut level that in dangerous situations their buddies must be protected almost at all costs and that a fallen officer must be revenged, on the spot if possible. Ordered on campus at the behest of others, they are spat upon, assaulted, cursed, and called pigs and motherfuckers. They are perceived as the invading, repressive arm of the establishment, not as peace officers. Some have sons and daughters in the college.

The lack of empathy police display toward a disorderly crowd is not surprising. Their inability to distinguish a rock thrower from an onlooker in a frenzied crowd may not be malevolence. Campus Robin Hoods who charge into a melee to free an arrested student should not take it personally if the Sheriff of Nottingham's threatened men become violent. Campus confrontations frequently become brutal situations fostered by experienced crowd manipulators. A part of citizenship education in our time for the great majority of nonviolent people is learning how to resist suggestion in a crowd setting and how to exert a stabilizing rather than a hysterical influence in tense crowd situations. We will be in large crowds with increasing frequency. The campus is as good a place as any to look critically at the factors of crowd conflict and the severe costs to participants and to the institution. For activists—even for radicals and revolutionaries—to bait and scapegoat police as a category of nonhumans is dysfunctional in the long run. Police, too, increasingly feel their powerlessness. Most *are not* the power structure. They are functionaries and symbols. They are also men with jobs—agents, if you will, of the power structure, acting under orders. A good revolutionary would encourage policemen to defect rather than force them to emotional commitment against the dissenters and with the status quo. The rapid rise of the police in the ultra-conservative political apparatus of large cities should be a tip-off to moderates and liberals alike who feel the urge to throw police off campus while subjecting them to savage abuse.

Despite some baleful results, our analysis of the San Francisco State experience, and our less intensive review of college and university disorders in this nation and many others reinforces our conclusion that large scale use of outside security forces will be required in conflict situations in higher educational institutions in the future. Colleges have become focal points of intense struggles for power in conflict ridden societies. Resistant to change yet vulnerable to disruption, they are marked as arenas of struggle among proponents of competing ideologies, including individuals and groups who are honestly willing to use force in pursuit of their goals. Particularly in large institutions, interlinked in the web of large urban centers, the security problems of campuses must be equated more closely with like problems in the larger communities, already pockmarked by major rebellions and with great potential for further escalation. Urban colleges must plan constructively to reduce the random elements that are loosed when large numbers of law enforcement personnel come on campus. Paradoxical as it may seem to many students, faculty, administrators, and others, emergency police assistance is an increasingly crucial requirement in keeping open the options within which much needed changes can be made. If mismanaged, police on campus can readily close options as well. Sudden change made in deference to coercion or unchecked violence is probably little more promising than is a stubborn, static posture toward powerful pressures for change.

Efforts must be made, prior to or between major campus confrontations, to come to grips with the problems created by divergent perceptions and attitudes, and by commitments to divergent ad hoc strategies for coping with campus disruption. Campuses should not be closed at the drop of a hat to avoid calling for outside police assistance. Campuses should be closed temporarily (a) when in the judgment of college officials available police forces in a particular situation are insufficient to control violence against persons, and (b) when major property damage cannot be avoided without police assistance and its great potential for escalating disorders. More importantly campuses should be free to suspend the conventional instructional program at the discretion of the responsible campus authorities when they think promise exists for resolving or reducing conflict through conferences, negotiations or convocations. This assumes that real bases for conflict do exist and that serious disruptions drawing wide support indicate a breadth and depth of real grievances for which police repression is a wretched answer. It also assumes that an improved level of police work on campus can hold accountable for their actions individuals and groups that behave malevolently and destructively. It assumes that college and university presidents are apt to be as courageous and as conserving of tax dollars and of grantors' funds as the next public official, and at least as committed to the maintenance and development of an educationally productive institution as are the proponents of instant order. *For these reasons, discretion for suspending the class schedule or closing the campus temporarily should rest finally and explicitly with the president.*

The resources and the authority needed to resolve the conflict should be placed at the president's disposal—and promptly. In such situations, adherence to a two-year line item budget cycle is perhaps the ultimate absurdity. Colleges and universities, especially state supported urban institutions, are becoming large and turbulent jurisdictions with populations of fifteen to fifty-five thousand persons. Many are linked with other institutions in massive and increasingly unwieldy systems. Augmented police assistance in times of crisis should be arranged for in advance by some variation of mutual aid now developing among cities in metropolitan areas. Such arrangements should be worked out with surrounding muncipalities and state law enforcement agencies, perhaps by a consortium of colleges and universities in a manageable area such as the San Francisco Bay Area. Police and court costs for state-supported institutions should be a charge on the state, not the city, thus spreading the costs over the state. More importantly, that might preclude the college's abandoning of large numbers of students to the courts with cavalier nonchalance while the city picks up the tab.

The campus should be viewed as a semi-autonomous governmental unit under control of its own government. Police should be called, and directed while on campus, by officials in the campus governance structure. An outside or distant official—whether mayor, chairman of the trustees, or governor—should have no more unilateral authority to call police on campus than does the president of the United States to call the National Guard without prior consultation with state authorities. A large college or university should have a highly trained, experienced, and professionally competent law enforcement officer on its staff. His role should be to develop a model program of enforcement of law and regulations on his campus and to direct all police activity on campus irrespective of the jurisdictions from which police are drawn during major disorders. Because the surrounding urban areas catch the ebb and flow of disruptive campus events and vice versa, the campus law enforcement officer should function for the college and its president in planning with the chief of the city police, just as the chief functions for the city and its mayor. (It is not our intent to propose the campuses become Vatican cities, although it is clear that we are dealing here with the centuries old issue of the "town and gown.")

General administrative officers of a college are responsible both for the educational welfare and the safety of the people involved. They must strive to support the law and function within it. Their professional reason for being is to participate in effective education. Maladroit police action on campus can destroy intended educational progress with dramatic suddenness and enduring consequences. The immediate assuaging of political passions and concern for the embarrassment of other public officials must not be the prime considerations in efforts to control campus disorder. The administrator's fundamental role as educator must persist, even if the crush of the emergencies in recent years leaves us somewhat uncertain as to what that role is during major police actions. Presidents are at least as apt students of campus turbulence and its dynamics as the general run of city mayors or governors and trustees. In any event, experience is gained quickly. The president's authority, his proximity to the campus, and his experience should not be brushed aside.

If officials outside the colleges preempt the president's authority by calling emergency police on campus and by directing them while there, the president and all members of his staff who are directly involved should be temporarily suspended, not to be restored to authority and responsibility for the remnants of his college until the president is permitted to resume the full powers of his office. To protect administrators from caprice and panic "in higher places," presidents should have term contracts for a minimum of four years, with renewals subject to review. Thus, one controversial episode would not mean a sudden changing of the administrative guard—perhaps one of the most damaging things that can happen to a large complex organization under stress. The rate at which California state college presidents are being forced to resign or are fired suggests gross incompetence at either the chancellor or the trustee level at which appointments are made. Smith has proposed that each president who leaves his position because of failure of trustee support should be able to designate the trustee most clearly an enemy of education and should select a replacement trustee.

A streamlined decision-making process, to be invoked under crisis conditions, should be established and should include a clear definition of the conditions that constitute a crisis. Emergency communications operations must be a corollary. The means by which emergency police are to be called and the approximate circumstances under which they are necessary should be open information, as should the names of persons authorized to call police. Provisions for external conciliation or mediation efforts during threatening buildups of tension should be seriously considered. In the midst of conflict, the task of legitimizing such personnel and processes with all parties is most difficult. A skeleton apparatus is needed for involving nonpartisan administrators, faculty, and students as nonparticipating observers of police and faculty-student interaction in emergency situations. Such a presence would be expanded as needed. The object would be to restrain extreme behavior and provide more accurate information for those who participate in conflict resolution.

A cadre of articulate and respected faculty and students is needed, to speak as "friends of the whole college" in the open verbal encounters that are so frequently a prelude to disorder. To some degree this happened on an ad hoc, spontaneous basis during several major campus disorders at San Francisco State, but most faculty let argument go by default. Such groups, with access to sources of accurate information, could attempt to dampen the rampant, unchecked partisanship and burgeoning campus mythology that is self-perpetuating. They could man an impartial rumor clinic and campus communication center. Such an ad hoc center was organized at State and operated for weeks during the campus struggle, manned by students and faculty. Its effectiveness, however, was hampered by implications of partisanship and lack of authorization by contending groups.

In the context of campus "struggle" described here, the formally designated leaders of the student groups, of the faculty, and of the administration steadily became more deeply involved in the roles—

as perceived by others—of adamant antagonists. While such may never really have been the case, those *perceptions controlled responses,* and communication quickly withered as police baiting and police action became more intense.

Well meaning "nonaccredited" groups attempting to find ways to help resolve impasses sprang up in profusion. With no alternate framework such as that suggested above available to noncombatants, the indigenous, alternate leadership that usually emerges in complex struggles became random elements, partially informed, with no way of accrediting their efforts to become an independent force in resolving the conflict. Police became the agents for winning a war of attrition, a baleful outcome.

In many ways, San Francisco State College experienced a loss of community over a period of years leading up to the 1968–1969 struggles. The multiple mismanagement of the gathering problems and of the crises further dismantled any remaining sense of polity. Two years after the struggle was stalemated, even the beginnings of a resurgence of morale are hard to find. The cues all point to further centralization of control and increasingly arbitrary decision making. The college, like a major city, is the antithesis of a therapeutic community. It is not a good place for young to mature in the direction of humane values. If the college cannot be rebuilt, and soon, perhaps it should be closed. Such are the consequences of massive, ineptly used force as an antidote to complex political and ideological conflict in one of the nation's leading colleges.

News Media

Colleges and universities have worked hard to devise ways of moving educational news from page thirty-six forward to page six in the metropolitan press, from marginal slots on television into time bands during which receivers are actually turned on. They have sought more effective personnel in the communications field in efforts to make higher education competitive in the scramble for public attention and positive support. Such efforts seek to explain the programs and services available through the college, highlight personalities and performances on campus and generally enhance the image of the college. The intent is to reassure the many publics that money is being spent wisely while simultaneously pressing home the unending need for more resources.

Prime time and favored space in the media have always come

hard to education. News of outstanding athletic teams, occasional campus skulduggery leaked into the open, the firing of a president, or charges of classroom heresy were the exceptions that received attention. In the latter instances college efforts turned to getting the stories out of the media as quickly as possible. During the last half decade the pattern of campus-media relationships has changed drastically. The politics of confrontation on campus and the ideologically rooted disruptions ebbing and flowing between the campuses and their surrounding urban areas have combined with issues of race and politics in an unprecedented alchemy. When the action starts, colleges are now dragged into the multimedia spotlights like reluctant virgins and raped on prime time in view of millions.

The term media is broadly defined here to include the metropolitan, state and national press, news services, radio, television, weekly and monthly periodicals, the campus press, the underground press, pamphlets, handbills, posters, graffiti, balladeers, agitprop theater, Hyde Park speaker systems, bullhorns, sound trucks, and loudspeaker systems. This assessment is limited mainly to the impact of the metropolitan radio, television, and newspaper media on the campus, on the trustees, and on public opinion in California. Of these, television has the most powerful impact on a campus crisis situation, on public opinion, and on persons in active roles in the crisis both on campus and off. The underground press and the veritable blizzard of fugitive materials introduce another pattern of communication of growing importance both on the campus and in responsive sectors of the metropolitan areas. Such media operate outside conventional campus communication channels, free of institutional supervision, yet with great feedback impact on campus problems.

As this study progressed, the media emerged as one of the most potent forces in shaping and escalating the cycle of crises and determining the shape of events at San Francisco State. We are convinced that the media require more intensive study than is possible within the plan for this study if we are to fully understand the dynamics of campus disorder.

Exploration of the impact of media in a cycle of campus tumult reveals paradoxes. The people's right to know about public affairs and issues is clear. The commercial media are at present the major agents for reporting and interpreting disorderly campus events. Media repre-

sentatives have broad access to campus personnel involved in conflict
and to action situations. Three such paradoxes are apparent.

Media efforts to inform and interpret escalate and widen campus conflict and delay solutions. Media efforts distort the roles of
parties to the conflict and also shift the pattern of leadership towards
persons skilled in media use. News media and colleges are both institutions presumably devoted to the search for truth and accuracy in reporting it in objective and reasoned terms. However, during a period
of sustained campus disorder, both the college and the media become
objects of manipulation by contending forces both on and off campus.
They become parties to a propaganda war steeped in ideological and
political content, while caprice grows at the expense of reason.

The paradoxical roles of the media in a persisting cycle of
campus disorder are explored through an examination of specific episodes during the year of the strike, 1968–1969. Some of the selected
illustrations have been described in previous chapters and in *By Any
Means Necessary*.

The 1968 controversy over George Murray is the prime example
among many of conflict escalation through media reporting. Ed
Montgomery of the *San Francisco Examiner*, a week before the 1968
fall semester began, broke a story of the hiring of George Mason
Murray as a part-time English instructor at San Francisco State College. The story reported Murray's role in the beatings of the *Gater*
staff a year before, his consequent probation, membership in the Black
Panthers, a summer visit to Cuba and alleged statements while there
in revolutionary rhetoric. The ensuing controversy grew along with the
furor over Eldridge Cleaver's role as a part-time lecturer at the University of California at Berkeley until they dominated the California
higher education news prior to the 1968 November general election.
Radio, television, and press coverage of the events following Montgomery's story carried counterpart treatment in the underground
media and helped polarize existing factions on the campus prior to
the student and faculty strikes. The impact of the controversy on
public opinion in California is shown in some detail in the next chapter. In October, when President Smith declined to remove George
Murray from teaching at the request of the State college trustees, segments of the radio and press reported that Smith had "defied the
trustees." This brought a cascade of angry mail to the trustees, to

Smith, and to political figures, most demanding action against Smith and/or Murray. A smaller volume, supporting Smith's action, demanded that outside interference with campus affairs be stopped. Murray spoke at Fresno State in late October, using extremely militant rhetoric. The speech, given on the same day the trustees were meeting on campus, assured broad media coverage and contributed to the pressure on the chancellor to force Smith to suspend Murray before campus disciplinary procedures could be completed. The press had picked Murray from a number of militant black part-time instructors, some perhaps more inclined toward revolutionary views than Murray. The others continued relatively unnoticed as college employees, well after Murray had been dropped from the college and jailed for violating probation and Smith had resigned.

The intent, here, is not to blame the media for the consequences of the Murray conflict but to illustrate the role of media in escalating campus conflict. Murray's hiring was a controversial act, as was the defense of his teaching assignment by Smith and his staff. The actions of the chancellor, the trustees, and Murray, rooted in value differences, generated further news. The news media made the statewide escalation of the conflict possible as various interests chose to exploit the controversy during a crucial general election campaign. The controversy helped beat a $250,000,000 higher education bond issue, and may well have enabled Richard Nixon to win California by a bare margin, assuring him the presidency.

It is apparent that the above discussion of media escalation of campus conflict also illustrates the power of the media to affect contenders on the scene and beyond the campus. Let's look at three examples of roles drastically altered by news media reporting as an active agent in shaping events.

The Tactical Squad charged into the BSU area on November 13, 1968, freezing the "nonnegotiable" position of the strikers after one of their leaders was beaten and arrested. A black man's assault on a media cameraman precipitated the event. President Smith reported inaccurately to the media on that incident on the basis of misinformation. Some groups attributed his response to duplicity and became more sympathetic to the strike. The presence of the newsmen drew the attack. The tactical squad response prolonged the strike. Smith's effort to report the facts through the media miscarried and added numbers to the strikers, while impairing his influence with students and faculty.

Many who had been ambivalent about the strike shifted their allegiances as a result of this incident.

A more dramatic example of media impact on an individual's role is reflected in the experience of California State Senator James Wedworth, who spent three weeks studying the disorders at San Francisco State. He enjoyed anonymity on campus from November 23, 1968 to December 3, 1968, including the transition between Smith and Hayakawa's administrations. Wedworth had asked Smith and his associates to honor his anonymity so he could more freely move on campus and among campus groups. He moved in and out of a great variety of formal and informal discussion groups. He reports that on December 3 1968, he could remain silent no longer about the violence and destruction of the college which he believed had been precipitated by the policies of the governor and Hayakawa. He traveled to Sacramento for a report to fellow legislators and a press conference. Arriving back to the campus at 4:00 P.M., he reports:

> The result of the press conference was startling—I had been on that campus for quite a long time, and although my identity was not known on campus when I arrived [on November 22, 1968], I was instantly *recognized by everyone today* [December 3, 1968] —students, the press, all people. I, therefore, lost one of the privileges—that of no one knowing who I was. My access to the many things in which I had been involved, while not limited previously, now underwent substantial change.

The senator immediately began to receive letters and telephone calls from all over the state and was constantly asked for interviews. One reporter asked him what kinds of disguises he had been using on campus, although he had worn conventional business clothes the entire time. He also reported that he was "frozen out of the administration building" as soon as he publicly stated criticisms of Hayakawa's administration.

This disturbing example of transformation from anonymity to mini-celebrity as the result of one news conference one hundred miles from campus describes well the impact of media on a person's role and on a situation when there is wide coverage of a campus struggle. The incident is not complete without considering the one-two punch of the media impact. The public response to media reports of his views shook Wedworth further.

As the campus disorders became more massive during Hayakawa's first weeks as acting president, Wedworth became more tren-

chant. In a further news conference he blamed the chancellor, Hayakawa, and Governor Reagan for the growing hysteria and violence
and called for Glenn Dumke's resignation. By the end of the week mail
and telephone calls were pouring in to his home, his district office, and
his office at the state capitol. When he challenged the tam o'shantered
Hayakawa and his massive police operations, Wedworth found himself plugged in quickly to a "feedback loop" provided by the mass
media and the direct public response. That abusive response shocked
him. He reported:

> Many of the words which are written in their letters are unbeliev-
> able. By now I have been branded about everything—including
> a "Jewish storm trooper." I have heard people wonder aloud
> many times where students pick up their foul language—they
> learn it at home.

The combination of provocative acts on campus—by dissenting
students, faculty, and media reporting—and officially expressed indigna-
tion generates a powerful counterforce of articulated public indigna-
tion. It brings demands that leadership personnel set aside notions
about due process and resort to any means necessary to suppress campus struggles. Hayakawa rose from anonymity in the campus struggle
to president and was the recipient of a national award as educator of
the year. It is the most dramatic example of potency of the media in
shaping roles of those immersed in campus conflict.

Hayakawa's dramatic, if illegal, assault on the sound truck
during his first week in office was caught by television and radio. By
personally attacking the truck and symbolically doing physical battle
with demonstrating students, he became a California folk hero. Many
viewed the performance as an act of impetuous bravery, earning him
adjectives such as "gritty," "gutty," and "feisty." The latent "ma-
chismo" in the nation that prompts President Nixon to telephone the
quarterbacks of winning football teams washed over Hayakawa.

Thus, one episode, whether contrived or impulsive, at which
the media were present helped give Hayakawa the leverage to carry
on a three month struggle for the control of the campus, a struggle
in which massive police action on campus—backed by public opinion
—eventually eroded the forces of the student and faculty strikers.

During the first month of Hayakawa's efforts to break or settle
the student strike, he was able to begin conversations with Roscoe
Blount, tough, moderate BSU member. Information about these con-

versations was seized upon by a reporter and promptly fed back to the public. The BSU then repudiated Blount because the fifteen demands were publicly held to be nonnegotiable. College officials spent the subsequent weekend worrying about threats that Blount would be killed. Nothing productive developed from the discussions between Blount and Hayakawa.

During the early weeks of the student strike, Hayakawa, speaking at a microphone on the open campus, urged the media representatives to leave campus because he believed their presence contributed to the disorder. After becoming president, he turned to the commercial media as his major avenue of communication, even inviting them against the advice of his deans and the Academic Senate to cover a faculty meeting that opened the 1969 Spring semester during the last weeks of the strike. During the weeks of the strike, the formal communication channels within the college were often overrun by reports of campus events by metropolitan media.

Efforts to capture the media and make them weapons in the conflict were aided by the workaday need of newsmen to bring in a story by the deadline set by a broadcast station or newspaper. News conferences provided opportunities on campus, as they did at trustee meetings, for minority opinion to gain wide distribution. With media representatives and their clearly marked panel trucks omnipresent or adjacent to the campus for weeks, almost any half dozen students, faculty, or administrators with a bit of moxie could precipitate themselves into the news on an otherwise slow day.

Deliberate attempts to disrupt news conferences were not uncommon, with the opposition shouting, jostling, and interrupting spokesmen. The broad awareness of the power of the media is apparent from episodes in which demonstrators smashed cameras and assaulted media personnel and in which police roughed up media men at the height of the violent police action. The practice of police or college officials reviewing media film of crowd action for identification of miscreants adds to the hazards for cameramen and to the likelihood of violence when media people are present. This practice also makes newsgatherers operational arms of police intelligence, a direct threat to newsmen's professional roles.

The second convocation, November 25 and 26, 1968, was televised by KQED, educational television station. The revolutionary rhetoric and abrasive language of the spokesmen for the Black Students

Union and the Third World Liberation Front provided part of the backdrop of public anger needed to support Hayakawa's paramilitary approach to crushing the disorders. The radical minority spokesmen were clearly directing their extreme assertions to their ghetto constituents and affiliated radicals. They seemed unaware that those who control the police, the funds, and the higher educational policies were also listening—already fed up with persisting challenges to their authority. This effort to use television in the push for power appeared to frighten more people than it convinced.

Newsmen, seeking mini-scoops and special angles on tense trustee meetings or campus events, persist in efforts to get hallway interviews with key figures in a dispute. This is done *away from the open press conferences*. The most astute, power oriented trustees and administrators know how to cater to such needs. So do a sprinkling of faculty and students. Governor Reagan, Max Rafferty, and others often sat almost silently through long, tense discussions of important issues and emerged from a long executive session from which newsmen were excluded only to launch a dramatic attack on an issue or person before a television camera that "just happened" to be in the hall. In such instances, the other participants, locked in the effort to solve a problem, did not know until the evening news report that a wayward member had attempted to shape public opinion on the issue by operating as a maverick outside of the decision-making structure.

Intensive news coverage of San Francisco State College's weeks of disorder contributed to skewed interpretation of campus events that, in turn, intensified the dismay and reaction of public opinion described in the following chapter. Two examples must suffice.

When campus disorders were severe, the "Ray Tannehill News" opened the six o'clock news repeatedly with scenes of disorderly or violent crowd and police action. After an hour's news, including commentary on the college's turmoil, the program sometimes closed with a replay of campus disorder. This form of double jeopardy was not designed to assuage public attitudes.

Shortly after his appointment as president, Smith agreed to a five minute interview with a local television station. He covertly timed the interview to avoid giving the editor too much leeway for editing. At one point the reporter asked President Smith, "Do you think the media contribute to campus disorder? If so what advice would you have for us?" Smith's response was approximately:

Yes, the media tend to expand the problems—but public education is public business and citizens have a right to accurate information about all public institutions. However, after a television
reporter films 27½ minutes of disorderly action by a group of
twenty-seven demonstrators trying to break into a building, the
cameraman should be willing to use his last *thirty seconds* of film
to "pan" the 2/3,000 students going their quiet ways to classes
and the sixth grade class, largely students from minority groups,
and their teacher, hiking across campus on an orientation visit to
college.

Smith's criticism of reporting imbalance was the main item deleted
from the broadcast.

Shortly after Smith's appointment to the president's role in
June 1968, he had breakfast with Robert Mendelsohn, a young, per-
sonable, liberal San Francisco supervisor. One aspect of the discussion
seemed especially attuned to a sense of the power of the media as well
as the fragmented roles expected of public figures in that context.
Mendelsohn's friendly advice to Smith—given shortly after the May
disorders that ended Summerskill's term as president—was to use the
news media deliberately to project to the public a hard, unbending
line against campus activists and dissenters, and to use a flexible,
conciliatory approach seeking workable compromises when working
with those groups on campus beyond range of the media. (Much of
Mayor Alioto's style reflected this thesis. And it was essentially the pattern adopted by Hayakawa during his early weeks, as a number of
major concessions were proposed *off camera*. The segmented posture
worked, after a fashion, although once Hayakawa gained the initiative,
his line on campus tended to harden to coincide with his public posture. For example, he was able to say to the media, "If they act like
pigs, treat them like pigs.")

Smith reminded Mendelsohn that an educator in a highly
publicized leadership role could not espouse one ideology for public
consumption and another for dissident student and faculty without in
the long run damaging both education and public service. The prescription highlights the disparity of value norms between campus and
television viewers and also the schizophrenic role some expect of the
college president when he is working in full view of the media.

Faculty and administrators at San Francisco State were not far
removed in time from a partially self-imposed discipline in which press
statements originating outside of the college administration were

cleared—or at least advance information was provided—before their release. Not so during a modern campus struggle. The groups that accepted the thesis of "any means to the end" attempted to exploit the media as often as possible. The first presentation of the ten demands of the BSU was made to the metropolitan press in a student lounge press conference before the demands were presented to college officials. Two weeks later an ad hoc AFT group went to Mayor Alioto and persuaded him to call a press conference to propose "his plan" for a three-day convocation. That meeting helped shoot down Smith's efforts to keep the class schedule in operation—certainly not Mayor Alioto's intent. Smith learned of the meeting through a telephone call from the mayor.

The Convocation Planning Committee, given clear responsibility by the president to plan the second convocation, had fourteen members. Half of the committee members were BSU-TWLF students, and half were faculty and administration people. Two of the latter group sympathetic to the strike gave that view of campus events a majority. The committee bypassed the college press officer, Harvey Yorke, and selected a young faculty member from the business school to manage the press relations for the convocation. Yorke was outraged at being bypassed as part of the administrative establishment.

As the disruptive conflict persisted all groups sought to coopt the media. Media presence on campus even established the general time limits within which disruptive campus action occurred. Television and press deadlines almost guaranteed that police could be withdrawn by 3:30 P.M. each afternoon. Even at the height of disorder, evening classes scheduled from 4:10 P.M. met almost without incident even though few outside police were available.

Had the disruptive, violence-threatening students been the fanatic thugs and revolutionaries the law and order proponents asserted they were, they could have wrought real destruction and extensive injury during the evening hours or the late afternoon. Smith's administration accepted the fact that the prime media hours for gathering stories marked the apex of campus action, and the additional fact that even the most trenchant disruptors were at that time more concerned about an impact on campus and public opinion than on violence against persons or grave destruction of property. The strikers, however, misestimated the public and college response. What the strikers deemed necessary, controlled pressure, was viewed by many as terrorist atrocities. Despite the broad awareness of the media role in campus crises, most participants in the campus struggles during three years of campus crises—including the writers—appear to have misestimated the potency of the news media in shaping the outcomes of their struggles.

The raw impact of televised reports of crowd action, strident rhetoric, and scenes of property destruction and occasional violence clearly exceeded other means of communication to citizens beyond campus. Yet we have concluded that the interpretation of campus events beyond the firsthand reporting also did much to consolidate thought and polarize opinions about persons and issues involved in the tumult. If an accurately informed public was an objective of parties to State's conflict, the several adversaries failed on two major accounts: the dramatic, fragmented television and radio reporting skewed the messages to the public; and the subsequent interpretive treatments tended to contribute further to the public mythology about campus disorder and institutional response. Talk shows, editorials, and feature stories focused on a person or an angle. Television specials, letters to the editors, and speeches before civic and partisan groups cast up a barrage of conflicting interpretations that overran campus partisans' efforts to tell their story to the several agitated publics.

The San Francisco Bay Area is the cradle of the radio and television talk shows. Communicasters preside for several hours a day over a mishmash of expert opinion, telephoned questions, vested interest pitches, ignorant dogmatic statements, and the moderators' personal opinions. The phenomenon is an extension of the cracker barrel tradition, the back fence gossip session, and the neighborhood bar. Thousands of those who feel too much alone can involve themselves. Some stations, following in the tradition of metropolitan newspapers' stables of syndicated columnists of varying views, now maintain a stable of communicasters who reflect varying social and philosophical positions, from moderately liberal to arch-right wing, abusive types.

During college disturbances, issues, personalities, and actions become open game for almost totally unaccountable charges and judgments, often involving character assassination, while the person ensnared is going about his own affairs totally unaware of such discussions. So abusive were some of these programs that three individuals from widely dispersed areas in California contacted President Smith, urging him to respond to particularly invidious treatment and offering to finance a libel suit on his behalf or to attempt to block a broadcaster's license renewal.

As stated elsewhere, the George Murray issue was broken into the metropolitan press by arch-conservative Ed Montgomery of the Hearst owned *San Francisco Examiner*. It was then aired at length by the right wing communicaster Pat Michaels, and pushed home within the state college trustees by the arch-conservative Dudley Swim, Reagan's right hand on the Board. That sequence *is also a pattern.*

A few days after Smith's resignation, an alumnus wrote him reporting an attack on Smith by Bay Area radio communicaster Hilly Rose. The writer states:

> First he denounced the militants with which we agreed. Following that, he made a rather personal, unfair and stupid attack on Dr. Hayakawa which betrayed his own (Hilly Rose's) ignorance. And finally he came to the most important point, namely an all out attack on you. The tone of his remarks was condescending, patronizing, sarcastic and utterly obscene. He finished by saying: "Poor Dr. Smith, where will he go now? Will he go to Ethiopia to join Dr. Summerskill? Perhaps he should stay in the Gater's office so that someone could hit him over the head. Perhaps he should work in the men's room."

The writer considered the comments to be "an open invitation to violence" against Smith and, in his opinion, "open slander." He gave an unlisted number at which he could be reached, and suggested Smith consider legal action. He closed with a statement that whether or not Smith chose to take action, he felt obliged to write, not willing to sit idle "as a concerned citizen while intellectual prostitutes slander your good name."

A week after Robert Smith's resignation, he received a letter from Robertson C. Scott, Program Director of radio station KPOL, Los Angeles,[3] including a script of a commentary broadcast *three days* before. The statement was highly critical of Smith's efforts to manage the campus crisis. Scott wrote, "We would be pleased to have you or an appointed representative present an opposing viewpoint," and suggested Smith get in touch with him "within the next two weeks." It appears to be another version of printing a retraction or rebuttal to a front page newspaper story on page ten a week later—with the added difficulty that in this instance a statement required an appearance several hundred miles away for a five minute broadcast.

---

[3] Capital Cities Broadcasting Corporation.

On December 4, KTVU of San Francisco-Oakland Television distributed a summary of the station-sponsored "Tele-Vote" for the weeks of November 18–22. The first date corresponds to the state college trustee's emergency meeting at which they ordered President Smith to reopen the campus "immediately" (while he and other top campus administrators *were in Los Angeles*). Questions to the viewers asked whether the campus should open even with police, whether the trustees should assume direct control of the campus (yes, 59 per cent), whether the president should resign, and ended the week with "are you afraid of flying?" Smith was pleased to see that 61 per cent did not wish him to resign—the same proportion as those who were not afraid of flying.

In January 1969, a month after Smith resigned as president, he made a speech to businessmen in which he criticized Governor Reagan for "exonerating himself as a prime cause of the disorder in higher education by indiscriminate attacks on the university and state college systems." These modest criticisms of the governor, reported in the media, were followed a few days later by press reports that San Francisco State College had admitted forty minority students at knife point and under threat. The account of this alleged cave-in was attributed to former President Smith as reported by Governor Reagan at a luncheon speech in Southern California. Of course, Smith's telephone began to ring as media men followed the fast-breaking story. Since Smith had not heard of the alleged episode, he suggested that as usual the governor appeared to be misinformed, especially on incidents that disparaged members of minority groups, including college presidents. The " 'tis, 'taint" pattern held for a few days while persistent reporters checked other trustees for verification. The box score gradually grew leaving only *Dumke* and *Reagan's press officer* as the governor's supporting witnesses. All other trustees contacted reported no knowledge of such an incident. Nor could any campus administrators recall such a memorable episode. Smith dismissed the effort at character assassination as routine, the kind of thing that happens when a nice boy falls in with a bad crowd.

While Smith was working at his desk one morning, the telephone rang. It was Jim Dunbar, San Francisco radio and television communicaster, on whose show President Smith had appeared shortly after his appointment. Would Smith comment to the radio audience on Governor Reagan's charges? Smith asked that the charges be stated specifically and then briefly summarized the above information as a flat denial. He then pointed out that the governor was apparently making luncheon speeches in which he was citing unverifiable charges of minority group felony on campus. Smith turned the radio on at the close of his comments and was astonished to hear Dunbar flatly misquote him, then ask his audience to judge for themselves who was right and who was wrong. As for himself, Dunbar said he believed the governor was telling the truth.

Smith called the public affairs director of Dunbar's station and bluntly reported what had happened, saying he wanted immediate access to Dunbar's talk show. Less than a minute later he was restating his position on the air, noting that he had been tried and convicted by Dunbar before a radio audience, in absentia, without a shred of evidence. Dunbar apologized and ruined the remainder of his program reiterating the apology.

As campus turbulence endures and more and more factions and individuals "rise above principle" to use any means available to gain an advantage, the communication distortions themselves become a major block to conflict resolution. The incessant circulation of false reports, half truths, big lies, threats, and rumors nurture anger, fear, and hysteria. The growing underground press both on campus and in the urban community also plays a role in interpreting events and reporting strategies among dissidents. It operates largely out of the field of attention of administrators and official faculty leaders. Just as the commercial media tend to support the establishment, so the underground press and the campus student press tend to reject it and uncritically support dissenting movements. Repeatedly, accounts of the same incident in the various media were so disparate as to make identification of the event difficult.

Efforts of the college administrators three months before the fall 1968 disorders to secure special funds and personnel for a quick retooling of the college's archaic information apparatus were unfortunately unsuccessful. Attempts to recruit volunteer help from departments instructing in radio, television, and journalism were overrun by the cascade of events. The invasion of dozens of media people, by sheer numbers, overwhelmed the two-man information office and helped transfer too much of the initiative in reporting and interpreting events to the commercial media and the underground press.

Difficulties in coping with the multimedia while trying to reduce campus conflict to workable levels can be attributed too easily to the random elements operative when large numbers of reporters and cameramen roam the campus during tense times. It is easy to identify examples of reporters' or editors' bias, distortion or misinformation but there is another side to it. The media escalated the conflict, but several parties contributed to that process. Much confusion *was generated within the campus and within the state college system*. Messages garbled at the sources are not apt to be clarified in transmission by the media. For example, Smith had clear positions on most of the major issues. However, that fact tended to be obscured by countering public statements from the governor, key trustees, the chancellor, faculty cliques, individuals in the administrative structure of the college, and students. In short, if clear messages cannot be conveyed, a communications system will promote confusion no matter how elaborate the system is and how much potential it has. Issues of student discipline, faculty ethics, the meaning of black studies, and the locus of administrative responsibility were already disordered and confused before Smith and Hayakawa's appointments. The media representatives on campus probably performed as well as any other involved personnel, all floundering in a setting with few precedents.

Hayakawa reduced the number of issues sharply, repeatedly enforcing order on the campus, condemning the strikers, and keeping the college open at all costs. Thus he marched in cadence with the governor and trustees, reducing the complexity and the uncertainty of what was communicated. The actions of several hundred uniformed, armed police supporting his positions helped clarify the messages. Yet, the campus conflict continued to escalate even as the approach to the media was shifted with President Hayakawa's adept use of the media as a direct instrument for mobilizing public opinion in support of his all out efforts to suppress the student rebellion and break the student and faculty strikes. Public opinion, mobilized for such a purpose and yet ill-informed about the complexities of the conflict, may have become a club with which to maul higher education following the suppression of disorder.

The college or university that is propelled into the public spotlight in the midst of its travail finds that the media themselves may become a controlling factor shaping and escalating the conflict. We have developed some perceptions concerning the impact of the media in a period of campus disturbances, as follows.

Dramatic reports of events will repeatedly determine the next cycle of events, thus drawing attention away from efforts to resolve the initial conflict.

Media reports expand tremendously the numbers of individuals and publics who involve themselves in the dispute—especially those who are threatened by, or who hope to profit from, continuing conflict—thus distorting the problem and widening the context within which it must be resolved.

The entire pattern by which the college relates itself to the media shifts drastically as contending on-campus and off-campus groups fight to coopt the media as tools to be used in every possible way to gain advantage in the struggle.

When metropolitan media are drawn into a campus struggle, the established formal systems of communication within the campus are quickly overrun. Partisans and onlookers alike within the campus community turn to the off-campus media for information and for interpretation of campus events.

As media reports broaden the arena of conflict, the appropriate locus for resolving a dispute is lost to the campus. Efforts on campus to ease the stress give way to efforts to manage public opinion and to influence those who may act on the situation from outside the campus. The media aid such distractions. Corrective measures are formulated far from the context of the problem, by people who are less concerned with educational aims than are those in the college community.

The media play a potent role in determining the style of leadership that emerges among the several parties to the struggle. Articulate persons with charisma and a flair for adamant statements and arbitrary action move into leadership roles as the camera picks them out and their rhetoric is reported in the press.

Fragmentary and slanted reporting combines with campus confusion to project a disconnected and partial story. Highly complex issues on the campus are cast into the public arena through the media and generate outrage and simplistic solutions. They are fed back to trustees and administrators through direct public pressure, legislators, and city and state executive officers.

Once the contending groups on campus push the conflict into the metropolitan media and public response becomes intense, mediation or resolution of the disputes is blocked as the several parties struggle to shape public opinion to support their cause. The ideological and political character of recent campus conflicts contributes to this strategy. The strikes at San Francisco State were negotiated only after it became clear that the strikers had lost the propaganda battle off campus. Restoration of campus order becomes an urgent end in itself as concern and anger spread to legislators, to the governor's office, and to the trustees, who take actions designed to quell the tumult, often unrelated to educational consequences.

When the campus is stabilized and the media depart, the vast work of healing and rebuilding is often in the hands of leaders cast up in the media context, carrying the legacy of struggle before a transfixed public. The talents that brought them into leadership may have little to do with the talents or stomach needed for the stubborn work of putting the institution back together. Their political potency and the fervent support of the victors hold them in leadership roles, nonetheless.

The continuing struggles on college and university campuses are dramatic and newsworthy. When such events are amplified by the media, the majority of citizens are forced for the first time to come to grips for themselves with many of the central issues of higher education. Most of the nine lives of the college described briefly in the opening chapter of this volume are driven to the fore in such times of stress, and each involves complex issues within its own sphere, let alone in relation to each other and to a conflict-ridden society. The lag in public information and understanding of higher education threatens the future of the state of California's multi-billion dollar complex of colleges and universities. The breakdown of communication and trust within the state college system during San Francisco State's crisis added to public confusion about higher education.

A time of stress and conflict is not, perhaps, conducive to reasoned consideration of higher educational issues. It has the advantage, however, of *public attention*. It is strongly apparent to the writers that caprice plays too great a role in the management of campus conflict when the mass media are heavily involved. There is a great need for radically new and more sophisticated communications within the massive campuses, among the institutions interlinked in higher education systems and between the campuses and their many constituencies and publics. The people of the state who wish to support rather than destroy higher education deserve a better chance to understand than the commercial media afford them as the media struggle to report the morass of events confronting them of which campus crises are only one. Each campus should be a major initiating center for a diverse, coordinated system of communication interchange with the people in its area. A colloquium of institutions in a metropolitan area should have broad access *under their control* (especially in times of controversy) to radio, television, newspapers, and other emerging means of communication with attention to provisions for interchange with the public.

This could perhaps be done by providing major resources to defray costs of commercial time in which programs could be projected, supervised by a representative task force from the institutions. We would favor media networks financed and managed from within higher education with capability for both closed and open broadcast and circulation within a region or statewide when deemed advisable. In times of struggle such as that described in this study, the people of the state should be well served if no more is accomplished than some reductions in higher education's losses. Further, the groundwork might well be laid for critically needed reexamination of the educational status quo and the conventional wisdom, as circumstances change and deep tensions persist. In times of relative calm, educational, cultural, and informational programs directed at the qualitative aspects of life in California could be projected. In times of crisis, a piecemeal, sporadic treatment of issues and events controlled independently of those directly involved—trustees, students, faculty, administrators and parents—is not enough. The avenues to a McLuhanesque, media-sensitive world must be open when needed to those with high stakes in the future of higher education.

In the following chapter, impact of campus disorders, administrative action, and media reporting on public opinion is explored, as citizens' responses to media reports of events grew steadily more intense.

NINE

The Public Reacts

The conflicts at San Francisco State College in which student and faculty dissent were major factors repeatedly drew the chancellor and the trustees into the fray very early in the cycle of each major conflict. This had the effect of inserting the trustees' views of the world and higher education directly into the struggles: views reinforced by angry mail from an increasingly distressed public.

A pattern of chancellor-trustee intervention has been repeated at other California state colleges: at Long Beach in 1968 the struggle was over "pornographic" sculpture, at Fullerton the controversy was over production of a play, *The Beard*. At Fresno State, a controversy over radical theater in 1968 and the proposed hiring of a Black Muslim in 1969 reflected a similar pattern of quick involvement. Sonoma State was caught up in a struggle—in which the dismissal of the college president was seriously discussed—over an elected black student body president with a record of conviction on a drug charge. Within two years five state college presidents resigned during or a few months after such struggles.

The chancellor and trustees through special meetings, executive sessions, and public statements to the mass media—both as a board and as individuals—added fuel to the controversies both by transmitting public and political pressure directly into the decision-making process and by further arousing the public through agitated statements for the media. Amplification of noise and escalation of conflict were the baleful results. Deep concern among trustees is understandable when difficulties on a campus become public. They assume they are discharging a public trust and that trust must reflect their view of the world as appointed agents for the public interest. But their almost convulsive response of grabbing for the steering wheel in every crisis obstructs conflict resolution for three reasons: local leadership is quickly undercut; the locus of solution is removed from the campus and ensnarled in state politics; and trustees' values and sense of prerogatives, rubbed raw by pressures from political figures, media people and aggressive public pressure, become the determining factors in efforts to resolve the conflict. Such direct involvement becomes increasingly disruptive because conventional trustee assumptions in California are increasingly at odds with the directions of movement on campuses. The value conflicts become so serious that every major controversy becomes a test of power. Campuses then end up with arbitrary controls imposed through "executive orders" backed by "all necessary" police assistance.

Earlier chapters set forth the ideology of the radical student reform movement and the ideology of those who have rejected the status quo in favor of revolutionary themes. The purpose of this chapter is to note some of the values from which the majority of trustees view campus disorder and to trace more extensively the deeply felt views of some of the public that are thrust upon trustees, pushing them toward intervention in specific campus controversies.

Hartnett's study[1] of the backgrounds, roles, and attitudes of 5,180 college and university trustees describes a control system for American higher education representative of the elders of one socio-economic class and largely of one ethnic pattern. Cast against the diversity and pluralism represented in large urban institutions, the stuff for conflict is built in. When the preponderant pattern of trustee views is cast against the ideology of the Experimental College, the campus radical activists, or faculty views, a no-man's-land emerges almost devoid of areas of value consensus within which educational disputes can be resolved. Yet California state college trustees, cudgeled by arch-conservatives Max Rafferty and Ronald Reagan, have deviated even further toward political and educational reaction than the norms described by Hartnett for the national sample.

The "typical" trustee was found to be in his fifties, and viewed

[1] R. T. Hartnett, *College and University Trustees: Their Backgrounds, Roles, and Educational Attitudes* (Princeton, N.J.: Educational Testing Service, 1969).

educational problems from an annual income above thirty thousand dollars. He was white (fewer than 2 per cent of the sample were Negro) and came from the upper range of professional and business roles. Over 35 per cent were business executives. Four-fifths were Protestant. While two-thirds of the sampled trustees believed faculty members have a right to free expression, more than a fourth did not and more than half believed a loyalty oath should be required of faculty. Three-fourths of the trustees in the West believed campus speakers should be screened. (Our campus had an open speaker policy for several years.) Although most agree that opportunities for higher education should be expanded, over 90 per cent still saw attendance at their colleges as a privilege, not a right. The notion that higher education is a necessity and a right, so prevalent among young adults, is not acceptable even among two-thirds of junior college trustees sampled.

Half of the trustees who were business executives agreed that running a college is "basically like running a business," although executives from higher levels of business management were less apt to argue that parallel. Increasingly, the alleged dominance of higher education by business and industrial interests is a catalyst for campus struggle. Leftist students and faculty get good mileage from the charge that colleges are not run for the education of students and the broad benefit of the society but as tools of the business and industrial segment of the nation.[2]

Evidence also accumulates that both faculty and students are becoming more insistent—perhaps strident is a better word—in demanding a stronger voice in policy formation, faculty and administrator selection, and program control. The chances for conflict resolution diminish as the value orientations of those who involve themselves in campus conflict reflect wider gaps in assumptions about the rights and powers of contestants to participate in decision making. Hartnett's study reports strong conservative tendencies among regents and trustees, sharpened in California by an arch-conservative state administration and by polarization bred in a running series of confrontations and campus disruptions.

Hartnett found that trustees generally favor a hierarchical system in which decisions are made at the top and passed "down."[3]

[2] See Chapter Three.

[3] In a memo to state college presidents dated September 13, 1968,

About three-fifths of the trustees believed faculty should *not* have major authority in choice of academic deans, awarding of honorary degrees, or faculty leaves. Faculty should have greatest authority in academic affairs dealing with courses offered and admission criteria. Students' authority is judged relevant only in matters of student life, housing, cheating, fraternities, and so on. Trustees generally prefer an arrangement in which faculty and students do not have major authority; neither do trustees want to "rule" by themselves. They expect to be "singularly authoritative" in choosing the president. They expect major decisions to be made by administration alone or by the administration and trustees jointly.

About three-fifths of the trustees viewed themselves as moderates in their personal ideology. Most identify themselves as having views similar to Richard Nixon (62 per cent) and Nelson Rockefeller (68 per cent). *Only one in six* viewed themselves as liberals. The hierarchical, bureaucratic model of college organization and control from the top down conflicts sharply with the continuing drive of faculty during the past decade to share in all aspects of institutional governance. Their growing active rejection of an authoritative bureaucratic model cast against trustee beliefs means a period of conflict in the governance of higher education. The attrition among college presidents speaks to the point. As this study has repeatedly shown, trustees expect college presidents and their administrative staffs to make decisions—*but in a manner consistent with trustee views of higher education.* (Hartnett also concludes that "Trustees do not read . . . indeed, have generally never heard of . . . the more relevant higher education books and journals."[4]) The disparity between the working value norms on campus and those which guide trustees' images of the campus provides the president and administrative staffs with little or no "demilitarized zone" in which to operate as creative, independent forces in today's campus crises in California.

If the conflict between emerging faculty views and the traditional trustees' views poses grave problems, the disparities between trustee and emerging student views have even greater implications. Apart from trustee willingness to support student voices in the area of traditional student activities as mentioned above, Hartnett reports

---

Chancellor Dumke wrote, "There must be no twilight zone of ill-defined authority, responsibility or accountability."

[4] Hartnett, *College and University Trustees,* p. 51.

that the students' potentially significant role in academic and institutional policy hardly appears as a possibility on the fringe of trustee perception. And yet one campus after another across the country has been disrupted or had its programs halted by student protests directed at gaining a major voice in institutional governance. There has been steady movement on a number of campuses recently to bring students actively into the central decision-making process in campus governance. However, most trustees do not accept such practices; those who do accept them do so with serious reservations. Only 3 per cent agreed students should have a share in adding or deleting degree programs. (In 1968 two degree programs, black studies and community services, were approved for San Francisco State by the trustees, both resulting from student impetus.) Only 1 per cent believed students should share in selection of academic deans, establishing admissions criteria, or determining tenure decisions. (At State, students have participated effectively in various ways in each of the above tasks.)

The most aggressive campus rhetoric includes concepts of absolute autonomy for campuses, for departments within a college, and for faculty and students. The refusal of this demand by presidents Smith and Hayakawa deepened the conflicts at San Francisco State.

Such ideas, coupled with "one man, one vote" proposals (including the student and the nonacademic staff votes), represent approaches that are almost totally alien to trustees as viable approaches to campus governance. The college president is viewed as *their* executive agent directly responsible for carrying out their policies. In adversarial situations, the president is expected to hew to the position of the chancellor and the trustees without equivocation. The colleges are caught, in crucial ways, in a growing struggle affecting many American institutions. There is a contest of power within massive organizations in which computer assisted centralized decision making within one value framework is transmitted through bureaucratic channels to thousands of persons—of distinctly different orientations—who are expected to be compliant. At the same time there is a surge toward an existentialist, radical individualism that rejects hierarchy and demands accountability to self rather than to external authority. As such movements surge through institutions built on neat conceptions of hierarchical authority, the differences separating styles of commitment and perception guarantee unremitting conflict. Traditional campus administrative roles are shredded between the two millstones. The internal governance structure and processes of San Francisco State reflected a disorderly mixture of both conceptions at the close of Summerskill's term as president.

Crisis situations on campus widely reported by the mass media tend to highlight the most dramatic rhetoric of students, faculty, administrators, trustees and political figures. Administrators and faculty leaders are caught trying to work with the fluidity of student and faculty movements, many of which are aggressively anti-bureaucratic and appear bizarre enough within the resistant institutional structures supported by administrators and faculty leaders. A patina of trustee judiciousness can easily dissolve in a stark struggle for control. Neurotic distortion of issues and behaviors moves toward generating social pathology and evoking cries of doom. "Our young are threatened by a deadly conspiracy"; "the President is a Fascist pig!"

Polarization in the San Francisco State struggle during spring and fall semesters of 1968 was sharpened by two forces at work in California. Those among the public who were disgusted or frightened by campus disorder acted to bring sharp pressure on the trustees, the president, and other public officials involved; and the self-styled revolutionaries among students, faculty, and community groups moved to destroy the college if they could not control it as a means of forwarding their revolution. The ingenious, aggressive efforts to push the activist students and faculty toward the radical left are described in previous chapters. The impact of mass media reporting and interpretation on campus events and on citizen opinion was explored in the preceding chapter. The remainder of this chapter will describe the patterns of public pressure on college administrators, trustees, and elected officials, pressure that reinforced most heavily the position of the most conservative trustees.

At the same time campus partisans, locked in severe infighting, seemed largely oblivious of citizen response to campus disorder. Efforts by administrators, trustees, or legislators to remind the campus adversaries of growing perplexity, disgust, shock and fear among the public were impatiently brushed aside. Many involved in the campus struggles believed they were attempting to improve the college by trying to force it to respond on their terms. Unsolicited mail addressed to President Smith from individuals and groups outside the college, expressing strong opinions on campus issues, began the week of the opening of the fall semester, 1968, about seven days after the San

Francisco *Examiner* story reported the rehiring of George Murray, a militant black man, as a part-time English instructor.[5] One of the first unsolicited letters set the tone of one pattern of response reiterated in an increasing volume of mail during the next three months.

> I am a businessman, taxpayer and citizen. My wife and I are very upset with the administration of San Francisco State College. It is a disgrace to the community and a haven for hippies and communists. What service or purpose is that nut hut you are running there doing for the community, serious students and this country? My business associates are writing to every member of our Government in protest of the activities of that college.

Another letter expressed concern that the unqualified were achieving power to shape the minds of the next generation and it was the president's responsibility to prevent it.

> I do not believe that these individuals are fit to teach in prison, where they surely ought to be. This country cannot endure if we let our enemies and detractors form the conscience and morals that will guide future generations.

A senior military officer asked by what reasoning the president could justify hiring Murray.

> You are accountable to me, among others, to run your college in a proper manner. "A proper manner" is defined as the way the majority of the citizens want their colleges administered. We don't want traitors teaching our sons.—now that this matter is called to your attention it would be incredible if you didn't realize that merely in your own self interest you cannot allow this man to become a member of your teaching staff—. However, if you feel it is proper to hire these individuals to teach our children, I will use every means I possess to have you fired.

The insistence that Murray be summarily fired on the basis of one newspaper report of his background bluntly bypassed such traditional American virtues as the need to prove malfeasance before judging a man guilty, the legal base of his employment, the right of an employee to due process and an opportunity to answer public charges, and the broad limits of political belief allowed teachers as long as those beliefs are not imposed on students. Membership in the Black Panther party and involvement in the *Gater* beatings seemed to many people evidence enough to justify arbitrary action. In blunt language still another writer refers to a militant instructor as a Black Panther and hater of the United States and says,

[5] See *By Any Means Necessary*, Chapter Seven.

This son-of-a-bitch has no more right to teach at San Francisco State than the president of the Hells Angels or some other radical of the right or left wing. I protest this sad state of affairs at San Francisco State or any educational institution that hires such riff raff! Am hoping that who ever is responsible for this boner will have his ass kicked off the campus.

A person, noting that she was a native-born Californian and a long-time taxpayer, wrote,

I think I have as much right to voice my demands as any one on or off your guerrilla-run campus and in addition I speak for a dead member of my family—giving a good life to the likes of your campus misfits may safely destroy institutions of learning. However, all such permissiveness must end—either by the vast silent public majority who have just about had it, or, God forbid, the *election* of another extremist, such as a Wallace, as an only answer to your extremes.

She respectfully requested dismissal of "this avowed communist." In this first trickle of mail further questions were raised about President Smith. Was he insane? Was he a part of a communist conspiracy? Was he merely a coward? Another letter demanded that all faculty involved in hiring Cleaver and Murray be censured and put on probation for "an incredible lack of judgment." This letter to President Hitch of the University of California, with copies to the governor, the regents and a number of elected officials opened thus:

The subject is Eldridge Cleaver, George Murray, Black Panthers, racism, riots, illegal acts, kidnapping, civil disobedience, drugs, shootings, murder, suicides, police, communists, blackmail, black, white racist pigs, police brutality, baiting police, long hair, dirty faces, hippies, on and on and on, any subject of which exemplifies the qualifications of Cleaver, Murray and the Black Panthers, and which also headlines the activities at the U. C. campus. There is no U. C. headline that infuriated me more than *"Eldrige Cleaver, Black Panther To Teach At UC!"*

He pledged "no" votes on higher education ballot issues until "persons in authority regained their sanity." The process of review of George Murray's appointment and the rationale of President Smith and his staff are described in Chapter Seven of *By Any Means Necessary*. All the groups on campus—student, faculty, and administrators—who stated their position supported retention of Murray and his right to teach in the face of the trustees meeting the last week in September, 1968, and supported as well President Smith's refusal to remove him from the classroom after trustees had voted eight to five to request his reassignment. Faculty organizations, academic departments, and individuals both within and outside of the state colleges wrote resolutions and wired their support for Smith's courage and commitment to academic freedom, due process and to the struggle for campus autonomy and self-determination. In the meantime communications from the public increased. One said,

> Being from the old generation who really sacrificed to make our U.S.A. and now to have people who have never given anything to it but trying to tear it down using our freedom. Free speech is a gimmick to teach everything but what we stand for. One wonders if you are one of the communists representing and teaching in our schools today? . . . It will all end by we real Americans having a "civil war" to end it all. . . . Mr. Smith: Are you crazy or just stupid? *You and Murray* have to go . . . fired!

A memo from the broadcasting arts faculty stated their complete accord with Smith's support of Murray, indicating that that was the only course of integrity for the administration and faculty of the college. They thanked him for his courage, fairness and consistency "in this matter that truly involves us all." More than a trickle of letters from individuals outside the college struck the following note:

> I am *so* proud of you! Please don't *ever* bow to politics in running our public institutions. I would gladly pay taxes upon taxes as long as you and ones like you let your conscience be your guide. Don't weaken! Don't fire Murray!

A minister wrote:

> I know that because of your stand you have opened yourself up to attack. However if our nation is to survive more men must take such risk. . . . to maintain an open and free society.

A professor of anthropology in Southern California wrote, "No matter what comes you have become a rallying point for all those who do not fear Socrates or his descendants."

A citizen from southern California wrote between the trustee meeting "requesting" the removal of Murray from his teaching assignment and President Smith's public announcement that he "declined" to honor this request:

> I commend in the utmost your actions in regard to the case, as I understand it. If a faculty member is performing his job and there is mutual agreement to continue his employment, so this should be. If you were to bow to the current mob calling for his dismissal, the college and all of us would have lost a vital part of

our freedoms—and this must not happen. The thing that the
mobs (and I use this word purposefully) never, never understand
is that freedom taken from one is freedom taken from all. You
are on constitutionally sound ground, Mr. President, and I can
only hope that you realize that there are many more of us who
concur with you. By the way, I am not exactly a radical, having
been a twenty-year Republican until this year!

But at this point in the controversy, an equally strong thrust of the
communications to Smith showed a deep revulsion against action re-
taining Murray as a part-time instructor. One student wrote Reagan
stating that the retention of Murray was unbelievable, referred to
him as a demented idiot, and accused the English department of
political indoctrination and intimidation of students and with obsession
with sex. One writer strongly urged the trustees to relieve Smith of his
duties and to appoint "someone who recognizes that he must be
responsible to the general public as well as the trustees and other
administrative bodies."

    At the trustee meeting that precipitated the request for Murray's
removal, the chancellor of the state college system credited Smith with
a "superhuman" effort in managing the college since his appointment
three months before, but as early as mid-September individuals and
groups had already stated their intent to "get his job." The belief that
a college president is obligated to carry out trustees' wishes to the letter
was stated in various ways. The unquestioning assumption that a
board of trustees always spoke in the general interest of the public
frequently showed through. The notion that a college president, presiding over a campus of twenty thousand persons, must feel a direct
professional obligation to that community—an obligation that tran-
scends alleged public opinion—is not reflected in letters such as this
one addressed to President Smith.

    I feel it my duty to inform you that you are my employe. You
    seem, in your arrogance, to have forgotten the fact that you live
    by exploiting my labor, and I will no longer tolerate such ex-
    ploitation. Along with my fellow taxpayers employed in private
    enterprise, I own San Francisco State and all the other public-
    supported California colleges. My grandparents paid for Cali-
    fornia school system, my parents paid for the system even though
    their children attended private schools, and now I, childless by
    choice, am being forced to pay the costs of other people's chil-
    dren. I did not hire students to officiate at San Francisco State,
    I employed Mr. Dumke, Mr. Meriam and other trustees to do my
    hiring and firing for me. If they cannot hire adequate help to

administer to the needs of a tax supported school, we shall have
to have a complete investigation including efficiency experts who
can keep the costs down and operate the schools in a businesslike
fashion which does not tolerate insolence in any employe.

The next writer became a bit nasty.

After seeing you on the television defying the trustees' orders it
was plain you are another spineless, gutless, and mean-looking
cuss for those who don't believe your way. What's the matter have
the Panthers got your scared? Coward! Better wake up and beat
it. No name so you can't retaliate on my relatives. They are not
black so you wouldn't stand up for them.

The theme of lawless and incompetent citizens gaining the
upper hand through privilege and assistance provided by public
officials was expressed repeatedly.

Now you may say that the real conflict is between you and the
trustees, but I say that the conflict is between the law-abiding
citizens and taxpayers of this city and state and the elements that
are destroying the very foundations of American morality!

The writer requested that Smith examine his conscience under pain
of her determination and that of other taxpayers to withhold further
support for the university and state colleges. She noted she was pro-
testing to Reagan the use of her tax monies for their support. A copy
of a full page letter to then Congressman John Tunney with copies to
other public officials pushes further the thesis of special privilege for
black people, criminals, and poor people, claiming that the taxpayers
have "more legitimate reason to revolt than any other." Referring to
Cleaver and Murray as anarchists and criminals, the writer asks, "What
does that kind of person have to bring to easily misled college persons . . . ? I am sick and tired of all the injustices being forced upon
the American taxpayers in the name of education, help for the poor
(most of whom would not work if they were paid a salary equal to
mine since they can make more on relief without working), and all of
these way out programs for the betterment of conditions in the
ghettoes." The writer asserts that whites are now the ones discriminated
against, that the teeth have been pulled from the law in favor of
rioters, and that Mayor Richard Daley of Chicago has shown us the
way. An excerpt from another letter reported,

One California assemblyman said that the universities and colleges are run by a bunch of intellectual freaks. This I believe. It
is hard to understand how this bunch of intellectual freaks could

ruin a wonderful university and college system in a few short years. I am telling all my friends to vote "no" on Proposition 3.

A professor of social science at a southern California college wrote to the *Los Angeles Times* with copies to several public officials saying that the case of Murray "reveals the kind of dry rot that is eating at the foundations of our social order."

> Liberal ideologues, unscrupulous politicians, and gutless public officials encourage acts of violence by tolerating those that occur, and by trying to rationalize them in terms of alleged "injustices" suffered by the offenders.

Many faculty, students and some administrators have lamented for years the kinds of controls the legislature and the trustees have imposed on the colleges and have crusaded sporadically to fend off aggressive onslaughts from outside the campus. Typical of taxpayers who saw it otherwise is the man who wrote several public officials, including his state senator and assemblyman, "fed up with filth, sedition, and anarchy being promoted under the name of 'academic freedom.' "

> It seems to me that the school administrators have had many, many years to work without interference from the legislature or state administration. This has certainly been academic freedom and what has been done with it? A mess has been made that sickens me. . . . I urge you, Mr. ——— and Mr. ——— to consider immediately legislation that will somehow put the brakes on the runaway trend to anarchy; restrict the absolute free hand of a red-infiltrated faculty; keep outside troublemakers off the campuses. . . . The two latest fiascos, one at San Francisco State and the other at Cal. . . . were the last straw for me. I will not willingly go on paying for this sort of thing.

A man from Southern California informed Smith by postcard, "You are a disgrace to the people of California. . . . I suggest that you go drown yourself."

During the week after the trustees' request that Murray be removed from classroom teaching, the deep distress reported above was balanced by an equal number of statements supporting Smith's refusal to act in a summary way in response to pressure to remove Murray. Those correspondents cited as things to be resisted in the controversy racial bigotry, violation of due process, penalties because of political beliefs, the closing off from students of significant viewpoints, political invasion of decision making in education, and McCarthyite attacks on the Black Panthers. One writer from northern California commended President Smith on his decision to retain Murray and his diplomacy in handling the problem, closing:

> My daughter has lived nineteen and a half years in the comfort-able womb of the WASP establishment. She chose San Francisco State, with my hearty approval, specifically because of the oppor-tunity there to get something more than a spoon-fed predigested education.

Another argued for Murray's retention, although she disliked the Black Panther movement, because the campus was "one of the few places in which a rational dialogue can take place." Another noted "the singular kind of courage that is *unpopular* today" involved in the defense of Murray's teaching assignment. Perhaps the charge of abject cowardice on the one hand and the plaudits for singular courage on the other best demonstrated the potential for polarization among the people of the state over an issue such as a Black Panther's right to teach college students.

Following the chancellor and trustee action requesting Murray's removal from the classroom and President Smith's refusal, Murray responded to the publicity with a series of statements through October that left no doubt of his capacity for violent rhetoric directed at the establishment and officials identified with it. Once caught in the lime-light as a militant black man, Murray gave every evidence of assuming he would be dismissed either through arbitrary action forced on the president or through the more tortuous process of academic due process. Smith's defense of Murray's teaching role was unconvincing. If a militant is to be sacrificed, he feels obligated to make his mark on the way out. As Murray's public statements gained publicity, cor-respondence in support of his right to teach withered. Outraged tax-payer and patriot mail began to build, especially after Murray's speech at Fresno State College on October 24, parallel to a meeting of the trustees on the same campus, thus assuring broad coverage by the news media. Although faculty disciplinary procedures had been in-voked *two weeks earlier,* the process was not paced to cope with the rising anger and fear of some sectors of the public. The result was in-creasing pressure on the college president, the trustees and other state officials. The tone of responses during the last week of October is captured in a letter from Los Angeles including a news report of Murray's Fresno speech.

How can anyone justify employment of this individual by a California state college in ANY capacity? The continued ineffective vacillation by the trustees of the California state colleges and the regents of the University of California is an inexcusable dereliction of duty. Your own stand in refusing to comply with the orders of the trustees in the above matter is offensive to all loyal Americans. How much of this do you think the working citizen-taxpayer can take?

The dilemma of the trustees and regents grew in the Cleaver and Murray cases because, for most, their views opposed condoning the operations of either man on campus, yet they sought to avoid giving flat orders to campus administrators to fire Murray or totally exclude Cleaver from the respective campuses. The trustees also saw a growing threat to the $250,000,000 bond issue scheduled for the November election. Outsiders who saw no link between due processes in handling personnel issues in college employment and judged the stance of President Smith and his colleagues as rank irresponsibility therefore judged the trustees as weak and vacillating. Though campus groups began to express second thoughts as Murray's rhetoric became more militant, their most trenchant statements were directed at trustee interference with what they viewed as an internal campus problem. Smith's mail during the last week of October reflected anger and dismay at the college's willingness to harbor a "traitor" on the faculty and a determination to campaign and vote against the bond issue in the general election a week away. An increase in postcard mail from the Los Angeles area, reiterating similar protests, suggested that opposition to Smith's policies was being solicited. For the most part, the growing volume of daily mail appeared to be rooted in deep feelings of concern of individuals and groups of acquaintances. One short note said, "What a pity men have given their life for this nation, back across the years, and today an educational institution *sponsors* a radical like Murray." The writer did not note that some who gave their lives were acknowledged revolutionaries, now deeply revered. The black-white issue began to surface more sharply:

You should realize by now that you can't placate those minority groups. Their demands never cease and become more ridiculous every day! Close the school if necessary—expel *all* the protesters —get rid of *Murray* and start over. You have a cancer in your midst!

In the face of growing threats of violence and an occasional unexploded bomb discovered on campus, Smith issued a blunt warning to those experimenting with violence. To the critics of the president and the college, this "small evidence" of backbone was worth encouragement. But Murray was suspended November 1 on direct orders from Dumke over Smith's protest. The BSU struck on November 6, the day after the general election, and precipitated enough disorder and threat to prompt Smith to close the campus briefly. A picture of Roger Alvarado, Third World strike leader, was appended to a letter. His full beard, long curly hair and "shades" prompted the writer to label him a disgrace to the students of the college:

> In the first place it is my opinion that no student should be permitted on campus unless his hair is trimmed normally, and there should be none allowed on campus without clean shaven faces. All those who display such hirsute adornments are merely endeavoring to attract attention, in fact, their minds are certainly lacking stability. In all probability they are not college material.

It was hardly an accurate picture of Alvarado, the man and student.

Those who created disturbances were to be dismissed without possibility of reinstatement. Some correspondents, noting the progress of disorder, attributed it to outside political interference in campus matters but more believed it was inevitable without summary expulsion of troublemakers. A few believed President Smith's public questioning of the chancellor-trustee decisions concerning Murray actually sanctioned disorder. The fact that Smith was attempting to follow established personnel procedures while the chancellor chose to set them aside was lost in the clamor on campus and in the news media. One citizen wrote to suggest establishing a university court comprised of students, faculty, and administrators to arbitrate disputes ahead of demonstrations, noting that such disputes wind up in some conference setting *after* disruption.

The fervor of the public response to Murray's behavior was coupled with the BSU-Third World strike for fifteen nonnegotiable demands and the ad hoc strike of some forty faculty demanding Murray's reinstatement. The November 13 Tactical Squad operation involving arrests and beatings moved Smith to suspend classes "indefinitely." Classes resumed the following week. Some supported the action to close the campus to protect safety, or to shake up the students and faculty. More letter writers were angry. One woman (sixtyish) recounted in some detail the hard work and sacrifice the eight children, of whom she was one, submitted to in becoming successful without the luxury of college degrees. She observed that in Smith's photo he looked like an intelligent man "But many of us wonder. . . . Hard work never hurt anyone."

> Why are *you* and many like you bending backwards for the lazy, spoiled, long haired, stupid, dirty kids today? Give the earnest hard-working kids a chance. Please excuse paper—I wanted to write this, because I felt so darn disgusted with the whole college situation. Civil rights, "the establishment"—God help these kooks —they will end up—all on relief that the "establishment" has provided for them. It's a shame Proposition 9 didn't pass. So you must cut enrollment. Well—then take only the qualified, deserving, decent, law-abiding kids. Please excuse the mistakes—remember I didn't have the privilege of a college education.

Some mail reflecting outrage charged: President Smith was capitulating to anarchism; administrators lacked the guts to fight communism; the rights of serious students were being trampled "by a tiny minority"; the college should stay closed "with the faculty and the anarchists off the backs of the taxpayers!" Smith's "well meaning but futile efforts through the normal channels of faculty disciplinary committees were subverted by an irresponsible and exhibitionist faction of the faculty allied with the student militants."

By mid-November, with the BSU-TWLF strike in its second week and the campus closed for the second time, voices of moderation wrote eloquent statements seeking to preserve working room for response to real needs but rejecting the tactics of the most aggressive militants. The faculty began to appeal to President Smith and their colleagues to check the violence while moving quickly to adopt programs where possible. Smith had pushed this approach since the day of his appointment. The Mission Coalition Organization, representing a heavily Mexican-American constituency, rejected the tactics of "a small minority of San Francisco State students or those used by members of the San Francisco Police Department," but stressed their belief that these excesses "should not be used to hide the major issue of the ethnic studies program and the recruitment of minority students and faculty to San Francisco State College." Pleas to restrain the police also were made by others:

> Honest I just saw on television that awful, cruel, bully tactical squad *clubbing* students. It always upsets me so and sure doesn't do my respect for the San Francisco Police . . . any good. Dear

> God! Do we live in Chicago? Why did the tactical police run to
> their prey? They could just walk onto the campus and scare any-
> one to death. Please do all you can to avoid this. You look and
> talk like a kind man. I do wish you and all well there. Look out
> for Reagan and that tactical squad.

Some wrote whose margin of resources was too thin for them to risk
losing a semester of work and hope for a better life.

> I waited for sixteen years for the opportunity to come back to
> school and it is very valuable to me. Only if I get my credential
> and teach can my five children have the higher educational op-
> portunities that they need. I commute sixty miles each day. I
> resent, more than I can ever express in a letter, that I have to
> depend on the radio to tell me if school is open or not. I resent
> even more that when I get there classes are cancelled. I resent an
> atmosphere in which it is impossible to study. Why can't you get
> me (and seventeen thousand other desirous students) back to
> classes? Why can't you put your foot down on that jelly-fished
> faculty and tell them if they want to teach, teach, if not, leave?
> Why don't you tell those spoiled brat, rude, badly reared young
> people that if they don't want an education, to get out? There
> are plenty of other students who do (including black students).
> Why don't you put a steel bar up your backbone and start acting
> like a college president? I know you will think this is pretty high-
> handed of me but I feel it's about time somebody got high-
> handed. The majority's rights are being completely ignored.
> Some students, under the guise of "democracy" have brought the
> democratic process to a complete standstill. You are in charge
> and I beg of you to get this deplorable mess straightened out.

Another letter began: "I am one of the millions in this state, the taxpayers who are sick of anarchist students, idiot teachers, and spineless
administrators. The large majority of lawabiding students should unite
and make their presence felt. Where are the good guys?" Yet another
informed President Smith that his "soft, foolish, irresponsible acts"
were building a civil war in this country. "America will never integrate
peacefully, but it appears there will have to be a civil war to prove it,
and it will be the fault of the leaders and educators, not the common
people!" Racist themes became even more frequent and were stated
more bluntly: "You can take Niggers out of the ghetto, but you can't
take the ghetto out of Niggers!" "Today our colleges and even the
Federal Government is 'blackmailed' into unhappy situations." A
psychiatric nurse applauded closing the campus saying that after forty
years of nursing she believed "the behavior on your campus was more
violent than any violent day room in such a hospital."

Among the many who applauded Smith's action closing the campus were those who thought it would settle down the militants, would avoid a violent catastrophe, and perhaps "bring the faculty and the majority of students to their senses." One person wired the governor and several public officials requesting immediate action to insist Dumke reverse the order to suspend Murray and "let Smith handle the situation." By November 15, letters began to state sharply opposing views. "Dear Dr. Smith: Please don't resign! Hang in there!" and "Please do one remaining public service. Recognize your own incompetence and resign!" The press had already begun raising the question of whether President Smith would resign or be fired. A newspaper account of Reagan's comments reported:

> For a school administrator to deliberately abandon the leadership invested in him by the people of this State—at the expense of the vast majority of students intent on receiving an education—is an unprecedented act of irresponsibility, Reagan said.

Dumke and Trustee Chairman Merriam had initially agreed that Smith's action was necessary. Reagan ordered all campuses of the university and state college system closed following the Kent State killings in May 1970. The same article quoted professor of economics William Stanton as saying disciplinary procedures against Murray meant "They are going to try a black man for a cry of anguish."

One correspondent wrote,

> I *support* your effort and the faculty to make a *reasonable stance* between the right and left, and with the nonsupport of a weak chancellor. You are dealing with long overdue civil rights problems and politicians with superficial understanding and over fondness for demogogery. Our "dear" governor seems to *confuse* education with that approach used in a factory. If our society were not so RACIST there would be no BSU or SDS. I applaud the students *care* but not their *carelessness* even though it's very understandable.

The chief of a metropolitan department of psychiatry wrote to Dumke on November 15, urging him to support Smith and stating his regret that Dumke had acted against Murray. "This adds substance to the legitimate aspects of the grievances that the administration and the faculty were trying to work out together." He believed further interference would only have far worse consequences.

A long letter castigated President Smith for earlier administrators' decisions and named Dumke "the real campus hero." The letter concluded, "You certainly bungled this situation royally right from the beginning. By your demonstrated inability to cope with Murray and his BSU/Black Panther's demands for instant everything, you have sold out the entire campus and given an anti-American racist the upper hand."

Next in the two-inch thick stack of letters on that day was one letter signed by two alumni. "We fully support your principled, level-headed handling of this explosive situation. The principle of academic democracy and faculty control is at stake in this confrontation with Mr. Dumke. . . . The unconscionable police brutality is another instance of police presence *increasing* dissension and exposes the staff, students, and faculty to personal harm." And another: "I want to thank you for your *cool* in handling the disturbances on state college campus. I think you are to be admired for your understanding and compassion as well. . . . P.S. *I dig you!* From a concerned parent."

Then: "I believe college should be opened and if necessary to have national guards there to keep the Negroes in their places. Shoot if necessary." A teacher, alumnus of San Francisco State, after urging severe treatment of troublemakers on campus, wrote: "I also urge you to abandon the benighted, sentimental, and immoral policy by which unqualified students of racial minorities are admitted to the college when thousands of genuinely qualified whites are being turned away." Two experimental groups of such minority students were doing as well or better in achievement than the ordinary run of those admitted under conventional standards. They did require extra resources, increasing the cost per student. Another writer said, "These Negroes never should have been admitted to a white college in the first place. What San Francisco needs is a Negro state college. . . . It has been the communists that have insisted on them mixing and it just hasn't worked and never will." A retired veteran of two wars wrote:

Anent these rabid lawbreakers, uprisings and riots, Rudyard Kipling would appear as right as the Constitution when he wrote: "Whatsoever for any cause,/Seeketh to take or give/Power above and beyond the laws,/Suffer it not to live!/Holy State, or Holy King/or Holy Peoples Will/Have no truck with the senseless thing/*Order the guns and kill!*" If Americans fail to heed Kipling's words, we stand to lose our homes and heritage. Encouraged by "liberals" . . . plus Washington's weakling stand . . . America's black primates have waxed ever-more vicious and kill-hungry. Anthropoids of their ilk will fear and obey one thing FORCE, in the form of Hot Lead. Mow them down without

mercy. . . . Carpet the streets with their dead. . . . And the
remainder will become "good niggers." Law and order must hold
. . . whatsoever the cost . . . if our nation shall survive.

The above letter was written the day Smith attended a special trustee
meeting in Los Angeles at which he was directed not to negotiate with
the strikers, except through "normal channels," and to open the campus immediately—whatever the cost. (He had previously announced
resumption of classes on a designated date.) Another letter said:

> As a taxpayer—as a part owner of your institution, I would like
> to ask you President Smith, where do you get the nerve to shut
> out of classes approximately sixteen thousand good and true stu-
> dents because you are too yellow to bring in sufficient police
> forces to put down a revolt by several hundred communists, radi-
> cals, rats, pigs, and swine who have no right to even be on your
> campus—pardon me, *my* campus? President Smith—it is only
> a few days after the defeat of Proposition 3. DON'T YOU
> PEOPLE GET THE MESSAGE YET? Just what do we, *the
> people you work for* have to do to get some backbone into you of
> the chicken-livered set? Throw those disruptive bastards out of
> school and off the campus. Forget about negotiating with them—
> they're smarter than you are! Get rid of them completely, even
> if you have to declare martial law and station a permanent police
> garrison *on campus*. I have three children coming up and before
> they get into this mess I want it cleaned up. I demand law and
> order on your campus and I demand that you keep it open.
> Do you hear this? I'll repeat it—as a voter and a taxpayer I
> DEMAND THAT YOU ENFORCE LAW AND ORDER and
> KEEP YOUR CLASSES OPEN. If you have to kill several hun-
> dred useless red bastards to do it then kill them! There are
> several million other people watching how you are going to be-
> have in the days to come—watching to see whether or not you
> have any guts.

Ironically, this cry of rage and demand for counteraggression came
from an address on *Warbler Lane!* An attorney, father of a student at
State, reported himself "infuriated" by the situation. He sharply raised
the issues of the proper definition of an educational institution and the
use of force as a routine matter, sending copies of his blunt statement
to the governor, Rafferty, and Dumke.

> I wish to remind you of certain basic facts which in my opinion
> have become obscured, if not completely lost sight of in the cur-
> rent struggle. San Francisco State is, or is supposed to be an edu-
> cational institution. It's sole reason for existence is the education
> of its students through its instructors and facilities, and this is its
> primary function. It is not an experiment in school living or so-

cial democracy designed to test social revolutionary concepts or changes in the body politic. It is not a political football for any cult, creed or sect, regardless of color, or idea, but is supposed to provide education in all subjects at college level. Anything that interferes with this prime function, to the extent of lessening its purpose, or completely nullifying its educational mission is wrong and dangerous to the college, as well as to the entire higher educational system, and should be met, challenged and confronted by any means necessary. . . . May I also remind you that as President of this college, the actions, decisions and solutions are finally and ultimately your responsibility, and no amount of hemming and hawing, and passing of the buck to the regents, trustees, faculty and students can disguise the fact that it is your college and your job to keep it operational as an educational institution, and if force is a necessary ingredient to the solution, it should be applied firmly, in the proper amount, to preserve the prime function of your college, without regard to the maudlin, sob sister approach to the use of force which is so prevalent in the educational society. The BSU has closed down your college with threats, violence and intimidation. What do you propose to do about it?

By November 18, twelve days into the student strike, mail to Smith concerning the campus problems reached as many as seventy communications a day.

The startling fact reported elsewhere in this study that onefourth to one-third of the students at San Francisco State acknowledge force and coercion as acceptable means for pushing policy and program changes becomes less surprising as one reviews the proposals for solution that welled up from a large sector of the public during the disorders. Twin themes of rage at the interruption of the education of "well-behaved students" by "uppity blacks" and "long hairs" and charges that restraint in the use of counterforce meant gutlessness suggested that violence had deep roots in the California culture and explained the honest acceptance by some students of violence as a means.

During the week of November 20–26, classes were resumed with a parallel convocation where discussion focused on the "fifteen nonnegotiable demands." The discussions were broken off by the BSU-TWLF on Thursday and violence revisited the campus. On Friday afternoon classes were dismissed in favor of faculty-student department meetings and a late afternoon faculty meeting. A new convocation was called for Monday through Wednesday. Smith resigned November 25, and newly appointed Acting President Hayakawa closed the campus Wednesday until after the Thanksgiving holidays. The mail during Smith's final week opened up few new issues. It was approximately balanced between those who blamed the administration and faculty for the disorder, for permissiveness and gutlessness on the one hand, and those who rushed support to Smith for his wise, courageous, and level-headed efforts to manage the crisis. The convocation brought Smith more strong expressions of support from students, as well as a few trenchant demands from others that the "talkfest" be knocked off so their education could be resumed. The polarization appeared sharper between those who demanded law and order by any necessary means and those who were willing to seek a return to order through minimum use of police, continuing discussion of the issues and a search for conciliation. Aggression against the striking minority students became more harshly stated.

> It took many, many thousands of years for the white race to reach its present state of civilization. Cannibalistic people do not become civilized in the short span of three hundred years. The actions of American Negroes plainly show that—although they dress like white people—they still are savages. Please help spread this message.

The open circuit televised convocation on November 25 and 26 brought statements of sympathy and admiration for Smith's restraint as well as new charges of letting the public down by absorbing abuse from black and Third World students in his role representing all of the people.

Mail continued in a diminished flow following public announcement of Smith's resignation. With few exceptions, communications expressed sympathy for him and his family, thanks for the battle fought, appreciation of the values for which Smith stood, and dismay at the impending probable destruction of the college. Enough fervent, hostile expressions of condemnation, combined with relief at Smith's resignation, were included in the mail to dampen any runaway tendencies of the ex-president to develop a swelled head. It is doubtless true that more proponents of counterviolence as a stand-in for courage were already swelling the sacks full of mail to Acting President Hayakawa. A comparable analysis of Hayakawa's mail has not been attempted in this study. The massiveness of the task precluded it, as did the authors' sense of propriety in not requesting access to that mail. All public reports indicate a massive outpouring of telegrams, letters, and other kinds of communication overwhelmingly in support of the "hard line, no nonsense" approach of the "gutsy" professor suddenly turned dragon slayer. His dramatic countercharge into the ranks of the dissidents with a paramilitary task force drew statewide and national applause. The lightning campaign did end the strikes three and a half months later with a student body, a faculty and a state more sharply polarized than they were when Smith resigned. There can be little doubt, however, on the basis of the data reviewed in this and the preceding two chapters that such polarization was well under way, if not critically so, before Hayakawa faced a situation of severe disorder on extremely short notice.

During the fall, President Smith's unsolicited mail ran approximately one-half sharply critical to abusive, about one-sixth analytical and nonpartisan, and about one-third supportive to laudatory. Multiple signature or petition-type communications were counted as one. Those who stated the strongest, negative views of campus disorders and administrators' efforts in the crises more frequently asserted that "all with whom I have talked feel as I do." Many believed it possible to bring quick peace to the campus by dealing summarily with disruptors, and that permanent peace could be achieved by restricting admission to students who would abide by the rules and concentrate on serious study. One correspondent wrote, "Get this straight! *Students* do not demand! If anything, they plead, from a *kneeling position!* Resign yourself to this—or resign, yourself!"

It was noted earlier that correspondence received by ex-President Smith following his resignation was largely but not exclusively supportive of his policies. The following letters quoted in full, and similar communications, seem significant for the flat contradictions in perception they reflect as citizens view the same situation and personnel.

> As a member of the student body of San Francisco State College, I would like to express the admiration and respect which I hold for you as the president of this institution. I feel, as I am sure a great many students and members of the community do, that during the past weeks of crisis upon the campus, you have shown yourself to be a sincere, competent, and courageous administrator. I want to thank you for being present at the convocation (instead of down at Los Angeles), for your mere presence has indicated to many your deep sense of obligation and love for this college. When I see the horribly uncivil and disrespectful abuse, which has constantly been hammered at you, I feel the deep hurt which

you and your family must now be feeling. I respect you for the
patience and emotional restraint which you have shown toward
those people who have only brought about a disservice to their
cause and to their race by means of their behavior. Most of all,
President Smith, I admire you for being able to keep your sense
of humor in the midst of the surrounding pressures. I see in the
future a hope for saving our college from destruction; and this
hope shall become a reality because of the great faith so many
of us have in you and in your sincere concern for us. No matter
what arises in the next few days, I shall respect your decisions,
which, as I have seen in the past, can only reflect your desire for
justice and unity upon our campus.

From the campus,

As a graduate student at SFSC I have been a close and concerned observer of your efforts throughout the current crisis. I
have only admiration for your sincerity and dedication to your
task, and your obviously deep commitment to restoring the viabil-
ity of the college. It is with regret that I—and many others—see
you vacate your administrative post, and I would like to convey
my appreciation for all that you've done at this time.

And from southern California,

I should like to inform you that your handling of the crisis on
San Francisco campus was outstanding. You always projected on
television your willingness, your concern for *everyone's* welfare
and the fact that there isn't anyone up there that could have nor
would have done a better job than you did. . . . I'm very upset
that you were forced to resign from your position. My husband
and I have had our ups and downs when dealing with stupid
people . . . unfortunately there are just too damn many of them
in high places. We are blacks and this letter leaves a lot unsaid.
. . . Most of all I wanted to tell you we're concerned about you
and your welfare and that we really CARE!! Please remember
that there's no doubt in most of our minds that you were and
are right! Thank you for a fight well fought!. . . . You are on
the winning team.

A letter from southern California, dated January 8, 1969 (written on
executive stationery of a business firm carrying the signer's letterhead),
read:

If I didn't express my utter contempt for you I would be remiss
in my responsibilities as a citizen. The people of the state have
your abject cowardice to thank for the anarchy current at San
Francisco State College. Your lack of backbone and patriotism
are largely at the root of all of the rottenness and depravity with
which the foregoing division of the state university system, and
some of the other branches, are infected. You appear to represent

that class of scum which has gained a foothold in California's educational system to the vast detriment of it, society, law-and order
and decency. If you had any pride or sense of honor you would
have left the state when you were relieved as head of the school.
But, such action is probably too much to expect of one as yellow
and spineless. Why don't you make at least one gesture in the
right direction and get out of California?

On March 25, 1969, the following graffiti from a men's room in the
Education Building:

Actung Niggers! This is *White Man's* country. If you don't like
the way it's run *GET OUT!!* Or, better still, try to change it by
fighting us. I just hope you try. But you won't—no your lousy
kind won't attack unless you have at least 10-1 advantage.
SPONGE. SPONGE strikes again. *Society* for the *Prevention* of
Niggers Getting Everything.

With the immediate shift to Hayakawa, the hardliners had
their way. As the strikes dragged on, literally millions of dollars of
community and state funds were diverted from their intended purpose
to strike-related activities. Most classes that continued to meet turned
to strike-related discussions, and the jails and courts were clogged. On
February 20, approximately three months after Smith's resignation
and Hayakawa's appointment, and before the strikes had been terminated, Theodore Merriam, chairman of the California State College
Trustees, sent each faculty member in the state college system thirty-
nine letters received by trustees and state college officials. They were
reportedly representative of approximately 186,000 written communications received concerning campus disturbances. Also included in the
mailing were brief summaries of twenty-five of "the numerous punitive
bills now pouring into committees of the Legislature." The letters span
the period from mid-October through January, covering the period
of heaviest mail during Smith's last weeks in office as well as the
period of a massive flood of mail marking Hayakawa's first months in
office. The sample of letters was distributed to faculty "at private
expense" (unidentified) because "the trustees feel strongly that all
faculty members should be aware of the public hostility that is being
generated by campus disturbances." The sentences advocating arbitrary action against dissenting or disrupting students and faculty were
neatly underlined. Only one of the thirty-nine letters was critical of
the trustees, and it was from a San Francisco State student criticizing
the governor for refusal to assist the college in the solution of its prob-

lems. Merriam wrote, "More than 98 per cent of the communications support the stand taken by the trustees, Governor Reagan, Chancellor Dumke, and Presidents Blomgren and Hayakawa." (A number of black students had been indicted on felony charges of kidnapping at San Fernando State College, Blomgren's campus.)

Disparities in value norms and frames of reference among various campus groups, trustees, and sectors of the public are becoming so great that there are few core values related to higher education acceptable to all power groups, traditional and emerging. The strongest impact from an aroused public during campus disorders appears to be the further reinforcement of the most conservative trustees and the proponents of quick suppression. Equally critical is the growing need of disparate groups, including recently emerging groups, to deny the legitimacy of power and authority held or aspired to by all other groups. College administrative officers work nervously in this increasingly hazardous no-man's land as conflicting groups drive each other even further toward polar positions. It seems certain that new ways must be invented for the successful sharing of power in a common enterprise.

Daniel Ritter, successor of Theodore Merriam as chairman of the trustees, spoke about the problem of leadership to the California Conference on Higher Education held, perhaps appropriately, at the Disneyland Hotel in December 1969. Ritter believes leadership is as critical to higher education as recruiting and keeping good faculty. "The problem I'm referring to is the shortage of good administrators. Without top-flight deans and presidents, our institutions don't even have a fighting chance to survive the turmoil from within and the attacks from without." He cited a reported two hundred vacancies among college and university presidencies. Ritter quoted testimony before a congressional committee that "there are hundreds of deanships and college presidencies going begging because no one wants to stand up in a shooting gallery." He continued, "Yet some administrators have gone out of their way to put themselves there through either a lack of understanding of public reaction or a lack of concern for it." Ritter did not acknowledge a third possibility, that of a professional view of his administrative role within which a president believes he must work even if it means standing up in the gallery.

The sixth state college president in less than two years had recently resigned, all but one caught in the squeeze of chancellor-trustee directives for specific administrative action on the one hand and campus rebellion on the other. Trustees had responded in ways consistent with the stated anger and fear among the public illustrated in this chapter. The syndrome of trustee perceptions summarized by Hartnett has been driven further toward sharp conservatism by the real challenges from the radical left and radical movements among ethnic minorities. Ritter, whom we believe to be a serious, well-intentioned trustee, seemed unaware that he and many of his trustee colleagues were among the most deadly gunners in the shooting gallery of higher education when campus crises generated by student or faculty dissent splashed into the metropolitan news. It is increasingly apparent that college presidents who have not learned to administer campuses from a prone position are being shot down among the accumulating ideological debris piling up in California higher education. It is a time of serious struggle. Elbow room for an independent professional role in college administration so basic to moderating conflict and projecting long-range goals has all but disappeared. The crucial traditional functions of trustees as buffers between colleges and public passions has been increasingly anemic, in some instances nonexistent, when political and social turmoil spills onto the campuses. We have noted elsewhere the failures at San Francisco State among students, faculty, and administrators to manage with elan the urban and academic revolution as well as the strident dissent against national policies related to the war in Vietnam, poverty, racism, and limitation of educational opportunity.

The governance of higher education as a social and political problem is one of high national and international priority. Colleges and universities at the apex of educational systems are increasingly important as potentially creative centers during a time of rapid social change and sharpened conflict. It is doubtful if even the contestants can afford to have these institutions knocked out of action. This study traces the destruction, for the time being, of many of the morale building, innovative functions of one college. That destruction was accomplished in the best brawling tradition of the old West translated into a modern setting: the city streets, the campus, the trustee headquarters as command bunker, the state house, the news media and the letter writers as onlookers.

TEN

Unfinished Agenda

This volume was written with the basic assumption that San Francisco State College experienced in the years 1966–1969—especially during 1968–69—a convergence of forces and value conflicts that promise to be endemic to large urban campuses during the next decade. We believe that a delineation and analysis of the issues and experiences etched in that period of duress will be of value to others concerned with higher education, be they administrators, faculty, students, lay board members, legislators, governors, media executives, police personnel, or concerned parents and citizens, as they gird for troubled times on other campuses.

An earlier volume traced in detail the rush of events and the conflict among power groups that disrupted our college during the administrations of John Summerskill and Robert Smith and the year of S. I. Hayakawa's acting presidency. This volume has concentrated on selected issues and conflicts shaping the cycle of crises that we believe have grave implications for higher education in metropolitan areas. We have tried to abstract from the welter of events possible learnings for those responsible for governing and supporting our colleges at this critical juncture in their history. In this final chapter we present a summary statement about the status of the college in the context of California higher education in two years after the upheaval; recommendations; conclusions of broader applicability to American higher education; and analyses and proposals we think would strengthen institutions of higher education while making them more responsive to young people and more responsible within society.

We agree among ourselves that the upheavals of thought, perception and circumstance of the past decade run deep enough to cast doubt on self-appointed prophets. We also believe we have revealed enough of our own value frameworks, and have presented enough data and analysis, to make clear the bases of our summary and recommendations. Despite the contingent nature of our times and of the future, we think that what we offer here is more promising than random chance or common sense.

San Francisco State, a large urban college, cherished the rhetoric of democracy, individual freedom, human values, and community consensus. Closing out two decades of surging growth in the face of severely limited resources, during 1966–1969 the college was caught in the urban revolution, the black and ethnic rebellion, and the antiwar movement. These pressures coalesced at a time when authority and responsibility on campus were dispersed and fragmented, when college leaders were insecure and mostly new in their jobs, and when a hostile chancellor and a conservative board of trustees were shifting toward the ultraconservative right under sharp pressure from Reagan.

The short-lived efforts of Summerskill to give substance to the liberal rhetoric and mood of the college in its programs foundered in the crush of conflicting forces of rebellion and reaction. Smith's intense six-month effort to restore stability and thrust never got off the ground. Support of the board of trustees had been withdrawn and the fragmented faculty and student body were in disarray when Smith resigned and was succeeded by Hayakawa. Most of the problems inherited by Summerskill had deepened during his two-year term and were passed on to Smith and then to Hayakawa, although by then more experience and stability had developed at the vice-presidents' and deans' levels. Smith had insisted, even during crises, on broad consultation, public discussion of issues, and minimum police support. These policies were discarded by Acting President Hayakawa. During four months of struggle, he crushed the disorders with heavy police action and legal sanctions, and, using the mass media to separate enemies from friends, built public support for his efforts.

The administrations of Summerskill and Smith left legacies of very severe frustration, polarization, bitterness, and bad morale. These conditions have become more acute under Hayakawa, and pervade the institution three years after the end of the strike. The authors see little resurgence of the institution's long cherished tempestuous vitality and venturesomeness.

Open conflict among faculty and between faculty and students has successfully stymied program development. Efforts to avoid severe conflict results in absenteeism from staff and committee meetings. Program planning has come to a standstill. Units almost in the college that did forge ahead to meet demands for change and new services were blocked by the retaliatory budget for 1970–1971, as passed by the legislature and signed by the governor. That budget funds no newly proposed programs, increases the already heavy faculty teaching load, and reduces research and faculty leaves. College and university professors alone among state employees received no salary increase in fiscal 1971 in the face of continuing inflation and a deteriorating position of the California system in relation to other state higher education systems.

In 1968 failure to gain increased funds needed to finance overcommitments and unmet needs helped precipitate the cycle of campus disorder. The gap between current need and available resources has grown in the intervening two years. Public and legislative support for higher education has been eroded by continuing campus disorders in the state, and attacks on administrators, faculty, and dissenting students have continued to undermine public confidence in the colleges. Reagan has led the assault. In present circumstances there is little chance of boosting San Francisco State College back into the front rank of the nation's colleges. The regressive educational policies of the state administration preclude that. The polarizations within the faculty preclude it. The active rejection of Hayakawa as an educational leader by major segments of faculty, administrators, and students precludes it. The student government and faculty organizations, including the Academic Senate, were smashed during Hayakawa's early months as acting president and have been eliminated as centers of initiative and creativity; they remain impotent. All the full-time faculty in black studies were dropped at the end of the 1969–1970 academic year. The black director of the educational opportunity program was also dropped, wiping out the last of seven black and Chicano administrators hired during the Summerskill and Smith administrations.

Monthly meetings of the trustees and the regents bring a steady progression of rules, regulations, and actions taken independently of recommendations arising from the campuses. The college continues to turn away thousands of qualified applicants. Perhaps symbolic of the developing autocracy, the last conference rooms in the administration building have been converted to office use—appropriately, the once heavily used president's conference room has become the headquarters for the public information office.

The college, aspiring in the mid-sixties to a broadening role in easing the educational and social stresses of the community and society, itself became an arena of conflict and a target of groups contending for power in the social and political upheavals of the late sixties. Yet the hard facts are that the needs of California and the Bay Area for higher education continue to grow. San Francisco State College is not alone in its loss of initiative and its retrogression, but its plight may be as acute as that of any college or university in California. Increasingly, the institutions of higher education are being forced back onto themselves and forced to defend themselves in the face of a cacophony of critics, many making incompatible demands. The precedent shattering struggle is in reality not ended. This complicates the problem of achieving perspective and balance in attempting a summary and recommendations. The sense of paradox and dilemma is strong.

The college must be a major source of expertise and creativity in an explosive, conflict-ridden time. The fundamental institutions of the nation must not ignore the crises that threaten to destroy the college and the society. Yet to some, the college as an institution must pose as a neutral in convulsive social conflicts, lest it come under incessant political attack because of its posture toward issues with political potential. Others assert that neutrality lends de facto support to the status quo, and aspects of the status quo threaten our lives and the future: environmental pollution, racial conflict, war, the collapse of the cities, and the rise of totalitarian movements committed to violence. Great pressures are exerted to force the college to retrench, to withdraw from areas of social needs and conflict, to return to a more objective stance, to avoid moral and ideological controversy and commitment: in short, to become less directly relevant to the problems of life around them. This runs counter to the stubborn perception of growing numbers of students and faculty who are convinced that every ounce of an institution's energy and intelligence should be invested in improving the qualitative aspects of life. The argument came to a head in the spring and summer of 1970, following the invasion of Cambodia and the Kent State and Jackson State student killings. The widespread reconstitution of classes on many campuses—to free students and faculty to study and act directly on the issues through political action projected toward the fall general elections of 1970—placed the issue of the role of higher education in relation to public policy and social conflict and change bleakly in the open.

It is the in thing to call for drastic reform in higher education both in curriculum and in the teaching-learning process. One archconservative trustee, Dudley Swim, resonates to the cries of campus radicals who demand relevance in the curriculum as a condition for peace on campus. Swim joins the attack on stultifying teaching and learning. Yet he is adamantly opposed to the objectives of the left. Even the silent majority break silence and join the chorus of criticism. But while critics with divergent views lustily join the attack, they want drastically different reforms. The chapters describing the rise and fall of the Experimental College and the traumas that grew around the drive for black and ethnic studies lead back by another route into the paradoxes and dilemmas suggested above. The thrust of such innovations distressed some trustees and faculty more than the allegedly sterile courses the programs were designed to replace. Much of the content of conventional college instruction engages only the marginal attention and commitment of students because it deals only vicariously with the world. The curricula of the media, the streets, the political arenas, the counter cultures, and current social problems are more vivid and demanding of the whole person. Such involvements can raise in a real way the toughest intellectual, ethnical, moral, and economic problems that face the individual and the society. They reveal the major failures of the society, its skewed priorities, and the seeming indifferences of its leadership—which are deeply alienating to the energetic and idealistic young, especially those responsibly engaged in assisting the poor, the ill, the uneducated, or those suffering discrimination. Distress evolves from student and faculty powerlessness to effect basic or lasting changes, and this radicalizing process impels people to novel patterns of action in the face of torpid institutions content with other priorities.

Change is hampered by power groups of diverging perspectives increasingly capable of checkmating others. The trustees and many critical of the colleges assume that colleges are maintained as a service to society and that trustees serve the electorate and those who provide basic financial support. In this view, faculty are hired to do the trustees' bidding. Students are extended the privilege of attendance on the institutions' terms as to qualifications, programs of study, campus conduct, and expected levels of achievement. On the other hand, faculty insist that they alone are competent to design programs, set qualifications, and evaluate students and colleagues. They want to be independent professionals, well paid by the public, on a guaranteed career basis. Increasingly students demand freedom from restraints, a major voice in institutional policy, the right to select or reject course content and instructors, and the right to self-evaluation. During the decade of the sixties students became a third source of power, upsetting the nervous balance between trustees and their executives and faculties.

As racial and ideological themes become more overt in the struggles for control in higher education, contending groups multiply and share fewer and fewer values in common. Administrators are badgered by each Balkanized group to commit themselves unconditionally to one or another of the positions advocated. They must follow trustee orders to the letter. They must go down fighting in behalf of faculty autonomy or student demands. They are held accountable on all sides—especially by chancellor and trustees—for every provocative event that adversely affects one of the several contending groups. College and university presidents have become prime scapegoats when social conflict invades the campus and expectations diverge among and between politicians, students, trustees, and faculty.

The president's first obligation, beyond that of maintaining his own integrity, must be to his role as educator. His basic obligations are to his students, to the faculty and staff, and to the welfare of the college as he perceives it both in the immediate crisis and in the long view. He must resist the hysteria implicit in the cry "all power to the people," whether it comes from the throat of a reactionary trustee who purports to speak for all the people of the state, a governor with his latest opinion poll in his pocket, a spokesman for an aggressive faculty, a black militant, or a white revolutionary. When forced toward adversarial roles, presidents, administrators, and faculty leaders must take their stands in relation to specific issues—not in wholesale support of or opposition to one power group. A president who cannot speak and act forthrightly in the best interests of the college and the people who are directly served by the college is worse than no president. A major

responsibility of a board of trustees is to encourage the president to
speak and act forthrightly and to weigh his views carefully. Publicly
reported flaunting of a president's recommendations or reversal of his
decisions by the trustees destroys his effectiveness as president. This is
especially true in times of crisis in which the president and his advisers
function in the glare of the media cameras and adversaries seek to
erode his position as a part of the struggle for power.

In the sixties California missed a historic opportunity to engage
its most talented and socially concerned young adults in improving the
deteriorating quality of life in the state. The colleges and universities
were the potential instruments. The political and lay educational
leadership of the state preferred to nurture a taxpayers' revolt, a scaling
down of commitments to higher education, an assault on college
officials and faculty, and suppression of student rebellions by all
necessary force. As student and faculty provocateurs deftly invited
retaliation against the college, many in the college and community
missed the urgent sense of the time—and joined one or another wolf
pack or withdrew from the conflicts. As a result of these failures across
a broad front, higher education in California begins the decade of the
seventies plagued by patterns of suspicion, fear, rage, retaliation, arbitrary decisions, isolation of individuals, and character assassination.
The well of higher education is badly polluted: it may in fact be
poisoned by the garbage from self-indulgent groups of limited perspective and vast capacity for hostility. Added to the malaise that pervades
higher education in California is an undertow of continuing disorder
at San Francisco State. It is not well described in this study because
limited emphasis has been placed on the aftermath of the 1968–1969
struggles.

The polarization within working staff groups blocks decision
making, from the redefinition of grading policies to the appointment
of deans. Inaction, or arbitrary decisions violating agreed upon procedures, are the result. Students and faculty and administrators are
subject to a web of caprice, not all of it intended. A faculty member
tries for months to determine the reason for her dismissal and, discouraged, tries with little more success to energize the grievance
machinery. A student persists for six months to gain a decisive review
of a questionable grade. Another student suddenly smashes his fist
through a glass partition because he is defeated in efforts to clear up
a mistake in his transcript of academic credits. Some of the writers' col-

leagues in both the state college and the university systems of California are estimating that little of creative importance will happen in California higher education for at least five years to a decade. Thus has the sense of urgency of the sixties been throttled. The California Master Plan for Higher Education is dead. It is time that fact is noticed. The university regents and the state college trustees have clearly demonstrated their incapacity to govern in ways that gain the confidence of the public, the legislature, faculty, or students. Faculty, in the areas of their discretion, and campus presidents and chancellors have done little better. Local campuses, caught in crisis and controversy, desperately needing flexibility and immediate authority, are trapped. Existing patterns of absentee management, systemwide norms, and rigid positions are seized upon by politically vulnerable elected state officials and used to tighten their control.

Governance of higher education under the Master Plan was designed to work from the top down. The upheavals on the campuses have greatly intensified centralization. But the Master Plan has been carried into an era of growing insistence that authority be built from the ground up, from the students, faculty, and community to state-level coordination. The trustees and the chancellor issue one call after another to students and faculty for compliance, for assumption of responsibility, and for acceptance of authority. Yet in instance after instance the trustees themselves behave in a "lawless" way, violating established practice and existing agreements while becoming more arbitrary and restrictive in their approach to campus problems. One can argue that acts such as those described above are no more than questionable practices within a potentially excellent framework sanctioned by the people of the state. But this is to miss the accumulated evidence of the past decade. Faculty continue to serve under a chancellor whose leadership has been repudiated by 65 per cent of faculty on the state campuses. Student representatives are even more disenchanted. Hayakawa was appointed first as acting president and later as president in violation of consultation processes jointly agreed upon and in operation. An appointment of a school dean by Hayakawa was made in violation of the process of selection when the faculty committee and the president found themselves in disagreement. In such circumstances, calls to duty and for assumption of responsibility become empty exhortation. Worse, they evoke a contradictory reaction. Some thoughtful people conclude that responsibility requires not submission to authority but *"obstruction* and if possible *destruction* of the system." How else can we interpret the statement of an administrator-faculty member of a school who concludes that the situation in the college is so contrived that only a "self-destruct" approach to one's college role can be justified? That statement made before a campus audience drew expressions of approval and was not challenged.

Insights

But we cannot let the matter rest at that point lest we further jeopardize the future of the young and of the society. Below are major insights—derived from the San Francisco experience—that we think are relevant beyond San Francisco State College. Some of these conclusions are merely brief repetitions of statements made eleswhere; others represent views and interpretations not previously recorded.

Colleges in a disturbed society, unsure of their leadership and role, are fragile institutions ideally suited for revolutionary activities. A mass constituency is available; containment of guerrilla assaults is extremely difficult and the struggle to do so is apt to magnify radical support. The liberal ethos resists repression or discipline; and the concept of academic freedom can be distorted in a confused climate to tolerate revolutionary license.

Once a campus is embroiled in acute crisis, initiative for the institutional response to this conflict rests with the college executives. Faculty can create appropriate policies in stable periods, but they cannot administer a campus in ferment.

Vacillating leadership by a college president—despite the most admirable of motives—serves to reinforce militant student power, invite public and political intervention, undercut administrative authority, and provide an unsatisfactory solution. Parties involved in intergroup campus conflicts tend to see mediation as vacillation.

In the short term, a hard line can pacify a major rebellion on campus by resort to massive police presence and intermittent use of force; by reliance on arrests and criminal prosecution of large numbers of those in rebellion be they students, faculty, or other citizens; by injunctive processes; by tight control of student funds; by abrupt suspensions and dismissals; by minimum compromise with demands.

If a rebellion is crushed, then determined, postrebellion efforts must be launched to alleviate the causes or revolt will continue.

Educators can gain the powers and public support necessary to repress campus rebellion by using promotional techniques and the mass media in ways well tested in selling deodorants, cigarettes, and political candidates.

On occasion there appears to be no administrative alternative to using police to contain destructive confrontations on campus. Use of the police increasingly swings students to the left.

Despite energetic administrative efforts to maintain police liaison before and during confrontations, once police from jurisdictions beyond the college campus are brought on a campus to contain student disruptions, ultimate power rests with the police—yet the president is held responsible.

Radical student protests can frequently exploit: administrative counter-responses under pressure; faculty-administrative friction; and administrative overinvolvement in containment, which leaves the college exposed in other basic areas.

Faculty are loath to be critical of student excesses or to defend their own conceptualizations, institution and colleagues from radical student attack. The most trenchant contradictions of current academic assumptions launched from political and ideological stances tend to be ignored as the faculty pursues business as usual.

Faculty have yet to learn how to maintain a balance between protecting the institution, protecting the climate for liberal learning, and protecting themselves from both hostile external forces and destructive internal forces. All too often in the past the focus has been upon the outside enemy.

In the current academic and political climate, a faculty strike will fail unless a heavy majority of the faculty supports strike action and is willing to endure major career and financial risks.

The basic faculty responses to traumatic strike and poststrike conditions are apt to be withdrawal, polarization, and impotency.

Student government, as practiced even at enlightened institutions in the recent past, is not a viable organization that can satisfy emerging student demands for control of their own lives. Inevitably it seems to encompass a basic subordinate status and an attitude of benevolent paternalism on the part of faculty and administration.

Student influence on the educational operation of the college can have its greatest impact at the departmental level. Because faculty values are vested at the departmental level, student involvement in academic governance also will obtain its greatest resistance at this level.

The student movement for liberal educational reform is apt to run afoul of radical student hostility and faculty and administrative lethargy in instituting desirable reforms suggested by the students; deficiencies within the student movement in developing a broad, continuous base of involvement and control; and active administrative or trustee opposition.

College operations and college teaching are, and have been, essentially authoritarian. The modern student will no longer endure this disparity between national democratic principles and actual educational practice.

Neither the faculty, the administrators, the public, nor the legislature has yet faced up to the reality that, if student constituencies for urban colleges were even proximate reflections of ethnic urban distributions, many state colleges and universities would (and should) have dominant ethnic populations of color.

Traditional college practices, teaching, and curricula speak with little cogency to the militant concerns of black and Third World students. On the other hand, some of these same militant imperatives violate many fundamental academic principles.

It seems likely that: any radical student venture involving both ethnic and white students will be dominated by ethnic students; during crises involving student movements, students will not commit themselves to involvement in student disciplinary procedures, especially if ethnic students are involved; and a majority of students believe our academic institutions are racist and sympathize with the efforts of the ethnic students to obtain redress of their grievances.

Short of revolution, neither the body politic nor the academic community appears to be willing to implement the full consequences of the radical student slogan "Power to the people!"

Until students, faculty, and administrators agree to formulate and enforce codes of conduct appropriate to both the emerging student and faculty values and the imperatives in the academic milieu, external agencies such as the legislature, the governor, lay boards, and law enforcement agencies will impose their versions of such restrictions and their enforcement on campuses.

During campus disruptions, the mass media escalate the conflict and the public response and compound the polarizations.

At some point in even a complex cycle of disruptive campus struggle, nonpartisan mediation or arbitration becomes acceptable to warring factions.

In a statewide system, emergency sessions of a statewide board of trustees called to deal with a campus crisis are dysfunctional and inflammatory. Local advisory or governing boards have a better chance of aiding efforts to reduce conflict. Once into a crisis, a college needs support and counsel, not direction. Systemwide intrusion into these difficulties has repeatedly exacerbated the frictions, not aided in the resolution of the differences.

Proposals

American higher education must begin a prolonged, committed, painful reassessment of its internal governance and its fundamental relationship to the American society, its values, its power sources. We must take seriously the radical critique of our society and of the manner in which our institutions of higher education serve that society and reflect its values and commitments. This does not mean we must ally with this critique or adopt its solutions. It does mean we must reexamine basic assumptions that have become a part of the conventional wisdom now being tested by the young, the ethnic groups, many of the faculty, and some of the silent middle. By the same token we must take seriously the conservative analysis of our institutions. For too long faculty and administrators have cultivated a mythical conception of their enterprise, a conception that they have not been willing to see tested by either their constituencies or current imperatives. Until this cooperative reexamination begins, public support will diminish, the purposes of the institutions will be confused, conflict will be the order of the day, and critical concepts such as liberal education, academic freedom, and professional ethics will be considered self-serving academic rhetoric rather than agreed-upon values to be defended.

We may take it for granted that a reexamination of higher education and American society will be complicated by the generation gap—by the fact that the values of young people and growing numbers of faculty appear to be moving rapidly in a direction opposite from those of both the taxpaying masses and the conventional sources of power. This wide disparity in points of view underscores the urgent need for dialogue and the skill and patience with which it must be undertaken. Faculty must abandon the aloofness of the professional who is beyond criticism and instead become a vital part of the public reexamination that redefines the purposes and governance of the institution. If such professional communicators and teachers cannot become persuasive in this arena, they should have no particular claim to hegemony. Unless ways are found to begin a joint process of reexamination, we believe public confidence and support are apt to be further eroded, and campus morale is not apt to improve. These conditions, in turn, will fail to gain student commitment, will threaten campus peace and stability, and will block needed innovation and reform. The remainder of this chapter projects a beginning of that process of reexamination.

It is no longer enough to talk about college administration. Large urban colleges and universities must be viewed as major jurisdictions deeply involved in governing people. For example, the California state college system controls and guides the energies of more people scattered over a greater geographic area than many medium-sized cities, some states, and some nations. We are dealing with a crisis in governance. Colleges and universities are also focal points for the sharpest conflicts raging within the broader society. The substance of this study urges us to make some blunt statements. The existing corporate system of governance of higher education is as ineffective as are the systems of city government now leading progressively to the collapse of the qualitative aspects of life in large urban centers. The stresses have merely converged on the colleges a bit later than they have on the central cities.

In the opening chapter we pointed out that the college often lives the life of a corporation. Perhaps one of the most significant insights which we drew from our analysis of the college in crisis is that during a crisis the illusion of an academic community tends to be quickly displaced by the reality of the corporate model. The heady and satisfying feeling that the faculty in the academic community are masters of their own destinies is rudely shattered by the crisis-revealed truth that faculty are workers in the academic corporation. As the attempt is made to bring the unruly factory under control, the faculty suddenly realizes that the power it has exercised on matters of curriculum, budget, personnel, selection of leaders, and so on, has been theirs through the benevolent delegation of the president, the board of

trustees, and the chancellor. Stripped of the outergarments of cooperation and supposed mutual interest, the academic corporation stands
as a naked model of a hierarchical organization that is reminiscent of
the business corporation or factory before the onset of organized labor.
The new grievance procedures, the near abandonment of advice and
consent procedures in the selection and removal of administrators, the
insistence that the president has the ultimate authority and responsibility on the campus at the pleasure of the board, and the public's
conviction that the faculties are "their" employees should remove any
doubt about the basic nature of our organizational structure.

All this is not to say that a passable education and even some
exciting scholarship cannot be accomplished within the framework of
this model. Past history confirms that it can. Yet, one wonders whether
the nineteenth-century corporate structure is really the most appropriate, productive, and effective way of organizing the academic
enterprise and whether it would draw wide public support if critically examined. Curiously, the corporate model that now comes to the
fore in higher education is in the tradition of the paternalistic time
when the boss hired and fired, unchecked by anything except his own
wisdom and sense of fairness and perhaps an upward obligation to a
board of directors. Ultimate power to the executive seems now to be
the message, but it is a message that for this time and place is anachronistic. As industry after industry has discovered, at best this
system promises low morale and the rise of a spirit of noncooperation
and covert resistance; at worst, it threatens the very freedom which
makes the college enterprise productive and possible. One can expect
that this unveiling of corporate power will precipitate a renewed drive
for countervailing power on the part of the faculty and students. It
also may mean that open adversary proceedings will characterize the
relationship between the faculty, the students, and the corporate
management. Below, we make some recommendations in the event
this corporate model is to continue.

Trustees, faculties, and student groups have moved steadily
toward adversarial relationships and struggles for power. The concepts
of conciliation, mediation and arbitration by parties external to the
conflicts—concepts so widely employed in other sectors of the society—
should be provided both at the campus and at the state levels.

Teachers and professors throughout the state should join and
organize independently of any single institution or system, with three

blunt objectives: to support the educational needs of this society, especially the educational aspirations of youth; to make education a state and national priority, more urgent than military commitments; and to secure for teaching and scholarship roles that are secure enough to assure freedom of performance and that are responsible both to the profession and to society—as *determined by the profession*. Counter organization is one implication of adversarial relationships within a corporate model.

Students, including junior college students, should reject current models of campus student government and organize off campus, seeking a corporate structure able to function as an independent power group with local, regional, and state levels of activities. The objectives of these groups should be determined by students as they identify their educational priorities. Minimally, they should secure roles on all governing boards of higher education and maintain active roles in political processes of the state.

College and university administrative and supervisory personnel must face the necessity for organizing and for seeking allies who can compensate for their limited numbers and vulnerable roles. In the corporate model they are presently as vulnerable to arbitrary power as are students.

Other potential power groups (such as campus employees other than the above) and alumni must reconsider their relationships in the realignment of power in the corporate college and university community.

Contractual relationships, negotiation, arbitration, and litigation should be the objectives of all when basic conflicts arise. Guerrilla warfare and other tactics dependent on terrorism and violence threaten the academic community and should be rejected. Political action is a necessary aspect of the above model.

The adversarial model is not our favorite—and itself depends on processes inimical to our concepts of education as human development in a less power-ridden context. If it is to be the model, the elephants ought not to dance unchecked in the hen yard.

There is another model that we prefer—the community model. In this model the academic community is viewed as a relatively autonomous place devoted to the search for truth, beauty, and justice in a context of mutual confidence and complementary roles. While the academic community is obviously a part of the larger community, in this conception it also stands apart from the larger community. As a largely independent unit, it is to be manager of its own affairs. It takes responsibility for self-governance, for enforcing the behavioral codes of the community, and for developing a workable relationship with the patron public. It should pride itself in its willingness to protect dissent, in its effort to provide a model system of justice for students and faculty alike and in its desire to serve the cause of the free person. It regards all who enter this community—whether students or faculty—as people who are willing to commit themselves, if only for a short time, to that series of values summed up by academic freedom. These values should be clearly stated.

As in most communities, the members of the academic community share an equality in some things and an inequality in others. In the ideal academic community a basic equality rests on the observation that the college or university brings together a people who are interested in learning. Professors are learners. Students are learners. Their interest in learning brings them into an arena where the mere call to authority and status on the truth of matters must forever be muted by the recognition that error is possible even for the authorities. This means, among other things, that students have an equal right with professors to accept or reject the current theories and beliefs of the profession. In the academic community we cannot accept the contention that the evidence is all in and that we possess immutable truths unchallengeable by mere students. Therein lies our equality. It is an equality of challenge to the conventional wisdom.

Yet, there is also a basic inequality in the academic community. We might call it an inequality of intellectual experience. The professor and the student do not enter the classroom as equals in the matters of the mind in relation to the learnings sought by students. Not only are the intellectual experiences of the professor much broader as a general rule, but also they are likely to be more focused, more intense, and more considered. In this context, the students have come to learn something from and with the professors, and the professors are obligated to maintain a sense of scholarly integrity in their relationships with students. Significantly, in this ideal academic community the professor appears as no pompous pedant, but as someone who is his own man, able and willing to relate to students in a positive and supporting manner without compromising his basic role of teacher and scholar.

Despite the inequality of intellectual experience and perhaps because of the equality of the learning, inquiring mission, the community model for colleges and universities seems particularly suited to nurturing the growth of a spirit of free inquiry and concerned criticism of the conventional wisdom. Viewed as a viable community, ever watchful of those who threaten its integrity, the college becomes not a factory filled with academic hirelings but a unique societal unit packed with men and women committed to free inquiry, discourse, and challenging involvement as a life style.

Hierarchical authority responsible outside the community seems incongruous to this type of community. The need for governance is there; the need for adjustment of conflicting interests is there; and the need for mutually satisfactory relationship with the broader community is necessarily there. But intellectual and operational running room is needed, running room perhaps provided by a charter where certain agreements, rights, obligations, and responsibilities are clearly stated both within the institution and between the institution and the society outside. There is little doubt that an uneasy relationship between the patron public and the academic community will continue with this model, but there is a possibility that this relationship can be made more satisfactory if a responsible community model is accepted. It is more complex and demanding than is the corporate, adversarial model. Below, we make some recommendations for establishing and maintaining the community model.

The governance of higher education must be decentralized. State systems possess a remoteness from institutional operation that if desirable in the past, now handicaps the capacity of the institution to make the kind of sensitive decisions required as colleges become politicized by confrontations. These statewide governing boards have also become too responsive to state political considerations; they are too small, and they are too unrepresentative of the various constituencies in the state that have a stake in the colleges and universities. As a first step in decentralization, boards with real powers should be created for each state college. Such boards should reflect the community composition and should have faculty and student representatives, but might well draw personnel from beyond the service area of the college.

A new system of appointing members to the trustees, the regents and the boards of governors should be developed. This system would need to be extended to local boards as they are created. Power should be shared by the executive branch, the legislative branch, and the academic community through a system of choices from slates of candidates mutually acceptable to the academic community and the governor, with advice and consent authority vested in the legislature.

Governors and other elected executives of state government should have no direct role in the governance of higher education. In times of conflict and stress, elected government officials are tempted to make board meetings the arenas for state political and ideological struggle—while political figures on the governing boards wring their hands at the reciprocal politicization of the campus.

Many of the conventional relationships within higher education, between the campuses and their publics, and with trustees are gravely strained if not broken. Business as usual will not suffice. Employing any means necessary to shore up vested interests and quiet conflict is sure to distort the outcomes. Persons both within and outside the colleges who are concerned with the future of higher education should join in mutual efforts to diagnose needs and problems and should move on them together where possible. A major institute or study and development center, well-financed and open to students, educational professionals, and citizens, should make a deliberate effort to explore, with those who are subjected to them, the deepest and sharpest tensions in society and education; the purposes and processes that higher education is to serve; and the structures designed to support it. It is urgent that administrators, faculty, and trustees should all engage in intensive in-service education concerning higher education.

Faculty must develop a more clearly designed code of professional ethics and must devise much more rigorous and equitable ways of calling colleagues to account.

The traditional protections of academic rights must be extended to students, and procedures must be designed through which these rights can be served.

The chief campus executive officer must be better protected from the arbitrary assaults by sudden coalitions among his constituencies or by aggressive factions on his policy board. The president or chief executive officer of the college and state bodies should be on a term contract of three to five years.

A system of power shared among administrators, faculty, and

students for educational policy formulation must be developed to replace the conventional approach of faculty consultation, administrative
ultimate authority, and student isolation. Lay boards must recognize
that such a system offers greater promise for wise policy that will be
supported by the various campus constituencies, despite dilution of the
ultimate authority *for policy* of the president and his administration.
Stated negatively, colleges must resist a system of hierarchical, managerial controls despite the attractiveness of such a system to those
possessing power in our society and those who desire instant implementation of their views on the campus.

Assuming that such shared power will be channeled through
an academic senate, such a body must stubbornly resist intruding into
administrative implementation of policy decisions, especially where
administrators have been chosen with the advice and consent of the
faculty and students. The customary academic government focus on
checkmating administrators rather than creating progressive educational policy has been counterproductive. A community style of governance means that faculty cannot demand control of institutional policy
while devoting marginal attention to the grave and complex issues
involved. Their effectiveness in crisis and change depends on a clear
view of both the status and priority of an issue and how it emerged.

Each level of leadership can make major contributions to the
reduction of confrontational type conflicts by working in advance with
the concerned groups to create the kinds of conditions that minimize
disruptive conflict. The conventional decision-making processes and
structures dealing with program development and review must be
made more mobile. Groups dealing directly with disruptive pressure
groups must be invested with authority to *move* or to *resist*. But the
main task is to move positively. This requires resources and flexibility
in their allocation and use. In times of acute crisis, a given college
should have prompt access to reserve funds and added personnel.

The administration of financial resources and personnel should
be a campus responsibility subject to *minimum* strictures and *minimum* review beyond the campus. Allocation of personnel and dollars
from the state budget should be by formula or ratio of money per
student. Public interest and student interests should be protected by
strengthened accreditation procedures and provisions for a citizens'
select committee or commission for special inquiry and review when

grave public concern about a particular public college or university develops and persists.

The resources for institutional research should be sharply expanded or redirected toward assessment of areas of developing tension and definition of program and policy issues related to pressures both within the college and beyond. Well-staffed task forces of limited size should be assigned to deal authoritatively with the emerging problems of the college community and should be given a clear charge, including a calendar for expected performance. A task force may be as small as one person on special assignment. It should be only large enough to include the expertness, balance, and commitment necessary to get a trustworthy job done. The groups or interests apt to be in conflict over the proposed solutions should attempt to agree on the composition of the task force and its charge. Membership may often go beyond the college community and may well include students. It should work openly to extend communication and share information with concerned groups. Decisive action should be taken on its recommendations with minimum delay. Such actions, of course, could include rejection by a broader policy body or general administrator. Rejection should be no casual matter and the burden of proof should rest with those who would reject the results of a working task force.

A college requires an advanced communication system comparable to those developing in the sectors of society most sophisticated in the use of multimedia, a system adapted to a variety of educational and informational uses. It should be fully available in crisis situations. Campuses in a regional area should be linked together as centers for lateral communication about educational issues. Deans of students, student editors, heads of ethnic studies, or presidents should be able to confer among campuses, on their own initiative, without leaving their own campuses. In periods of urgency, broadcasts directly to the public, independent of control by commercial media, are critical. They are necessary on a sustained basis, as well, if the level of public information is to keep pace with issues growing from change and conflict in education.

A large college should develop an administrative unit to secure justice, peace, and accountability on the campus for all members of the college. That unit should handle grievances, discipline, and compliance. The chief administrator of the organization should function at a level equivalent to that of a vice-president for the foreseeable future. The unit should include personnel specializing in the following functions: ombudsman, prosecutor, public defender, judicial services, counseling and case reports specific to those found guilty of infractions, and police and security functions. The administrator should function under a policy board that includes students, faculty members, administrators, and citizens (perhaps trustees). Specific cases should be settled within the unit independently of the chief executive offices of the campus. This administrative unit should strive to reduce city police and criminal court involvements arising from campus behavior.

Failure of a campus to manage citizenship problems means external police, under external control, as a conduit to an increasingly overwhelmed community judicial and penal system. In the meantime the college carries the overtone of a garrison under harassment, if not siege. Basic responsibility for the maintenance of peace and freedom and the enforcement of law and regulations on campus should rest with the local campus governing body and its executive officers, even during periods of disorder. The chief campus security officers should be comparable in status and competence to the best police chiefs in neighboring communities. Effective peace keeping depends on the support and consent of the citizens in the academic community. If other agencies order city or state police, national guard or army units to a campus, without reference to the views of the president, an emergency should be declared, and the president and his staff given the option of abstaining from their duties as long as the occupation continues. Responsibility and authority cannot be separated in this crucial area of conflict and continuing confusion.

Campus personnel concerned with justice and security must be expanded in number, and means must be developed to assure some reserve forces, all of whom should be continuously upgraded in law enforcement and security functions. At some point in the build-up of campus dissent and disruption—perhaps at the point of active violence —an emergency should be declared to alert all members of the campus community to the growing crisis. At such times, for the period of stress, the authority for college policy interpretation and administrative action must be gathered into a small, administratively mobile group with the president as the key figure. The nature of the crisis must shape somewhat the membership of the decision-making group. The emergency should be terminated at the earliest practicable moment and conventional governance restored. This action should be followed promptly by a review by an impartial body of the decisions and events undertaken during the crisis, with access to the records and persons involved. This body should be charged with making recommendations for reconstituting the college and restoring academic freedom and due process and for a return to a distributed decision-making process.

It is important to be clear about what is involved in a declared crisis on the campus. Who can declare it? Who can terminate it? What extraordinary authority does it invoke? What circumstances justify it? Who determines what the circumstances are? What ordinary rights and responsibilities are set aside? Who monitors the crisis events?

Efforts must be made to determine the degree of militancy that can be accommodated within an administrative staff, what roles are practicable during confrontations involving racial and ethnic issues, and what patterns of mutual support are possible between black, Third World and white administrators. (Seven black administrators with college-wide responsibilities were unable to sustain themselves during a period of campus disruptions at San Francisco State led by militant black students. Two years later all had resigned or had been dismissed. Almost without exception, white administrators (other than the president) continued in administrative roles.)

We have discussed two models for campus government for large, urban, public supported colleges: the corporate model committed to a managerial hierarchy responsible to a statewide lay board of trustees; and a community model with campus governance the focal point for most policy making, executive action, and the securing of justice and accountability. In the former, higher education is directed from the state level. In the latter, the local campus governs, with regional and state level coordination among allied institutions. Severe pressures from Reagan and his appointees on the state college and university governing have impelled movement toward a highly directive version of the corporate model. Reagan was reelected for a second four-year term in November of 1970 with a reduced but decisive half million vote margin. Despite our preference for the community model, the drive for central direction of the massive California systems may be expected to continue until the consequences become more clearly apparent to the citizens of the state.

We have said earlier that the Master Plan for Higher Education is dead, although it is admired from afar in other states. But like the sturdiness of a redwood stump shorn of its powerful vitality, it does not fall over or disappear from the scene without generating a variety of self-stunting, competing progeny. Fear, suspicion, retaliation, and intensified bureaucratic bindings are examples.

A rigid, managerial, hierarchical system of governing the state colleges and the campuses of the University of California has been emerging in the past year in response to the new power structure in California, with its interest in controlling all critical aspects of the colleges' operations, and student and faculty behavior in particular. That system must be effectively resisted by all parties interested in preserving a climate of free inquiry, social usefulness, and human fulfillment. Such hierarchical control gives little promise for success of educational outcomes we can affirm. Coming in the guise of a rational response to student violence and faculty irresponsibility, and with widespread support from a suspicious public, it threatens the future of a system carefully nurtured over many decades by committed citizens, legislators, and academicians. Hierarchical control is creating more problems than solutions.

The ethnic bias of the tracking system in the California Master Plan has already become apparent. The need in the state for a system of such hierarchies of academic ability and function is questionable. By failure to fund facilities and programs, the executive and legislative branches of the government—with the complicity of the public in its bond issue votes—are seriously eroding California's commitment to quality mass higher education. If this is to be the new wish of the body politic, this policy should become deliberate and emerge from legislative debate. The doors to higher education are closing softly one after another.

A corollary to the needed Master Plan reexamination should be an analysis and subsequent reform of the state's financing of higher education. With student enrollments and costs accelerating, with the new injection of ethnic demands including student funding, with faculty demands for reduced teaching loads and increased salaries and fringe benefits, with the three segments challenging their respective shares of the available resources, the financing of higher education in California is in a serious dilemma. Financial problems, too long ignored, contributed significantly to the chaos at San Francisco State.

Federally financed schools of ethnic studies should be established, in various cities of the United States, in which both young and seasoned scholars could concentrate their efforts to develop and experiment with programs and materials. The nation should provide a student bill of rights based on a minimum for adequate financial support for all students. The steady trend of the past decade to transfer the costs of higher education to students and their families blatantly penalizes children of the poor and lower income groups, of whom a disproportionate number are ethnic minority citizens. As an economic investment in human potential a proposal for general financial support is unassailable. Its social and ethical aspects promise even greater returns.

Members of governing bodies should be paid salaries commensurate with the competence expected of them. Performance in policy formation in behalf of higher education is needed, not honors bestowed because of political obligations or great wealth or high performance in another field. Personnel with specific technical competencies—such as in architecture, land acquisition, and finance—can be contracted for or hired on a term or project basis. Whether or not the Master Plan for Higher Education is retained in California there is grave need for regional commissions charged with assuring equality and appropriateness of higher educational opportunity for the total population of a geographic area such as the nine urban and metropolitan counties of the San Francisco-Oakland Bay Area. A local campus within one of three separate public higher education systems is confined with its sister institutions to a defined set of functions and a hard limit on size and resources. To the citizens of the Bay area the systems appear tragically uncoordinated, and many students fall through the interstices. Each system's campus in an area can do its best to discharge its limited functions during a given year, but thousands of Bay Area citizens are turned away with no recourse except to a polymorphous state coordinating council for higher education.

Such are our summaries, conclusions and proposals. We hope that we have raised some of the most important issues stemming out of the disorder and confrontations of three years of discontent. We contend that the significance of the parochial events at San Francisco State reach far beyond the confines of California and to the nation and the world. We know that there are a number of issues we did not raise as well as a number of perspectives which we have not presented. We believe that our analysis provides important insights into ways of solving some of the dilemmas of modern higher education, but we recognize that almost all of the issues we have examined are controversial. Yet to be controversial is often to be important. Out of the controversy may come ways of attacking our problems that are creative and possible. We agree that the problems now capturing our attention are the beginnings of the problems that arise out of postindustrial America. We think that the colleges and universities will be looked to as never before to help solve these problems. It therefore becomes terribly important now to tackle the question of who we are and what we are to become. Without treating questions of governance, of student roles, of minority education, of faculty and student ethics, and of the relationship of the rest of society to the academy, it is unlikely that we can easily be a university where the struggle to gather knowledge and promote humane life is our central concern.

Index

Neocolonialism in treatment of minority groups, 63
New Left thought on campus, 26–30
New student ethic, 148–152
News media, 225–226, 239–256; and Cleaver at Berkeley, 241; effect of on public, 248–249; and Hayakawa, 185, 244–245; impact of on campus disorder, 253–256; and Murray controversy, 241–242, 250; and Rafferty, 246; and "Ray Tannehill News," 246; and Reagan, 184, 246, 251–252; and second convocation, 245–246, 248–249; and Smith, 246–252; and Tactical Squad during strike, 242–243; and Wedworth, 243–244
NEWTON, H., 79
NIXON, J., 32–33, 35, 153

O

Office of Internal Affairs, 170–171
ORRICK, W. H., 26, 108, 109, 110–111
Orrick Report, 26

P

PAULSON, S., 180
Peace and Freedom people, 74
PEEBLES, T., 77, 78
PENTONY, D., 104n
PERSICO, J., 153
Philippine-American Collegiate Endeavor, 108
PITZER, K., 61, 228n
Polarization, 67–71, 151–152, 162, 262
Police, campus, 159, 161. See also Police intervention
Police intervention, 160, 161, 225–239; activists' view of, 228–229; and arrests, 160, 161, 165–166, 172–176, 233; avoidance of, 235–239; effects of, 234–235; as outside authority, 231–232; purposes of, 233–234; under various presidents, 230–231
Politicization, 118–120
"Power to the People," 64–65, 144–145, 294

President, obligations of to college, 289–290
Progressive Labor Party, 58, 71–73
Propaganda in ethnic studies, 133–134
Public, reaction of to campus disorder, 184–185, 257–283; demands of for counteraggression, 275–276; financial backlash of, 286; letters from, 262–282; racism in letters of, 273, 275–276, 281; support of Hayakawa by, 278–279; trustees' view of, 257–262, 281–283

Q

Quality control, 8–9. See also Grading

R

Racism, 80–86, 101–102; dangers of in ethnic studies, 115–117; in letters from public, 273, 275–276, 281
Radical ideology, 52–98; and anti-Vietnam War Convocation, 57–61; and demonstrations and demands, 65–67; implications of challenges of, 93–98; against institutional neutrality, 62–65; isolation of individual as strategy of, 68; key premises of, 90–93; manipulation of majority by minority in, 87–90; polarization strategy of, 67–71; racism of, 80–86; search of for antiestablishment allies, 71–75; split between liberals and new left in, 58–60; stages of, 56–57; suppression of by reactionaries, 94–97; violence as a means of, 75–80
RAFFERTY, M., 182, 246
RAMSEY, T., 153
Reactionaries, 16–17
REAGAN, R., 161, 179, 182, 184, 246, 251, 286, 305
REAVIS, E., 154
Rebellion and revolution, J-curve theory of, 23
Recruiting on campus, 63
REDDELL, F., 159, 160, 164, 170

Reform programs, student-initiated, 22–51; activists in, 44–46; fate of, 25; financing of, 45–46, 48–49; involvement of in community, 26–31; problems and abuses of, 41–51; reasons for failure of, 46–51. *See also* Associated Students programs

"Revolutionary nationalism," 115–120, 135–137

RIDGEWAY, J., 149

RIESMAN, D., 8

RITTER, D., 282, 283

ROSE, H., 250

ROSENTHAL, A. M., 231

S

San Francisco State College: attitudes in in 1967–1968, 53; financial backlash of, 286; present status and morale at, 285–287

Scholarship and standards in ethnic studies, 117–121

School of Creative Arts, schedule of fees, 48

SCOTT, R. C., 250

SEARLES, R., 65–66

Select Committee to End the Strike, 171

Self-discovery role of colleges, 17–19

SHOUP, D., 94

Sit-in, May 1968, 160

SMITH, R., 72, 73, 86, 88, 166, 180, 230, 232, 238, 241, 242, 285; mail from public to, 262–281; and news media, 246–247, 249–252, 253; student discipline under, 164–166

Specialization, undergraduate, 6–9

STANTON, W., 274

STEWART, B., 74

Struggle, concept of, 64–65, 66

Student arrests, 160, 161, 165–166, 172–176, 233

Student conduct, limits of, 153–155

Student demands, 65–67, 168

Student discipline, 146–176; and AAUP-NSA-AAC student bill of rights, 167; and amnesty, 163; during cafeteria boycott,

157; and confrontation politics, 160–164; and double jeopardy, 163, 169–170; and *Gater* incidents, 157–159, 173; under Hayakawa, 166–176; and identification of dissidents, 161, 165; and lack of judicial process, 155–157; and lack of limits of conduct, 153–155; in liberal period, 152–153; and *Open Process* incident, 157; and penalties, 162–163; and personal fear, 162; and polarization, 162; in preconfrontation era, 152–160; and presidential delegation of authority, 167–170; during Smith's administration, 164–166; and student-faculty court, 162–163, 167–169; and trials of students, 172–176

Student-faculty court, 162–163, 167–169

Student government, 25–26, 293. *See also* Associated Students

Student Judicial Court, 152, 156, 159–160, 164

Student strike, 53

Student Union building, 47, 48

Students: criticism of college by, 26–30; exclusion of from due process by professors, 212, 215–216; involvement of in community and community problems, 26–31; radical, 16–17, 52–98. *See also* Radical ideology

Students for a Democratic Society (SDS), 58, 89–90; split in, 74, 91

SUMMERSKILL, J., 47, 49, 57, 81, 157, 158, 159, 180, 230, 232, 285; attacks on policy of, 53–54, 60–62

SWIM, D., 250, 288

T

TAYLOR, H., 25, 94

Teacher preparation programs, 29, 30

THELWELL, M., 66, 87

Third World Liberation Front, 53, 277; demands of, 100, 271, 272–